Lamborghini

BY THE AUTO EDITORS OF CONSUMER GUIDE®

Louis Weber, C.E.O.
Publications International, Ltd.
7373 North Cicero Avenue
Lincolnwood, Illinois 60646

Printed and bound in Yugoslavia

8 7 6 5 4 3 2 1

ISBN 0-88176-931-2

Library of Congress Catalog Card Number: 90–63958

Introduction
Italy's Other Fantasy

Exiting the last turn of a twisty road course near Verano, Italy, in September 1990, an American journalist lost control of one of the world's first Lamborghini Diablos. It slammed into the pit wall, "erasing the left side of the car," in the words of one witness. No one was hurt, but the shunt meant that European journalists—already chafed at being second in line to test-drive the new supercar—were forced to cool their heels several more weeks. Thus, the continent's motoring press joined its populace in waiting. For Lamborghini had chosen to publicly unveil the highly anticipated exotic not in Italy or even in Europe, but in the United States, in Chicago, of all places.

As successor to the planet's most-recognized exotic—Lamborghini's own Countach—interest in the Diablo was incendiary. The motoring community had argued and speculated about the form it might take. Artists conjured their own visions, and rumormongers prospered. But the calculations of the board room and the fortunes of the test track conspired against the very land that gave birth to the super-fast exotic. Europe, whose passion and protectionism allow these rolling works of art to run free, stewed until the Americans got their fill.

The uproar was not as sharp as it might have been, however. After all, "it was not a first-drive Ferrari," explained Luca Ciferri, a European editor of *Autoweek*. "It's not as big a deal as a Ferrari, so there was not the reaction there was in Japan when Lexus and Infiniti launched first in the United States."

Second fiddle to Ferrari has always been Lamborghini's lot. A younger company, with fewer cars, virtually no racing history, and a founder less skilled in self-promotion, Lamborghini is the *other* Italian fantasy. That it holds a lower profile in some circles does not mean Lamborghini's annals are less

storied, however. And for those schooled in ultra-performance automobiles, a Lamborghini hardly is less worthy, just different.

Indeed, much of the allure is that few aspects of the Lamborghini saga fit the conventional mold. All affairs automotive require a certain audacity, but Ferruccio Lamborghini's strokes were exceptionally bold. His birth sign is Taurus, and he lived up to its associated characteristics. Born a to a farming family, he trained as a mechanic, then made himself a major industrialist. When he decided to jump into the auto business, he did so wholeheartedly but with remarkably little egoism. Though called *Il Cavaliere*, he often worked alongside his men on the shop floor.

He also had the ability to draw out the enthusiasm and energy of creative people—and the rare willingness to stand aside for it. Lamborghini did not design his cars, but he was the instigator and spiritual director of those who did. He did not have their imagination, but he had the good sense to let them exercise theirs.

Lamborghini cars hail from Italy's wine country, but like truly fine wines, they are not necessary. Lamborghinis cope with everyday traffic, but they are not bred for mere transportation. They are creatures of passion—created for the wild centers of our souls. In specification, technology, appearance, even color sometimes and always in performance, they have been breakthrough designs.

But there is a dark side. The ambition and audacity that created these cars and made them unique, often demanded too much. Some Lamborghinis have more spirit than substance. New models were frequently released before they were ready. And they often were poorly finished or unreliable. Even now, owning a Lamborghini remains an adventure that defines "exotic car."

Nor is Lamborghini's corporate

history a model of success. After bursting into the automotive firmament, Automobili Ferruccio Lamborghini S.p.A. went into a long economic and creative eclipse from which it emerged only recently, and then only with the help of America's Chrysler Corporation, which purchased the company in 1987.

The history of these magnificent

automobiles—most so aptly named for fighting bulls—began some three decades ago. That's ample time for details to have been lost, for myth to have shaded truth. To tell this story we have sought out original sources and listened to people who were there. We have driven some of the cars and have read what others wrote and weighed their judgments.

We investigated famous tales with critical eyes. But we also attempted to learn from the legends. Truth often is found in myth. It is also our purpose to convey something of the personality of these fabulous machines. For whatever their shortcomings, inside us there stirs a love of wondrous things built purely for satisfaction and speed.

Casual observers identify Lamborghini primarily with the outrageous mid-engine Countach, like the '84 at the right in the photo. A deeper look reveals a rich legacy that includes a host of cars, among them the urbane 350 GT two-seater of '65, at left and the innovative 1973 Espada supersedan.

CHAPTER 1
Swords Into Plowshares

He was born on April 28, which made him a Taurus. That may not have had anything to do with his character, but he clearly perceived that it did, and that amounts to the same thing. Taureans are said to be born winners; aggressive and goal-oriented, determined to achieve material success and social dominance through initiative, tenacity, and plain hard work. Indeed, this is the substance of the life's work of Ferruccio Lamborghini.

Italy was still entwined in its feudal roots in 1916. A man's birthplace and birthsign were still important. Thus did certain things seem almost preordained for Ferruccio (fah-ROOCH-ee-ho), born in the spring of that troubled year at Renazzo, a rural village near Cento on the plains of Emilia some 15 miles north of the industrial town of Bologna.

The Lamborghinis were farmers, stolid peasant folk of the flat, fertile fields of the broad Po valley, so stocky little Ferruccio grew up with his feet in the soil. But this was the automotive century and, like numerous other youngsters of that time and place, he had engine oil in

his veins. Machinery of every type fascinated him, and he was not immune to the enthusiasm for fast cars that made Italy a major power in European auto racing during his boyhood. While he was still a boy, Ferruccio is said to have set up a primitive but workable machine shop, forge, and casting foundry in the family barn. The story has his enterprise once setting fire to the structure.

Acknowledging their son's talents and ambitions, Ferruccio's parents packed him off for formal technical schooling in the nearby "big city" of Bologna, where he reportedly earned an industrial arts degree. After that, young Lamborghini apprenticed himself to a Bologna mechanical shop.

World War II might have derailed his career, as it did for so many, but the Regia Aeronautica stationed Ferruccio at a base on the island of Rhodes, off the Turkish coast, and put him to work in the transport pool. Rhodes was not a theater of heavy action, but neither was it at the top of the military's list for replacement equipment, and Lamborghini soon became known as something of a wizard at keeping

decrepit vehicles running.

One tale has Lamborghini making an "improvement" to the braking system of his commanding officer's cherished Alfa—which promptly sent the car into the Mediterranean. It might well have sent Ferruccio to the stockade, but he seemed to have the kind of personality that made even COs grin and give him another chance.

Rhodes fell to the British in 1944, and some accounts have Lamborghini becoming a prisoner of war while others cast him as a free and valued employee of the Brits. Regardless, he stayed on the island into 1946, working his wizard ways on British military hardware. He then returned to the family home at Renazzo di Cento to resume civilian life at age 30.

In the late 1960s, Ferruccio Lamborghini was the hub of an enterprise pliant enough to build both exotic cars and tractors (opposite). Strength and resolution fueled his success, symbolized today by the figure on display at the auto works that bear his name (above).

8

Lamborghini's hands naturally fell on mechanic's tools again, and now his parents' investment in his education was repaid. Like other farmers in the region, they had urgent need of a new tractor, but no such grand thing was available in postwar Italy. No problem. Their son duly built them one—out of junk.

There is a story that Ferruccio got the idea for this on his wedding trip; that British forces in Italy were disposing of a small fleet of light armored cars, that the happy couple somehow stumbled across them, and that the bride abruptly found her honeymoon at an end. Whisked home early, she watched as her ambitious, determined new husband tore the armor plate off each car and turned it into a little tractor—a

carioche in the local vernacular.

Lamborghini wasn't the only *trasformatore* in Emilia then hammering such swords into plowshares, but he was evidently among the best. Certainly his tireless promotional enterprise was among the most effective. Bull-built Ferruccio would take one of his tractors to a town on market day and challenge other mechanics to a pull-off, back-to-back. It was a rare rival that could get the better of a Lamborghini carioche.

Mrs. Lamborghini soon found herself prospering. Her husband's little garage business grew to the point that by 1949 he could erect a new, specially designed factory at Cento. Three years later he was able to start building proper, all-new tractors using two-, three- and

four-cylinder diesel engines of his own design and manufacture. Then, in 1954, Ferruccio scored a first in his field by launching a line cf air-cooled, direct-injection diesel tractors. Soon, his Lamborghini Trattrice was one of Italy's largest tractor makers and Ferruccio was a wealthy man—respected and honored, and with the financial wherewithal to pursue new challenges.

He didn't take long to find them. A trip to America as part of an Italian trade delegation prompted thoughts of other products, and in 1960 he duly established Lamborghini Bruciatori, in nearby Pieve di Cento, to turn out home and commercial heating and cooling equipment. Ferruccio tackled this second business with characteristic

energy and enterprise. For example, he pleased customers with an innovative service plan. He also pleased both his country and his accountants by setting up in an economically depressed area. The Italian government, in fact, was an investor.

Before the age of 45, then, Ferruccio was on his way to a second fortune and to renown as one of Italy's top industrialists. Like achievers everywhere, he naturally acquired honors. Five years after the furnace factory opened, the government recognized his contributions to the national economy with an "Order of Merit" that conferred on him the title *Commendatore.* Italy's president also made him *Cavaliere del Lavoro* or "Knight of Labor." To his old army

buddies, the Brits, he would now be addressable as "Sir."

Lamborghini certainly could have been satisfied with his first two commercial empires and called it a career as early as 1962. But he had one more itch to scratch.

In life-loving Italy, the passion for fast driving is as abundant as grapes on hillsides. In setting up as a *trasformatore,* Ferruccio involved himself in a postwar hot-rodding movement that signaled Italy's return to sports-car racing. A mainstay of this impatient little industry was Fiat's 500 Topolino, the beloved "mouse." A simple, sturdy baby-car introduced in 1936, it was to become as important to its country's performance enthusiasts as Ford's Model T had been to America's.

Lamborghini turned the ruined machinery of war into farm equipment sorely needed in Italy during the late 1940s. By the early 1950s, his tractor factory at Cento was turning out engines of his own design (opposite). Clean, modern, and efficient, the plant was home to the latest in '50s agri-tech. What more perfect showcase for Lamborghini—on the left in the photo—to present another of his new products to journalists (above)?

The original 500 engine, which actually displaced 569 cubic centimeters (35 cubic inches), was an inline side-valve four that chugged out a claimed 13 horsepower. Fiat later improved the model with overhead valves, but Lamborghini was one of several entrepreneurs who catered to backyard racers by making up overhead-valve cylinder heads for the older engine. His was cast of bronze and bolted to a bored-out 750-cc (46-cubic inch) block.

Cut down and souped up with a homemade bronze cylinder head, this Fiat Topolino (top) was driven by Lamborghini in the 1948 Mille Miglia. He crashed it through the wall of an inn, convincing him that his rewards did not rest with race driving. Indeed, it was as an industrialist that Ferruccio first gained recognition. At left, he accepts a memento at a business banquet. But his passion for fast cars was undiminished, and by the early 1960s (opposite), he was a man with a new automotive mission.

Installing this package in a cut-down Topolino, Lamborghini set out to compete in the 1948 running of the classic Mille Miglia road race. Alas, he crashed after completing about three-quarters of the near 1000-mile distance. As he described it to a journalist years later: "I finished my Mille Miglia in an *osteria*, an inn—which I entered by driving though a wall." Neither he nor his co-driver were hurt, but it was Ferruccio's last race. He turned down orders for more OHV heads, concentrated on the tractor business, and waited to indulge his taste for rapid road cars until he could afford to buy new ones.

Just what prompted Lamborghini's turn to the auto business, his third career, has long been a subject of speculation. We know that he owned a string of exotic cars—certainly several Ferraris and, say various sources, the likes of Alfa Romeo, Maserati, OSCA, Jaguar, Aston Martin, Mercedes-Benz, even a Morgan and a Corvette. We can also be certain that running refinement was of prime importance to this professionally trained mechanic and that he found each of these cars unsatisfactory in this or some other way.

According to an oft-told tale, there came a day when Ferruccio grew so annoyed with a particular Ferrari that he drove over to Enzo's factory at Maranello, not far down the road, and tried to get in to complain to the proprietor himself, only to be turned away. No doubt Lamborghini was rebuffed. More than a few important visitors to Maranello—including some who'd been invited—have told bitterly of cooling their heels for hours in a narrow anteroom outside *Il Commendatore's* office. It would also have been entirely in character for Ferruccio to drive away in a fury, resolved to show that he, the successful major industrialist and self-made millionaire, could damned well build a better car than any of 'em.

Ferruccio has never been one to let a good story die in the telling. But Bob Wallace, the racing mechanic from New Zealand who was soon to become an integral part of Lamborghini's entire automotive operation, dismisses this bit of folklore with a snort: "Naw, that's all BS, which he himself may have helped keep alive, but nothing like that really happened. What motivated him was prestige, plus the fact he thought he could make money at it."

Prestige, of course: the gratification of seeing one's own

name on the front of an automobile. To this enthusiast born and reared in the home province of Ferrari and Maserati, the name Lamborghini would look much better scripted across a sleek, sexy *gran turismo* than it did on a diesel tractor or an oil heater. The urge has seized many, but few have found an opportunity to satisfy it. Ferruccio Lamborghini made his opportunity, and he made the most of it, charging into car building with no half measures. Shadetree days and

hot-rodded Fiat Topos were well behind him by 1962. Now he would fashion a world-class grand touring machine.

All that remained was to follow the formula that had already built two manufacturing empires. Accordingly, Ferruccio bought a piece of land, erected a new purpose-built factory and filled it with the absolute state-of-the-art in automaking equipment—and the best people in the automotive business.

CHAPTER 2
Tycoon

Had you accepted an invitation to one of the frequent lavish parties at *Casa Lamborghini* around 1962, there to extend a welcome would have been a most unlikely looking host.

He might preside over the gathering while "dressed in the rough clothes of a working man, and wearing carpet slippers because he was at home," in the description of British writer Chris Harvey. Secure, at ease, powerful, "Ferruccio Lamborghini was his own man," Harvey wrote, and one who enjoyed his success in his own way. He had a villa down on the Adriatic seacoast, where in later years he kept a Riva speedboat powered by a pair of Lamborghini V-12s. He'd get to it in one or another V-12 Lamborghini car—unless he chose to drive the family Fiat econobox.

Here was a man in the bloom of life, 46 and looking a decade younger. "He was short, stocky,

built like a young bull, handsome and tough, with an easy laugh but the air of a very strong and determined man," reported Griffith Borgeson in Britain's *CAR* magazine. In business, as at home, the fledgling auto magnate seemed to have balanced his personal scales of ambition and achievement. This Lamborghini was "a readily recognizable tycoon and definitely not one to get in the way of," Borgeson observed. "The charging bull which he had adopted as his symbol was a shrewd, accurate and poetic choice."

Countryman Athos Evangelisti wrote in *Road & Track* that Lamborghini was "the perfect model of the Italian tycoon—so different from the American type—always smiling, full of vitality, talking about his factory and his products, but also talking of women, good wines and good food. All in the right proportions, of course."

Visit his new car factory and you'd likely discover, as did American journalist Pete Coltrin, Lamborghini down on the shop floor in shirt-sleeves, happily wrenching away at an engine with employees. People found him an unusually democratic chief executive, one uncommonly willing to delegate authority. This last trait was particularly significant. Says Bob

"...Handsome and tough, with an easy laugh but the air of a very strong and determined man," was one writer's description of Ferruccio Lamborghini (opposite) in the early 1960s as the industrialist plunged into the making of exotic cars. A priceless talent was the ability to inspire his workers. These Countach craftsmen may have posed smiles, (below) but is there not also an air of pride here?

Wallace, who had earlier worked for Enzo Ferrari: "Basically, the two of them are very alike. They both have a gift of finding the right person for the right position and then letting him go to work. Ferrari himself is not the person that people make him out to be—of being heartless and this sort of thing—but he does keep himself very, very much apart from the average staff. Whereas Lamborghini's the typical farmer. He'd say 'Hi' to the president of Italy. He doesn't stand on ceremony. He's, uh, a little crude sometimes, but a very, very straightforward person. He's always been very honest and very fair."

These engagingly human traits, plus simple taurine vigor and audacity, were irresistible to young people of talent and ambition. Infused with creative fervor, they flocked to the heady, freewheeling climate that surrounded the new Automobili Ferruccio Lamborghini. Four in particular would prove to be key figures in the development of Lamborghini cars.

Prime among them is Wallace. As chief development driver, he was ultimately responsible for the performance, road manners, flavor—in a word, the personality—of every Lamborghini automobile.

Born in 1938 outside Auckland, New Zealand, Wallace grew up as much a gearhead as Ferruccio himself, and more of a racer. He says now that he'd been dreaming of joining the Italian auto racing world since he was 10 years old, but it wasn't until he reached 21 that he got on a boat and did it. That was 1959. Over the next four racing seasons he spent time as a factory mechanic with both Ferrari and Maserati, plus a couple of privateer teams. "In late '63, October or November, I had the choice of rejoining Ferrari or taking this job at Lamborghini as mechanic and trouble-shooter. I thought there was much more opportunity to learn something there, and I took it."

One of the men Wallace would learn from was a year younger than himself, a gifted 24-year-old engineer named Giampaolo Dallara. Born in a mountain village above

16

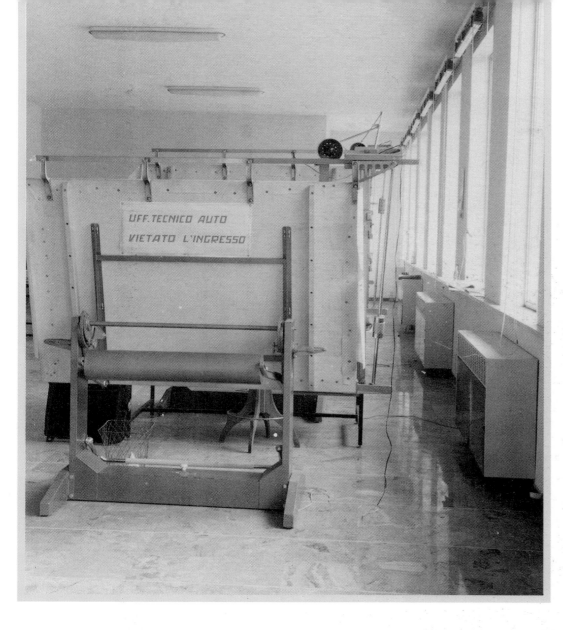

Ferruccio scoured the world of high-performance automobiles for the best talent in the business. To design his engine, Lamorghini snared Giotto Bizzarrini, former project director for Ferrari's immortal 250 GTO (opposite), which was just being introduced in 1962. Much of the early work at **Automobili Lamborghini** was done in a closed-off corner of the tractor factory (left). The engine that emerged in '63 was far from makeshift, however. Unlike the GTO's 300-bhp sohc 3.0-liter V-12, the one Bizzarrini designed for Lamborghini displaced 3.5 liters and had two cams per cylinder head. Below, Ferruccio shows off his new V-12, which in this pre-detuned form had 360 bhp. It made 270 bhp installed in the 350 GT.

Parma to a well-to-do family (his father was the mayor), Dallara had earned a degree in aeronautical engineering at the Technical Institute of Milan. Thanks to one of his professors, who moonlighted as an engine-design consultant to Ferrari, Giampaolo bypassed aviation on graduating and went straight into the automobile business. After 18 months as assistant to then-Ferrari engineer Carlo Chiti, he moved to Maserati to work with his cousin, Giulio Alfieri, before harking to Lamborghini's siren song in March '62. (Years later, Alfieri would also leave the trident for the bull.)

Wallace's assessment of Dallara is both interesting and pertinent, and generally mirrors that of other observers: "I think he's one of the best chassis engineers that have ever come out of any Italian factory. I always found him a very easy-to-get-along-with person. He's always had very clear ideas of what he wants to do and how he wants to do it. He's generally had a lot of fun doing what he likes to do. He comes from a fairly wealthy family, so it hasn't been a question of having to go work for wages to live."

With Dallara, whom Ferruccio named chief engineer, came another young Maserati engineer, Paolo

Stanzani. Then 25, he hailed from Bologna. Wallace, who'd previously worked with him at Maserati, says of Stanzani: "He comes from a fairly lower-income family. He struggled his way through the university and that sort of thing. He's always been very bright as an engineer. I think, theoretically, Stanzani might be the brighter one of the two." Stanzani would come to play two key roles at Lamborghini: factory manager and, on Dallara's departure, chief engineer.

Rounding out this formidable foursome was Giotto Bizzarrini. Then 36, he had an engineering degree from the University of Pisa and was already well-established in Italian performance circles. He had, in fact, just left Ferrari, where he'd been project director for one of Enzo's most memorable cars, the immortal 250 GTO that was just being introduced in 1962. He'd also spent time at Alfa Romeo. Now he was running his own business, and was full of ideas. One involved the pair of GT cars with American Chevrolet engines for Count Renzo Rivolta, the refrigerator king with a paler version of Ferruccio's dream. Another was a similar vehicle bearing the Bizzarrini name, which would materialize in 1963 as the GT Strada 5300. But Giotto was also an engine man, and it was for this talent that Lamborghini sought him.

Bizzarrini still had the drawings for a pure racing engine he'd designed while at Ferrari. It was a tiny jewel of a thing, having been intended for the 1.5-liter Grand Prix formula then in force, but in basic architecture it was precisely what Lamborghini wanted for his forthcoming street car: a modern short-stroke, four-camshaft V-12 capable of ultra-high performance. Ferrari, of course, had long offered V-12s, in displacements ranging from 3.0-5.0 liters by that point, but their basic designs dated from the early 1950s and the street versions had only a single cam per cylinder bank.

As Bob Wallace recalls, Ferruccio proposed something like this to Giotto: "Draw me up a version of your four-cam race engine for street use, and make it as big as Ferrari's 3.0-liter if you can. How much money do you want?"

"I'll make it bigger," Bizzarrini replied, "And I'll also make it more powerful—a lot more powerful. In fact, you don't have to pay me until the first engine goes on the dyno and it makes more power than the Ferrari. Then you pay me X-amount of lire for every extra horsepower. Deal?"

It was precisely the thing to say to an entrepreneurial car nut born under the sign of Taurus. But Bizzarrini had his own agenda—the same one burning inside the other prodigies on the payroll: They wanted Lamborghini to go racing.

"I hoped they would," admits Wallace. "Because I personally firmly believe that, for a factory of that type, racing does help the natural overall development of this type of car. So there was always the hope that we would. But the only sane person of all of us, initially, was Lamborghini himself. He said no. And he was right. To have divided things up at that stage would have been sheer insanity."

It was an edict the boss would stick to. Although his speed-minded youngsters continued their daydreaming, and in some cases their scheming, there was never a meaningful, official Lamborghini involvement in motorsports until

1989, when Lamborghini V-12s powered a pair of Formula 1 cars. (More on this in subsequent chapters.)

Still, Ferruccio seems to have been an almost magically fun employer. As Wallace remembers: "He had an enormous personal interest in the first years, before all the union trouble. That's what really got the company going, because people would work 'til nine, 10, 11 at night. It wasn't a question of money or overtime pay or anything like that. No, everyone was motivated, everyone had a lot of enthusiasm. He'd get stuck in and work too. It was very, very enjoyable. He had the gift."

He also had a vision of a great new Italian thoroughbred. Ferruccio was about to make his "dream GT," the first in a line of automobiles sometimes blessed and sometimes cursed, but always passionate, and frequently even quite important.

Bizzarrini's GT Strada 5300 had a Corvette engine (opposite, top). So sound was his original Lamborghini V-12 that its basic design was good for championship marine use (opposite, bottom) and as 48-valve 5.7-liter power in the Countach-Diablo era (above).

CHAPTER 3
"...A Perfect Car"

It towered over Sant'Agata Bolognese like some surrealistic Yankee Stadium. The pair of long, yellow-painted structures had more than half-a-million-square-feet of floor space. A scalloped cornice—reminiscent indeed of ornamentation at Yankee Stadium—crowned the roof of the main building. It was a temple of technology. It had the gift of geography. It was Lamborghini's new auto plant.

Ferruccio had drawn on all his powers to build the factory. His sustained interest in racing had put him on good terms with a number of top figures at various auto and motorcycle companies. From the winners he solicited advice about the latest in manufacturing methods and tooling. And when it came time to construct and equip his car factory, Ferruccio listened to everyone. He dug deep into his resources and didn't cut a single corner. The result was a production palace.

Perhaps even more important than being ultramodern, however, was

the plant's location. Sant'Agata Bolognese was a burgeoning development community along a road that threaded from Modena—a small city in north-central Italy some 22 miles northwest of Bologna—northeast through Ferruccios's birthplace, Cento, and on to Ferrara. That Lamborghini should build his plant here was no accident. If there is a geographical center of the Italian sports motoring industry, it's Modena.

"People in that area of Italy are a very innovative, industrious, hard-working people," explains Bob Wallace. "Not only as far as automotive manufacturing goes. Modena is renowned not so much for automobiles but small and medium industries, fairly high-tech products which they can make and develop extremely quickly and extremely well. It's sort of like the Brescia area is for gunmaking and armaments." In other words, in and around Modena were concentrated the specialized knowledge and skills required to launch the kind of enterprise Lamborghini envisioned.

In the strictest of terms, the actual birth of Lamborghini's auto-making enterprise didn't happen at Sant'Agata. The big new factory would take over a year to complete, and the tycoon in Lamborghini couldn't wait. Eager to get his automotive wheels moving, he went to his tractor plant, cleared out a corner—one reporter called it a "cubbyhole"—and got down to work.

Bizzarrini's V-12, displacing just under 3.5 liters (214 cubic inches), was ready for its first dyno runs on May 15, 1963. Per his agreement

Lamborghini built his automobile factory near Modena, the heart of Italy's sports-motoring community. Enzo Ferrari located his own plant in nearby Maranello. The region is known for its industrial craftsmanship. Unlike many auto works, Lamborghini's facility, shown in 1975 (opposite), was well-lit and orderly.

Lamborghini's original V-12 (right) first ran on the dyno in May 1963. The 3.5-liter unit churned out 360 bhp at 8000 rpm, though 370 bhp at 9000 rpm also is recalled. In this same basic form, it went on to power a variety of Lamborghinis, from mid-engine hotbloods to the four-seat Espada and the 2+2 Jarama (top), shown coming off the assembly line in February, 1974.

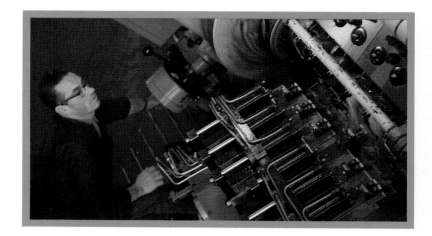

with Ferruccio, it had a very high specific output, with all the sharp edges of a racer, and was soon churning out plenty of power; some sources say 360 horses at 8000 rpm, though Wallace remembers 370 bhp at 9000-9200. Bizzarrini duly collected his check and, assured that Lamborghini had absolutely no intention of putting the engine in a track car, said *ciao*.

Engineer Giampaolo Dallara was duly assigned to re-engineer the V-12 into a civilized street mill and finalize the GT it would power. Let's be sure we understand the importance of that word "civilized." Remember that Ferruccio had raced (the little Fiat Topo in the '48 Mille Miglia) and was now surrounded by racers. But though visitors may have

heard him talk about racing from time to time—or wished they had—he was not out to build a race-and-ride sports car, let alone an all-out competition machine. By "GT," he did not mean prototypes like the Ford GT40 then being fostered by international racing rules. Nor was he thinking of the mundane stuff with those initials being hawked by mass-market makers at the time: mere sporty cars with bucket seats, GT badges and little else. No, Lamborghini was using *gran turismo*—grand touring—in its classic sense: a car that may employ the latest appropriate racing technology but always combining sports-car-like responsiveness and driving satisfaction with touring-car levels of

The ungainly one-off 350 GTV of '63 (above) was Ferruccio's first car. It was an engine-less mock-up, but launched the company. Subsequent Lamborghinis were seldom free from flaws in detail assembly, but the pride and skill that went into their mechanical componentry was never compromised. An engineer by training, Ferruccio sought the best workers and the latest equipment. Crates of gleaming crankshafts (top, right) attest to his high standards.

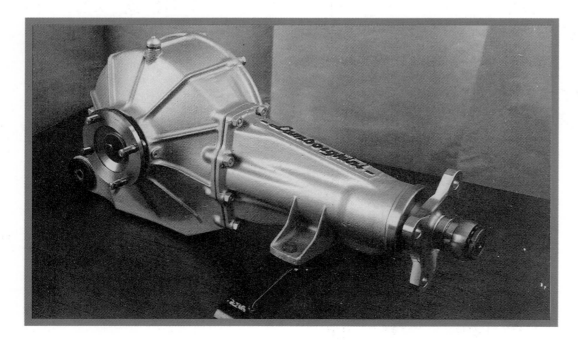

Lamborghini quickly cleaned up the styling of his 350 GTV, installed a polished powertrain, and unleashed the 350 GT (above) in 1964. If it wasn't the most beautiful car on the roads, it was nonetheless the most technically advanced GT of its day. Ferruccio desired an automobile with a "perfect" balance of speed and comfort. He came quite close. And today, the two-seater's looks are considered timeless.

comfort and refinement over long distances.

"It is very simple," Ferruccio told *Road & Track*'s Evangelisti. "In the past, I have bought some of the most famous *gran turismo* cars and in each of these magnificent machines I have found some faults. Too hot. Or uncomfortable. Or not sufficiently fast. Or not perfectly finished. Now I want to make a GT car without faults. Not a technical bomb. Very normal. Very conventional. But a perfect car."

Alas, his first effort was far from perfect. Called 350 GTV, a designation that also applied to its V-12 engine, the car was a raw piece of construction, and elements of its Scaglione-designed body were more than a bit strange. Press and public alike were lukewarm when the GTV bowed at the 1963 Turin auto show in October, prompting Lamborghini to postpone plans for immediate production. (Only one non-running prototype GTV was ever built.)

Ferruccio hustled, summoning the respected Carrozzeria Touring to clean up the styling. The result appeared five months later at the 1964 Geneva show as the 350 GT. A much smoother rendition of the GTV, it was greeted with sufficient enthusiasm that Ferruccio decided to proceed with production. Customer deliveries began soon afterwards,

though slowly and in small numbers at first.

The 350 GT was conventional in some ways, quite a breakthrough in others. A front-engine two-seat closed coupe, it was similar to certain Ferraris, Maseratis, Aston Martins, et al. But Ferruccio's intent had been to best these competitors in every respect, and by all accounts

Successor to the 350 GT was the 400 GT 2 + 2 of 1966 (top). Its transmission and final-drive (opposite) were the first made in-house by Lamborghini, an advance that marked his emergence as a bona fide automaker. The fact was not in dispute by the time of these Espadas and Isleros (above).

25

The Islero of '68 (top) was a big GT in the mold favored by Ferruccio, but dowdy styling deflated its desirability. More aesthetically successful was the Bertone-designed Jarama of '70 (opposite, top), which followed Islero as the 2 + 2 in Lamborghini's line. The most commercially viable model, however, was the Espada (right). It blended space for four with space-age styling and V-12 swiftness. Production began in '68 and continued for a decade. With 1,217 built, Espada was second in volume only to the Countach.

he succeeded. Even detuned to a claimed 270 bhp, his V-12 was superior to almost anything else in performance and refinement, while the all-independent suspension offered advances in both ride and handling.

Wallace, who test-drove and helped develop that original Lamborghini, remembers it fondly to this day: "Basically, Lamborghini himself wanted a very refined, high-speed, front-engined touring car. It reflected his own desires in a car, and I think it achieved what we all wanted. The car was extremely quick, and very, very quiet, and, for its day, was a very, very good-handling car. Whereas Ferrari was still building a very, very well-refined 1939 Chevy sort of thing. The difference was enormous. The difference in the weight of the cars, the way they handled—well, Ferrari was still playing around back then, still had his old live rear end and fairly crude old forged front suspension and the old, heavy

250-type chassis and so forth and so on.

"Oh, our car was not as well sorted out. There were the odd teething problems. Nothing major. Any car of this type, or any factory of this type, would have them. Even at Ferrari, the 275 series, the 330—you name it—had their teething problems. But the Lamborghini—shall we say design-wise—was a much, much more refined car. And the 350 would out-perform any of the then-current Ferraris by 20 kilometers an hour, just in performance alone."

Bear in mind that to Wallace, "performance" meant something more than mere standing-start acceleration, which was about all that most enthusiasts understood in speed-strangled America. In mid-'60s Europe, performance really did mean speed—top speed on public highways. Come to that, it still does, at least on the *Autobahnen* of Germany and much of the Italian *autostrada*.

The European driving public viewed the 350 GT much as Wallace did. There were detail manufacturing and reliability problems, and it wasn't quite the loveliest thing on the road, but it was notably quiet and well mannered. Ferruccio Lamborghini's first production car was generally well received. He was in business.

Other dreams floated around Sant'Agata in its earliest days: plans for eight-, six- and four-cylinder engines in cars of various sizes and types. But the 350's superb V-12 and basic front-engine chassis would remain Lamborghini's mainstay into the next decade. A year after introduction, the engine was raised to 3.9 liters and 320 bhp for a derivative 400 GT model. At the same time, Lamborghini started building its own transmissions and final-drive units. These, the 3.9 engine, revised bodywork and "+2" seating went into a range-expanding 400 GT 2+2.

In 1968 the same platform was topped by a new body to produce the rather blunt Islero. Two years later came its wedgy successor, the unibody Jarama. Neither was a hit, partly because of indifferent assembly quality by new body builders, though the chassis was becoming a bit dated by 1970 anyway.

Still, Lamborghini managed to stretch the life of this basic design by stretching it between wheel centers. It appeared along with the unfortunate Islero under the marvelous Espada, a ground-hugging GT with full four-place capacity. It was not only very fast but very attractive, with truly unique styling by the House of Bertone. There had never been anything like the Espada, and there has been little like it since. It was popular, too. In fact, the Espada arguably stands as Ferruccio's biggest commercial success.

The Miura was his greatest artistic success. Shown first as a bare prototype chassis in late 1965 and as a complete car early the next year, it was the most exotic road machine ever seen, decisively overshadowing every production Ferrari and quickly establishing itself as the favored hot rod of the rich and famous. Its competition-inspired design, particularly the unique mid-mounted transverse V-12, was the product of an enthusiastic—nay, fevered—collaboration between Dallara, Stanzani and Wallace, who were frankly hoping that this would be the one to take their company's colors onto the world's racetracks. But they were doomed to disappointment, for their boss was firm: Lamborghinis were road cars, and that was that.

But what a road car! Though the midships layout was already *de rigueur* for front-rank Formula 1 and Indianapolis racers, this was the first time it had ever been applied to a really powerful road machine. That

Lamborghini aimed to build faster, more refined GTs than Ferrari, and historians say he succeeded, at least at first. The ferocious Miura hardly fit his original **gran-turismo** *ideal. But today, Ferruccio says it was his favorite Lamborghini to drive.*

alone made the Miura the world's most technically advanced sports car. It also just happened to be the fastest one on the planet. And it was stunningly beautiful, thanks to the talents of another 24-year-old, Bertone's Marcello Gandini.

With the Miura, Lamborghini not only outdid all other automakers, he outdid himself. This was hardly the sort of car he'd started out to build. Hot and noisy inside, it wasn't very comfortable and, in the beginning at least, was as far from "perfect" as the GTV. Aerodynamic lift, for example, proved a problem near the incredible top speed of 170-plus mph. But more than any other, the

Miura was the car that established the Lamborghini name among motoring's greats—and Lamborghinis as cars to be reckoned with.

"The Miura basically was a car that got other people thinking, that forced Ferrari to do something new," observes Wallace. "As I've always said, the whole problem with the car is that it became a commercial success overnight. The factory was virtually forced to put out the car way, way before its logical development or its evolution was

ever, ever completed."

Like all too many Lamborghinis, the Miura was mechanically troublesome to begin with. It was finally debugged after constant fiddling and two formal redesigns, only to be yanked from production—a curious, capricious, and costly decision that began Lamborghini's decline as an automaker.

The Miura died in 1972 partly because Ferruccio's interest had. Although he still seemed to be climbing the ladder of success, having opened a fourth company to manufacture hydraulic equipment in 1969, the rungs had become rickety. Financial disaster struck when Bolivia cancelled a very large tractor order following a political upheaval there, forcing Ferruccio to sell off his first company. Then came labor unrest that plagued all of Europe but seemed particularly acute in Italy. Work stoppages and supply

disruptions began to cripple operations at the Lamborghini car plant, a plant whose health had never been particularly robust anyway.

Wallace, who was there, says lack of money was a chronic problem for every small Italian automaker: "All the factories, even Ferrari, pretty much struggled on from day to day, and it was only with the influx of Fiat money and the Fiat takeover [in 1969] that Ferrari survived, basically."

When it became clear that Lamborghini's son Antonio—"Tonino" to most—had no interest in the automobile business, Ferruccio must have begun to wonder why he was bothering. After all, he'd already proven his point: he'd turned out a GT car that was at least the equal of anything built anywhere in the world, and superior to most. It had been fun, too, but that factor had faded.

Today, Ferruccio maintains a small personal museum of Lamborghini cars at his estate in Italy's Umbria province (above). He also maintains vineyards that yield a deep-red wine called "Colli del Trasimento," or "Blood of the Miura" (below).

Moreover, this capitalist who was so very much a populist in his way, honored by his government for boosting the local economy, now saw pickets parading beyond his gate. So in 1972, while still working out the sale of Lamborghini Trattrice and strapped for cash, he accepted a bid for a controling 51-percent interest in Automobili Ferruccio Lamborghini by a businessman he knew from Switzerland, Georges-Henri Rossetti.

Many observers have speculated about Lamborghini's mood at the time, his motives for cancelling the Miura at its peak (Rossetti's role in this is unclear, but Bertone certainly urged it be continued), and the company's hour of greatest financial need. Only the man himself can say for sure. In any case, the last Miura was delivered in early '73. Later that year, Ferruccio sold the remainder of the car plant to another Swiss, Rene Leimer.

Neither of the new owners had any known background in the automobile field, and neither spent much time at Sant'Agata. Ferruccio stayed on for a while to run the place for them, but he was a *Cavaliere* now bereft of any real power. In 1974 he turned Lamborghini Bruciatori over to an administrator, put Tonino in charge of Lamborghini Oleodinamica (the hydraulic-equipment firm) and, at age 58, left the industrial world for good.

He retired to a vineyard near Perugia in the province of Umbria—the farmer's son returning finally to the soil whence he sprang. Today at his estate, La Florita—a lovely place graced by tennis courts, an Olympic-size pool, and a museum to house many of the cars he built—Ferruccio Lamborghini puts out a red wine called Colli del Trasimento, but known by everyone as "Blood of the Miura."

31

CHAPTER 4
Vanquished

Slang recognizes what formal language sometimes can't put its finger on. It's where we turn to express our most emotional circumstances, our earthiest feelings. And the real beauty of it is that slang can spring from a particular geographic region.

In Ferruccio Lamborghini's neighborhood there was a word that captured a certain sense of astonishment. It might be uttered in the presence of great power—a volcano, maybe, or the gait of a young woman. Those who first gazed upon Lamborghini's new supercar are said to have turned to this word. The word is Countach.

The Countach (say COON-tahsh) was already the most famous Lamborghini even before it went on sale. It's remained so ever since. Approaching 20 years from the day its primal shape first seared the world's eye, and no longer even in production, this outrageous land-based missile still literally stops traffic like no other car.

The spark for it was struck in 1968, when technical director Giampaolo Dallara left Lamborghini to pursue racing interests. Plant manager Paolo Stanzani took on the added role of chief engineer and set

about the painstaking refinement of Dallara's original Miura design, achieving virtual perfection with the 1971 Miura SV. That task completed, Stanzani, with so much control in his hands, must have begun to itch for something still better, something of his own.

Starting with a clean slate, Stanzani laid out a new supercar. It retained the Miura's midships format, but with the engine turned lengthwise for better weight distribution and improved shifting. The engine remained a V-12, of course, but was enlarged to 5.0 liters for more power. Suspension was altogether more modern. Last but not least was the strikingly futuristic, almost pyramidal styling, another triumph for Marcello Gandini.

The new Lamborghini was greeted with wild enthusiasm at the Geneva Salon in spring 1971. Surely, management thought, we won't be able to sell the Miura now that we've got this. But the Miura's execution was premature, for the complex new Countach wouldn't be production-ready for another three years.

Lamborghini had launched a number of other models in this

period, but none could really be described as successes. Take the Urraco. The result of an ill-advised interest in lower-cost, smaller-displacement GTs typified by Ferrari's mid-engine V-6 Dino and Porsche's rear-engine flat-six 911, it was a pretty and pleasant little mid-engine V-8 car. But to quote Bob Wallace, the Urraco was "overweight and underpowered"—by which he meant that it just didn't perform like a "real" Lamborghini. Unfortunately, it was very much a real Lamborghini in its initial teething troubles, which took years of heavy capital spending to eradicate. Yet, the company's new Swiss owners, Georges-Henri Rossetti and Rene Leimer, pressed on, committing a great deal of money on the Urraco idea to achieve highly unrealistic production goals. A redesigned engine and a conceptual rethink ultimately led to a pair of targa-top successors, the Silhouette in 1976 and the evolutionary Jalpa of 1981, but neither was any more successful. Today, the V-8 project is widely regarded as having nearly sunk the troubled company in the late 1970s.

The Cheetah was an even more curious aberration. For some reason, Lamborghini's owners became

enamored of the military market in 1977, deciding to build a series of fast and fabulously expensive off-road vehicles for an American outfit named Mobility Technology International. The first of these dune buggies had a Chrysler V-8, but later ones were powered by enormous V-12s designed for powerboat racing. These brutal behemoths made the same sort of impact on desert denizens that the Countach did on pavement peelers. Not too surprisingly, armies didn't show as much interest as the public, and the Cheetah was reoriented for the civilian market. But it, too, was a costly program that Lamborghini could ill-afford.

So was another 1977 adventure, this time with BMW. The German automaker had a mid-engine GT of its own, the M1, conceived mainly for production-class racing, and an imminent homologation deadline prompted its decision to farm out body construction to Lamborghini. But Lamborghini management used BMW's money, as well as a

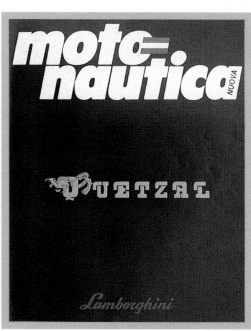

Lamborghini mainstays through good times and bad were the LM002 4x4 and the Countach, shown outside the factory in 1990 (opposite), and opened to the world in '75 (top). Winning V-12 marine engines also were one of the few constants (above).

substantial grant from a still-hopeful
Italian government, for the Cheetah
and perhaps other things. The
upshot was failure to meet BMW's
delivery dates, so the M1 contract
was yanked back.

It was a dismal hour. Most of
Lamborghini's money and all of its
credit were gone. So were its
"founding fathers"; Stanzani and a
disgusted Wallace had left in 1975,
though Dallara was back on the
scene, but only as a sometime
consultant. Meantime, labor-union
troubles continued.

Rossetti and Leimer launched into
desperate and by some accounts
rather inept negotiations to refinance
or sell the struggling company.
Canadian petroleum baron and loyal
Lamborghini fan Walter Wolf was a
prospect, as were various oil-rich
Middle East sheiks and, at one
stage, even British automaker Aston
Martin. But all these talks fell
through and in August 1978, the
once-great Automobili Ferruccio
Lamborghini was declared legally
insolvent by the Tribunale di
Bologna, the bankruptcy court in
charge, which installed a local
accountant named Alessandro
Artese to manage things.

This actually turned out to be a
positive step. Italian historian
Stefano Pasini notes that Artese was
"a leading expert with experience of
similar appointments with other
companies, and a car fan as well,
and thus exactly the right person to
realize Lamborghini's potential...."
Artese wasted no time. He retained
sales director Ubaldo Sgarzi and
brought in Giulio Alfieri from
Maserati to take over as technical
chief. Artese used his cost-cutting
knife to pare the aging Espada from
production, and he approved
development of the charismatic
Countach into an even more
wondrous S model, including an
emissions-control system to qualify
its engine for the lucrative U.S.
market. "The results were
immediate," says Pasini, "with a
definite upturn in the company's
fortunes toward the end of the year."

Still, the Italian court knew it
didn't belong in the automobile

Scrambling to jump-start sagging sales, Lamborghini's new Swiss owners shelved the Urraco for a targa-topped two-seater on the same platform. The Silhouette of 1976-78 (top) found only a few dozen buyers, but the derivative Jalpa (above, left) bowed in '82 and survived into 1988. Brochure aimed at Middle Eastern customers (above, right) introduced the Cheetah 4x4. Just one was built, but its LM002 descendent lives on.

business and began casting about for someone to buy this one. First to fall into the net was Hubert Hahne, former ace race driver and more recently the Lamborghini distributor for Germany. Hahne teamed with fellow countrymen Raymond Neumann and Klaus Steinmetz in late 1979 to acquire all stock from the Swiss partners and take over the Sant'Agata plant. Luckily, this was on a trial basis only. Neumann, at least, seemed interested only in pillaging what resources remained, and the court refused to complete the transfer of ownership. With that, Automobili Ferruccio Lamborghini was placed in liquidation on February 28, 1980.

"This was the worst period of Lamborghini's history," moans Pasini, not least because Countach production was down to "a trickle." It wasn't for lack of eager buyers with money but for lack of money for the factory to buy components. "It really seemed that the company had no future."

That Lamborghini has since come back from the brink is a monument to the stubborn determination and hard work of a handful of people who simply refused to let it die. Sgarzi and Alfieri were among those who kept the doors open, partly by taking on contract work for other automakers, such as Fiat. Meanwhile, two of their big Italian distributors boldly invested in the

future by actually buying Countachs before they were built.

And Bertone, despite past bitterness over unpaid bills, ran up a show car on the V-8 chassis. It was called Athon—"Hymn to the Sun." Derived from the name of the ancient Egyptian sun god, the appellation was especially appropriate for a neatly innovative little convertible that focused the public spotlight on Lamborghini in its darkest hour. More importantly, the Athon seemed to signal that the sun would indeed shine again on Lamborghini.

That sun rose in France. During the spring of 1980, an enthusiastic 24-year-old named Patrick Mimran approached the *Tribunale* about acquiring Lamborghini. As the court's investigation revealed, he was no fly-by-night dreamer. His family was extremely successful in a variety of commercial and industrial holdings, and inquiries made to the appropriate Swiss banks about the Mimran credit line came back with the answer ''*illimite*''—unlimited.

With a sigh of relief, the Bologna court incorporated a new firm, Nuova Automobili Ferruccio Lamborghini S.p.A., in July 1980. The Sant'Agata factory was turned over on a lease basis to Patrick Mimran, who would be the new firm's president, and his older brother Jean-Claude, who would continue as an outside advisor.

Under the direction of trusted deputy Emil Nuvaro, the Mimrans pumped in money, stepped up Countach assemblies, and assigned Bertone to design the Jalpa evolution of the Urraco/Silhouette. They even revived the Cheetah off-road idea, putting Alfieri to work on a series of improvements that were given type numbers beginning with the letters LM.

All this positive activity, as well as young Patrick's readiness to put his money where his mouth was, won the court's full endorsement. At an auction held on May 23, 1981, Mimran was the only bidder to appear, but nevertheless indicated that he had no intention of haggling over the price, and the company was his.

Over the next six years, Lamborghini was slowly and carefully put back on its feet. The Countach benefited from a series of engine improvements, culminating in a revised 5.2-liter unit with new cylinder heads hosting a grand total of 48 valves. The factory even found the time and money to play with possible Countach successors, including a prototype that looked very familiar outside but was full of advanced space-age materials inside. Meanwhile, the 3.5-liter Jalpa settled into its little-sister role, and the LM-series, with an all-new V-12 of no less than 7.0-liters, was readied for production. A four-door design

Master coachbuilder Nuccio Bertone poses with the Silhouette-based Athon around the time of its 1980 Turin debut **(opposite).** The show car was a partisan's demonstration of faith in a Lamborghini brought to the brink of death by inept management and other troubles. The car's name was derived from an Egyptian word meaning ''Hymn to the Sun.'' As it turned out, the future was indeed brighter, with such luminaries as the Countach, shown above in 25th Anniversary dress, and the LM002 V-12 off-roader **(right),** fostering a Lamborghini renaissance.

study of a long-awaited Espada successor was built, too.

Then, in 1987, a surprise, as the Mimran Group sold Lamborghini to none other than the Chrysler Corporation of Highland Park, Michigan. This was merely the latest round in a Detroit rivalry that had begun in late '85, when Chrysler invested in Maserati, with an option to buy a controlling interest. General Motors joined in a year later by acquiring Lotus in England (and since has established a partnership with Sweden's Saab). Ford Motor Company, not to be left out, took over Aston Martin at the end of '87 and Britain's Jaguar in '89.

Of course, one-upmanship wasn't Chrysler's sole motivation for buying Lamborghini. The Countach was certainly a tangible asset, as was the LM off-roader. And there was the undeniable prestige and excitement that still accrued to the charging-bull.

Chrysler, which underwent its own near-death and resurrection not so long ago, has thus far shown a great deal of enthusiasm for Lamborghini—including a pledge to its independence of both management and product. And with funds from the U.S. firm now in its coffers, Lamborghini's prospects are

even brighter than they were under the Mimrans. Diablo, the ultra-exotic 200-mph V-12 Countach successor, bowed in 1990. Due to replace the Jalpa in the early '90s is an all-new two-seater with a mid-mounted V-10.

Moreover, Chrysler capital has allowed Lamborghini to go racing for the first time in its history. Bolstered by a cadre of former Ferrari racing talent, Lamborghini engineers designed and built a V-12 for Formula 1. The 3.5-liter engine debuted in a pair of Lola chassis in 1989 and also powered two Lotus chassis in '90. An expected plague

of teething problems combined with Formula 1's cutthroat competition to keep the Lamborghini-powered cars well down in the points in their first two seasons, but all evidence indicates that the skill, commitment, and money needed to win is there.

So, 40 years after Ferruccio Lamborghini finished the Mille Miglia in an *osteria*, his name is again officially linked with competition—this time at the highest level. And at La Fiorita, perhaps, grow grapes for a wine that one day will spray the crowd in honor of a Lamborghini world championship.

Lamborghini and Chrysler celebrated their
1987 union with the Portofino show car
(below). *It foreshadows future Chrysler
four-doors rather than any charging-bull
sedan. Chrysler contributed detail work,
but the Diablo of 1990,* **(above)** *is the
essence of Lamborghini, from scissor doors
to the exquisite 5.7-liter V-12* **(opposite, top).**

Ferruccio Speaks

Ferruccio Lamborghini lives in Bologna with his second wife, Maria Theresa—21-years his junior—and their teenage daughter. Weekdays are spent at La Fiorita, a lush, 740-acre estate a few miles south of Lake Trasimeno. Lamborghini bought the land after selling his automobile factory in the mid 1970s and established there a vineyard and one of Italy's most modern wineries, from which flow 800,000 bottles annually. Ferruccio's latest enterprise is development of a golf course and an attendant recreational complex. He's also busy with the prototype of a golf cart of his own design. And Lamborghini was reported to be a behind-the-scenes ally of Paolo Stanzani in Stanzani's unsuccessful bid to take over Bugatti Automobile SpA.

Lamborghini was interviewed for this book by Mirco Decet, an Anglo-Italian photojournalist. Their meeting was in October, 1990, when Ferruccio was 74 years of age. Decet traveled from his home in Great Britain, arriving at La Fiorita after dark and in the rain. He discovered **Il Cavaliere** *aboard a tractor in a muddy field, leveling ground for his golf links. Approaching the machine, Decet said he noticed that Ferruccio ''seemed in some kind of trouble, and there were one or two lightweight Italian curses coming from the cab. It soon became apparent that he did not know the whereabouts of the (windshield) wipers and was grovelling in the dark to find anything that looked mildly like a wiper switch. I believe the cursing may have gotten stronger, but suddenly there came a cry of, 'ecco le qua (here they are!),' and all seemed in order.''*

Later, in an office overlooking a courtyard, a relaxed Ferruccio made small talk over coffee. ''He instantly made me feel at home, making comments like, 'Fire away with whatever you want, you've come a long way,' '' Decet said. After a brief tour of the estate buildings, including a small personal museum for Lamborghini cars and tractors, Ferruccio directed his visitor to an inn in the nearby village of Panicarola. ''He instructed me to a restaurant called 'La Cascina,' where, if I mentioned that he had sent me, they would feed me and give me a room for the night,'' Decet said.

Next morning, Ferruccio sat for the interview and posed for photos. Answering between draws on one of his frequent cigarettes, he was direct, jovial, and gracious—a patriarch satisfied with the world. ''He could easily be far more important in the hierarchy of Italian life,'' Decet noted. ''But here was a pleasant man who decided that all he needed was peace of mind and pleasure in what he was doing. That, it seems, is what he has.''

Q—During your life you have driven many different cars. Which one of these cars was your favorite?

A—Quite honestly, I would have to say Ferrari. No particular one—just Ferrari. They had 12 cylinders, were very powerful, very fast, and fun to drive. Ferrari is certainly the car I have had most fun with. Of course, they too have their faults.

Q—Is it true that you started making your own cars because Enzo Ferrari would not listen to you when you had a problem with one of his cars?

A—Yes. What actually happened was that we both were hardheaded in those days. We both got heated and so I started my own car company. The thing was, you see, I had some problems with the clutch on the

car. Every time I wanted to accelerate from standstill the clutch would take a bit of a beating and would smoke and smell. In no time it would wear out. I decided to confront Ferrari with this problem. His reply was that I only knew how to drive tractors and that I should stick to driving them. I was mad at this and said I would go and fix it myself, at which point he laughed. This made me even madder and so I told him that I would go and build my own car. And that is what I did. Before this though, I went home and took the clutch out of the Ferrari. To my surprise it was a Borg and Beck, the same type of clutch that I was using in my tractors. So what I did was replace it with the largest clutch I had. The car never gave me any further problem.

Q—Which Lamborghini was your favorite to drive?

A—The Miura. It was a very popular car. We used to ask for all the money up front and then build the car for the customer. It usually took 14 months.

Q—The Countach, when it came to the end of its run, was a very different car than it had started out as. It had a wing and all manner of flares added on. Was it still the car you had intended it to be?

A—It was still the car it started out as. All that was done was that a few bits were added and the engine was uprated. In fact, the four-valve-per-cylinder head was there at the beginning, but it just was not the fashion to have a four-valve-per-cylinder head, so we made do with the two valve. We could have put (digital instrumentation) in the car, but it would have cost so

much that in the end we decided just to put in the usual dials and instruments. The wing was put on later. Again it became a fashionable thing, just like the era of the turbos.

Q—Have you driven the Diablo?

A—Yes. They sent one down to me here in the country. I kept it for a day, and I was quite satisfied. I think the one I tried was too new to make a complete assessment, but I would say that I thought the Countach was slightly lighter to drive. As for the rest of the car, I was very impressed.

Q—Getting back to the older cars: The first few cars that you produced were luxury-oriented, not out-and-out sports cars. Then there seemed to be a sudden change with the Miura, a two seater, almost a sheer racer.

A—These first...cars were certainly sports cars. They were cars that competed in the market with the Ferraris of then. The 350 was born to compete with the Ferrari. Right from the beginning I had intended to build fast sports cars, be they 2+2 or two seater. And we must not forget the Espada. That was a good sports car for four persons and plenty of room for baggage. We had a lot of requests for this car. All the cars that I have wanted to build have been two seaters, though. All the cars that I have had—Ferraris, Mercedes, etc.—they were all two seaters...You also must realize that if there had been no Lamborghini, Ferrari would not have been improved. Competition like this is always good. Lamborghini made Ferrari get better.

Q—Getting to the Urraco, many people say that it wasn't as well made as the others, and also that it was underpowered. What do you say about this?

A—I wouldn't totally agree with that. The new owners of Lamborghini made the Urraco and also that other car, which was basically a Uracco, the Silhouette. A lovely little car, eight cylinders, well priced car. I believe they went well. I have one in my collection.

Q—Why didn't you get involved with motorsport? Was it because of the danger—were you were worried that perhaps your son would get involved?

A—No, I have never wanted to be involved in racing. As far as I can see, if you produce a car that the public is happy with, what is the point of spending millions of lire going racing? I was always being asked for specials, like the Miura Le Mans, or similar. Quite honestly, I was not interested. My son had nothing to do with my decision. If you look at racing today, there are probably four top men; the rest are just followers. What is the point of spending all that money to be a follower? Besides we did not need to go racing.

Q—There is a theory that the V12 you used was partly designed by Honda. How true it this?

A—The V12 was born at the Lamborghini factory, designed by Lamborghini designers and technicians. These technicians are now at the Bugatti works. It is they who have designed the new V12 Bugatti engine.

Q—Talking of Bugatti, how are you involved with that company?

A—I have been asked to be a consultant. I would like to say, though, that without saying any bad about anybody, I think that the new Bugatti engine is probably ten years ahead of anything around at the moment. Its mechanics are at the forefront of motoring technology...All their mechanical parts for the engine are lightweight materials. The engine they are producing will weigh almost half that of the Miura.

Q—Who is responsible for this new engine?

A—Well...certainly Stanzani is foremost in my mind. As I said, all the technicians that were at Lamborghini are at Bugatti now.

Q—Do you ever return to the Lamborghini

factory? Do you still have friends there?

A—I used to go on very rare occasions. But since they heard that I was involved with Bugatti, things obviously are a little difficult. It's understandable.

Q—Has there been anything in your life that you would like to change?

A—No. I have enjoyed everything that I have done. I am very happy. I have always worked hard: built up five factories, of which two I sold. Then I came here and built up this place, and I am very happy to continue doing this.

Q—What is your son doing these days?

A—My son is in Japan. He has several clothes shops there, all of which have the Lamborghini mark. I have nothing to do with it, though. They are his shops and his concern.

Q—It seems that you have always had good people around you: Good designers, technicians, etc.

A—Yes, I have. The way I have done that is by going out and getting the best. If you want to produce a good product, you need to have the best people producing it. Sometimes I have had to rob them from elsewhere. There was, I remember, a Swiss journal that had a photo of me on its front cover with the title of "Il ladrone dei uomini (The Thief of Men)."

Q—And for the future, are you going to be concentrating on your new golf course?

A—Yes, I plan to open the golf course in spring of next year. This is a unique course and will have a section fenced off for those people who are interested in playing but cannot afford to learn. There will be no charge for learning.

Q—Many people at your age would be happy to relax and put their feet up. What keeps you going?

A—While I can and while I am able, I will keep working and doing things that I get satisfaction from. If you just stop, well, you might as well just give up and say good-bye.

Lamborghini's vineyard estate in north-central Italy is a tourist haven, a working winery, and base for a unique entrepreneurial intellect.

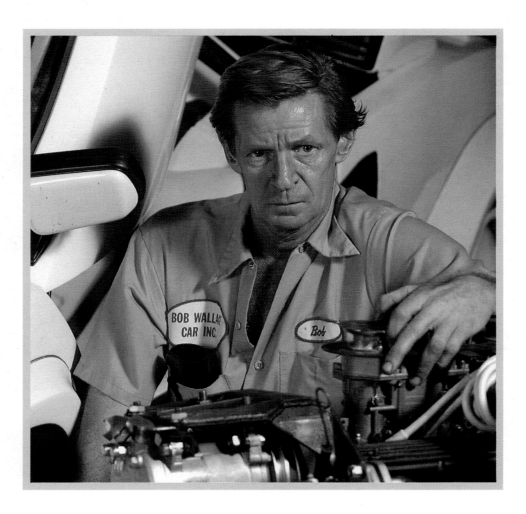

CHAPTER 5
"The Best Job in the World"

No one had a greater influence on how the original Lamborghinis felt than a taciturn New Zealander on an odyssey in the land of Italian exotics. Today, Bob Wallace's dour manner brightens when he recalls those ebullient early days of Lamborghini, when an all-star cast of young enthusiasts unreined their automotive passions and the cars of the charging bull rocked the motoring world. But the veil returns when he talks of the fate of his most beloved Lamborghinis, of promise unfulfilled, of miscalculation and wasted opportunity, of aim untrue.

There is no sign. Bob Wallace Cars in Phoenix, Arizona, presents a completely anonymous exterior—just a plain, single-story building among dozens on a quiet, tree-shaded street in a modern industrial park

just south of Sky Harbor Airport. Even once you've found the place, nothing confirms your success but the back door, and only if it's open, and then only if there happens to be coming from it the inimitable muffled growl of a thoroughbred Italian V-12.

You walk in to find a clean, well-lit, orderly establishment, filled with gleaming machine tools, brightly colored cranes and containers, sleek *gran turismo* bodies—and seeming mountains of gorgeous all-aluminum overhead-cam engines. There he is, familiar from so many years of magazine photos, bending over the open hood, hair blowing in the draft from the engine fan. Still wearing an intent frown, he straightens up to meet your intrusion and you see his name on the blue mechanic's shirt.

Now in his early 50s, Wallace is still a lean, lanky individual with a tendency to constant activity. He has faded sandy hair, pale-blue eyes set amidst knobby features, and a deepish, gravelly voice with an unrepentant New Zealand accent. He speaks slowly, but there's an obvious impatience—even a crustiness—to his manner.

Sensibly approached, however, he'll take time to talk about the old days. And as the memories begin to flow, he'll break into a wry, shy

As chief development driver for the company's first 12 years, New Zealander Bob Wallace (above) shaped the road manners of early Lamborghinis. Today, he owns an exotic-car service center in Phoenix.

smile, maybe even an engaging, open grin. Sometimes it's the unmistakable racer's grin, sly and savage. "Oh, yeah." he'll tell you, his eyes alive with it. "I had the best job in the world!"

As Lamborghini's test and development driver for a dozen years, Wallace is the man who, more than any other, stamped his personality on Lamborghini cars. An Aucklander by birth, he grew up fascinated by cars and racing. At 21 he journeyed all the way to Italy to be among the most passionately enthusiastic racers on earth, working as a racing mechanic for Ferrari, Maserati, Count Volpe's Scuderia Serenissima and Lucky Casner's Camoradi U.S.A. He was with Casner when the flamboyant American's "Birdcage" Maserati won the 1000-kilometer race at the Nurburgring in 1960 and again in '61.

At the end of the 1963 racing season, Wallace was weighing options. He'd been asked back to Ferrari, but he'd just heard about that new auto factory opening up at Sant'Agata and it sounded more interesting. "I thought there was much more opportunity to learn something there, and I took it."

Wallace joined Lamborghini just as the buildings had been completed and the first of the ultramodern manufacturing equipment was being installed. Ferruccio had already shown his prototype GTV and was now working hard to turn it into the series-built 350 GT. Wallace was hired as a mechanic and, as he says, "a troubleshooter." He helped ready the Lamborghini V-12 for production and assisted in assembling the first production cars.

That Wallace became the factory's test-driver seems to have just happened; remarkable, seeing as how he had little serious experience as a race driver. "I used to fool around with race cars as a kid. I've practiced on pretty much all of the world's circuits. I worked for Volpe for a while with a lot of the young Italian drivers—[Lorenzo] Bandini, [Lodovico] Scarfiotti and people like that. You'd get the job to take the car out before the race or the hillclimb and make sure everything is right, and if you do it for one you've gotta do it for the next guy, and it just sort of snowballs.

"Some idiot gave me a helmet in night practice at Sebring one year. He said, 'Go and see what's wrong with the thing.' It just started from there. I never really intended to pursue it, but then I got pushed into it full-time at Lamborghini. I

Wallace's most famous hot rod was his ultra-light Miura Jota (below). He modified the 3.9-liter V-12 (bottom) to give 418 bhp at 8800 rpm and fit wide tires and a race-car suspension, but never raced it.

inherited the job; I didn't really want it initially. My first years were quite interesting."

Bob "got pushed into it" because there wasn't anyone else, but he soon showed a flair for high-speed vehicle evaluation. Before he knew it, he was the de facto factory test pilot and eventually had four men working under him.

And it was in that role that he quite literally molded the character of every new Lamborghini introduced up to the mid-'70s. "We'd take a prototype car out and first of all evaluate what its actual possibilities were, and come back to

the design office with an initial list of suggested changes or whatever we felt was necessary.

"Not that I was in charge of the personality of the car, but it usually just ended up that way. Yeah, I was the development driver and, good or bad, you get some credit. But some of the mistakes were mine, too. You've got to remember, we were a bunch of very, very enthusiastic young kids."

He recalls that a typical day of test-driving began at 5:30 or 6:00 in the morning and lasted until about 3:00 in the afternoon. During those hours he'd range the entire length

The only Wallace-modified Lamborghini to race was the Rally Urraco, seen in an intermediate stage at left and in final form above. Built from a prototype of the 2 + 2, it was a two-seater lightened by aluminum panels, stiffened by a roll cage (opposite left) and eventually powered by a four-valve, 310-bhp version of the V-8 (opposite right).

and breadth of northern and central Italy. One day he might flash down to Rome or Naples on the *autostrada* at 130, 150, 170 mph. On another he might turn up into a twisting mountain road a lane-and-a-half wide, laying rubber around myriad bends that had once served the storied Mille Miglia. Some days he'd drive to a closed race course like Misano or Varano and spend hours sliding around in studied abandon. Occasionally he'd encounter one of his counterparts from Ferrari or Maserati and there would ensue a little gentlemanly contest—followed,

no doubt, by an hour at a cheery roadside *ristorante.*

"When you'd get back in the afternoon, you'd spend the rest of the time in the office or hashing over the problems with the design office, mainly. The rest of the time playing around. It was a unique opportunity, and probably a very, very unique job. The big problem was too much to do and normally never enough time to do it."

So he worked more than a typical eight-hour day? "Oh, yeah. Yeah." And he was probably in there on weekends, too? "Yeah. Oh, yeah."

So he didn't have any spare time for hobbies or anything else? "No. Spare time I used to play around with odds and ends of cars. Like the Italians said, I married the automobile. *'Aye sposato l'automobile.'*

"Initially, when everything was first laid down, everything was the most modern equipment, the best equipment you could buy. It was a very, very clean, very, very well laid-out plant. At that time—in '63, '64—Ferrari was *struggling* on with some of the stuff dating back to before the war, old machine tools. They basically had the same money problems that anybody else had.

"Whereas we didn't lack anything, and playing around with any of the oddball special cars that I built up in the evenings and on the weekends, I had virtually the full use of the equipment that the factory had. Very, very pleasing, very satisfying job."

Satisfying as few of us can even imagine. For in a manner not unlike that of the Renaissance masters and

their wealthy patrons, Bob Wallace was being paid by one of Europe's top industrialists to create automotive works of art to please, essentially, himself. When he set out with a new car, Wallace didn't have to think about its eventual buyer. "No, we never, ever developed a car or did any testing with a customer point of view in mind. Basically, it was what I thought the car should be. Oh, yeah. That's the only way any car can have any personality."

Such a job would have been remarkable enough in one's native land, but this Kiwi was working half-a-world away from his in what to him was a very foreign culture. "I didn't speak a word of Italian when I first got to Italy. It took me about two years, two-and-a-half years, to learn. It took at least the same time to be accepted there. They do not accept strangers very easily, especially someone like myself. When you boss someone around, you've got to be accepted and usually liked by them. But once they had seen that I worked just as hard as they did, and there was no BS and no problems and no sort of pulling rank anywhere, I got on very, very well with them."

He also "got on" very well with the boss, whom most respectfully addressed as *Cavaliere*. "I just called him Ferruccio," Bob says.

"Being a foreigner had its advantages in the fact that mainly I didn't have to follow the usual Italian bureaucratic way of doing things. If I had to, I'd bypass anyone and everyone. [That sometimes] created some hard feelings amongst the engineers, but normally it didn't create any problems at all. People would look at something I did and

shrug, because I was a foreigner. You know, I could pretty much get away with murder."

Lamborghini myth has become so intertwined with the truth that the two often are hard to separate. Wallace is the right man to solve some of the puzzles. As he freely admits, "I've never been noted for diplomacy."

For instance, what about Ferruccio Lamborghini's alleged love of the Spanish *corrida?* "Naw, that's a bunch of bull. That was probably something a PR man came up with. I don't remember who started those series of names—Miura, Espada and all this sort of thing. I think it was probably somebody in the PR department at Bertone or something like that."

What sort of driver was Ferruccio? Didn't he have a long string of exotic cars? "Oh, yeah. Anyone in his position as an industrialist would have. [But he was] a mediocre driver. A little rough and heavy-handed. Not a quick driver, and very, very sort of mediocre."

Was that in any way reflected in the cars? "No, no. He did not interfere in any way at all. He wanted to know the whys and wherefores of everything, but he never, ever interfered with the actual work in the factory."

Wallace takes fast driving seriously—after all, he did it for hundreds of miles every day—and is thus not easily given to ladling out praise. He strongly feels that there aren't many people—particularly many journalists—qualified to pass judgment on a very fast car's handling at its outer limits. To the glowing test reports on some of the heavier front-engine 2 + 2s, which he

still considers poor examples of the Lamborghini marque, he snorts, "Maybe they should have taken it to a racetrack and pushed it hard. A lot of motoring journalists could be much more critical than they are."

He might have been more diplomatic then than he realizes now, because he knew many magazine writers and all seemed to have liked and respected him. At most car companies, those in a position like Wallace's don't normally have much contact with either the public or press. But journalists found Lamborghini a very open-door place in those days, and most had a great deal of contact with the chief development driver. They went for very fast rides with Wallace, and most worked his name into their stories, usually in glowing terms.

Well, there was an exception or two. One French journalist felt a trifle less than glowing about a certain test-drive Wallace set up in a Miura—a rather special Miura, as it turned out.

Lamborghini was hardly the first automaker to cherish "good press," considering it important that motor-noters be impressed with its cars' performance. No surprise, then, that the firm occasionally proffered "special" press cars. Wallace admits as much: "Some of the road tests you can read way, way back, you can see they did not have a standard engine in half of the journalists' cars. That's off the record, but . . . ."

Jose Rosinski, a talented writer as well as an experienced racer (Wallace ranks him with Paul Frere as one of the few journalists who could really drive well), came down to Italy to

45

Wallace, shown above in his Arizona shop, left Lamborghini in 1975 disaffected by the low morale under its new Swiss owners. It's the "mental stimulation" of his Sant'Agata days he misses.

test a Miura for *Sport Auto,* the French enthusiast magazine. He climbed in and set off down the local superhighway for some top-speed runs.

"We clocked him at 288 k's an hour," recounts Bob, a glint of humor beginning to twinkle in the corner of each eye. That's 179 mph, Miura fans, but it wasn't enough to satisfy the factory man. He told Rosinski to come back in the morning and try harder.

Jose did. "He came out from an underpass on the freeway, and it caught a three-quarter gust of wind, and the whole car—the whole nose—lifted. The thing took off. All he could see was the sky." How high did he go? "I don't know. I never asked the guy. He's never spoken to me since."

Why? Did he think you were to blame? "Oh, yeah," The Wallace face begins to twist in one of those fierce

racer's grins. "He'd run the car before at 288, and we'd stuffed another engine in it with, I think it was about another 30, 40 horsepower more, and we didn't have time to try it. We just said, 'Here, take it out again today.' And he logically wasn't aware of this. He thought he was just driving a straight-off-the-shelf production Miura.

"And it did fly. When he came back to the factory he was still white. I don't know how he got the car down, or how the car settled down onto the ground still tracking decently." Sounds like a close call. "Very, very close." The 288 was done with a standard engine? "No." So you had a trick engine and a super-trick engine? "Aw, we had whatever you wanted."

A short laugh escapes him. "The name of the game with everyone there was to pick out the most attractive-colored car to photograph and back it up onto the assembly line and just tell the journalist and his photographer, 'Well, you pick out whichever one you want to drive.' And they'd all pick that one. The same thing went on at Ferrari. The same thing went on everywhere, so we were nothing

different."

A story that used to make the rounds in those days of open-road testing was that certain kilometer-stones along the *autostrada* were spaced a trifle less than a full 1000 meters apart, and would therefore indicate an artificially high speed if used for timing. "No. That's not true. No, we had a big enough variety of engines lying around that you didn't need to do that."

Fun-and-games was all very well, but there was a serious side to Wallace's job, for accidents and high-speed mechanical failures were not uncommon. The compact mid-V-8 Urraco emerged from one of the more troubled development programs: "On road testing I broke the first five engines, all within 5000 miles of each other. Oh, yeah, you'd get a crank that hopped out the side and rear subframes breaking and so forth and so on. Well, I'd complained the car was enormously overweight, and someone in the design office went stark raving mad and built up these real light subframes, and you had the radius rods pulling out and front uprights shearing off.

"In fact, I had a couple of journalists in a car once when we sheared a front upright up in the mountains and it was scary. Fifty yards of skid marks going toward the edge of the mountain and a thousand feet down the side of it, and...well, it was part of your job. It was what you were paid to do."

Were there other experiences like that? "Oh, yeah. A few bad crashes, but that was all part of it." Were the crashes largely due to mechanical breakage? "Hmmm. I'd say 50 percent of them, yeah. Testing a Chrysler automatic and shifting it at seven-thousand-five, and it grabs the drive band and locks itself in the secondary band and you skid down the freeway 'til the case breaks itself open....Oh, it was a lot of fun."

He's really warmed to his subject and that wry smile is constant. "Or you have one of the prototype four-cam Urracos and it drops the head off a valve flat-out down the freeway and bounces it back out into the next carburetor, goes down inside, puts a rod through the side and the oil catches fire and you head for the tollgate. And the attendant, instead of dashing out with his fire extinguisher, leaves his booth, jumps over the fence and runs down farmer's fields.

"Or, the end-of-the-world prototype Countach large engine, which explodes and reduces itself to scrap metal when you're running flat-out down the freeway. All you can do is slow the car enough to undo your harness and get out of the thing and *let* it burn. Oh, an enormous number of mechanical breakages and problems. But that was your job."

What's this about an "end-of-the-world" engine? "Aw, they'd been doing an enormous amount of dyno-testing on this engine. It was putting out a substantial amount of power, and everything was fine according to the design office and the dyno shop. And you take the damn thing out and destroy it after half an hour." He snorts a laugh. "It didn't make people very happy, but there was no intentional destruction on my part. That was just what I was paid to do and what I felt the car should hold up as."

If the thought of flaming Lamborghinis streaking down public thoroughfares at insane velocities offends your sense of social responsibility, rest assured that such antics weren't that public. "With that first Countach, speed limits actually had started going up in Europe and we did most of the flat-out testing up on Fiat's private freeway, where you had all the equipment you

needed."

Private freeway? "Well, Fiat's a fairly influential company and [when] they built the Milan-Turin freeway....They built 30 miles beside it for their own use. There's a guardrail separating you from the Fiat 500s and that's it." The old-boy network, Italian style.

And then there's the Varano de Melagari circuit. It comes up while looking at a snapshot of a younger Wallace and the original Countach prototype in front of a house on a village street. Where was that picture taken, Bob? Were you on a trip somewhere? "No, just Dallara's hometown, where he had a little racetrack and we used to use it." Dallara had a little racetrack? "Oh, his father was the mayor, and the town council decided the city needed a racetrack. A little country village way up in the mountains. That's family influence. It was a real little dinky club-racing track. We used it because it didn't cost a dime and it was always available. You'd stop at Dallara's house and get the key."

Fun days, fun job. But it never lasts. "At first, everyone was motivated, everyone had a lot of enthusiasm. [Ferruccio Lamborghini would] get stuck in and work too. It was very, very enjoyable. The whole thing was really enjoyable up to, I'd say '71, '72. That's when it started to go bad."

The high point probably was the Miura program, when Ferruccio Lamborghini, Giampaolo Dallara, Paolo Stanzani, and Bob Wallace were still together, working on the

*In between the Jota and "Urraco Bob" was Wallace's Jarama hot rod (above). Aluminum and plastic got the fat out, extra welding got the rigidity up. The souped 3.9-liter V-12 was moved rearward slightly, the back seats were replaced by a fuel tank, and the suspension was modified. It was quick, but never raced. Wallace's dour manner can sometimes conceal his appreciation for what was "the best job in the world." His talent, forthrightness, and **cojones** won over the insular Italians. And when others respectfully said **Cavaliere**, "I just called him Ferruccio."*

car that would secure their company's reputation for all time. Dallara would be the first to depart, in 1968, but Lamborghini himself had started withdrawing by then, too. That was the reason Stanzani was elevated from second engineer to factory manager—and one of the reasons Dallara quit.

"See, Stanzani ended up having to do that job because someone had to do it, when Lamborghini himself said, 'No, I don't even want to hear about running this place anymore. One of you has to do it.' Stanzani stepped in and started doing it. Logically [it was] Dallara: one, he wanted to go racing, and secondly, it wasn't very nice to be working underneath your sort of junior engineer. No hard feelings, and there never have been, but he just decided to go out on his own, and that was the end of that." And the beginning of the end for the "fun."

Ferruccio's withdrawal was complete in another five years. "The factory was making money when he sold it. When the Miura started production, the factory became a money-making concern, and was right on through until basically he lost interest and the eight-cylinder program started. But his son didn't demonstrate any interest in the

company, didn't demonstrate the sort of following-on in the father's image that the old man really hoped for.

"Plus, [Ferruccio] was like a lot of other Italian postwar industrialists. They could govern their business empire up to a certain level, but they weren't an Agnelli [Gianni, head of Fiat] or a Ferrari or someone like that. They had their limitations. And things started getting out of control and he just lost interest. In his other companies, too, to a certain extent.

"The whole problem with the company actually, when Lamborghini himself abandoned it, was lack of money for research and development. Complete and utter lack of money, and also with the foreign owners, basically a lack of direction and where they really wanted to go."

Wallace is scathing about the first post-Lamborghini owners, though he stayed on and worked for them: "Basically I think a lot of their programs were way out of whack—trying to develop the small eight-cylinder cars, trying to go into a bigger market. The Swiss owners then didn't really take any great interest in the company or get very involved with it. Some very, very

"You'd stop at Dallara's house and get the key..." to the Varano test track (left). His three years spent developing the Countach (right) over thousands of high-speed miles on both highway and raceway were the culmination of Wallace's career with Lamborghini. He'd climb in the new mid-engine supercar or perhaps the Rally Urraco (above) and, starting at sunrise, range the length and breadth of Northern Italy, deep into triple-digit speeds on the **autostrada**, dancing on the edge of adhesion up twisty mountain roads. Sometimes he'd hunt down a Ferrari or a Maserati with **Prova** plates for an impromptu contest. "You've got to remember, we were a bunch of very, very enthusiastic young kids."

49

serious commercial, long-term planning and that sort of thing with the smaller cars virtually broke their wallet and actually finished the place off. Tooling up with enormous costs of tooling to build thousands of cars a year when the market just wasn't even there.

"The little Urraco—that car had tooling and body dies and stuff specially [made] to build thousands. All the dealers said, 'Oh yes, we can sell 500, 1000 in the U.S. alone.' And it just wasn't true. No, it was the wrong type of car for them to build. Different clientele, a different price range, and the car was basically, I think, what finally broke the company."

The man who left his mark on every Lamborghini built through '75 has firm opinions on the entire range, and his criticisms begin well before the change of owners. "Well, a 2 + 2 was a mistake. I think the first car, the 350, made a lot more sense than any of the other 2 + 2s or the mediocre cars that followed.

"Later on, the Isleros and Jaramas—someone's crazy marketing ideas. I don't think Lamborghini had—or still don't think they have—any commercial direction as to what the hell the market wants or what people really want. You're pushing these 2 + 2s off onto people with badly built bodywork. The quality of the creature comforts and the body construction and so forth was abominable. Just innumerable little things weren't right, and it takes a lot of money to put them right."

As for the Espada, Wallace judges it "a very, very good concept of car. I think if they'd refined it further, they could have continued on with it as sort of their big flagship four-seater. Let's face it, the car was a lot lighter than a big 400 Ferrari, it handled better, and it was a lot quicker.

"But you're faced with the same thing there, with that type of car, where customers came to expect a lot more: a lot better air

conditioning, a lot better defrosting, and a lot better creature comforts than what the factory was really—I won't say 'qualified'—but what they had the money to do. That type of car is the wrong type of car for a factory like that, really." And what is the right type? "A performance-type automobile and that's it. Mercedes and BMW can deal with the creature comforts a hundred times better than a place like that."

So Bob Wallace unabashedly favors the true high-performance Lamborghinis. He's got plenty of company, of course, but does he have any particular favorites among the cars he helped develop?

"Not really. The Countach, because I had a lot to do with the initial concept, and I really believed in the car when we first started building it. Yeah, basically it was conceived to go like, ah— performance was everything and that was it, no other considerations in the car. Over the years, seeing the way the car has changed from a performance image to a macho, ego-trip sort of image, it doesn't make sense anymore. The car's heavier than hell, and aerodynamically it's like pushing a barn door down the road. Personally, I don't have much enthusiasm for the car any more."

Not so the Miura, especially in its later forms, "mainly because it was, shall we say, a milestone car in what a GT car should be. The Miura was a car that got other people thinking, that forced Ferrari to do something new." As for the Urraco, Wallace calls it "overweight and underpowered, but probably the most nimble-handling car that we'd built in a long time. Nimble, because even though it was utilizing four-wheel MacPherson-strut suspension, it was quite well balanced. We put a lot of time and a lot of work into making the suspension work properly, and it did. It worked quite well."

Bob Wallace finally left Lamborghini when he saw he no longer had a future there. But it took a while, and a lot of miles, to find a new challenge. "I went home to New Zealand for about three months and died of boredom. When I first left Europe, I thought it would be nice to go back there, but

unfortunately I ended up being disappointed."

With his wife (the widow of Gioachino Colombo, the great Ferrari engine designer), he again went halfway round the world, this time to settle in Phoenix. He worked there for a little while at an exoticar repair/restoration shop, then set up one of his own, to be his own boss again. Today, Bob Wallace Cars caters to both Lamborghini and Ferrari owners from all over the country.

Why Phoenix? "Get out of the cold! And, plus, it's a very rich area and you can do anything you want here in Phoenix, because you've got a lot of small and medium places that work for the aircraft and airspace industry—high-tech shops and stuff like that. You can do pretty much anything you want here. Plus our labor costs here are pretty much about 25, 30 percent less than Southern California."

One of the things you can't do in Arizona—or anywhere else in the U.S.—is enjoy running a big Italian GT flat-out. Does Bob miss the kind of driving he used to do? "Not the driving. I miss the work. I'm 50 years old now, and I miss the type of work I used to do. The mental stimulation of doing something, rather than servicing someone's car."

His hands were back in that "work" for a time as Wallace and one of his good customers campaigned a Ferrari 308 modified for SCCA GT2 competition. Wallace co-owned the car with the customer, who was the driver. It apparently was the class of its class in southwestern club-racing circles. "It was on the minimum weight and there was nothing that came close to it handling-wise. Plus the engine: If you build them properly, they'll run forever. I just wish there was a little better competition around in GT2, really." Alas, Wallace ended his involvement with the project in late 1989 to concentrate his resources on his business.

Finally, it wouldn't be responsible to drop the curtain without asking Wallace about the Diablo. Here is the heir to Lamborghini's ultra-performance legacy, a legacy handed down from the Wallace-influenced Miura and Countach. Wallace had seen only photographs of the car,

and so was hesitant to pass judgment, though he wondered how many of Marcello Gandini's original lines survived after Chrysler's styling revisions.

Wallace was firm about what the car must do, however: combine performance, reliability, and comfort in a blend about which his generation of exoticar makers and buyers could only dream. "Times have changed so greatly that what was acceptable 20 or even 10 years ago today is not." To achieve such a symbiosis, he said, it is imperative for Lamborghini to wholly exploit Chrysler's research and development resources. He wondered, however, whether the American company had come on the scene too late in the Diablo project for that.

Wallace likened the Lamborghini-Chrysler marriage to the union of Fiat and Ferrari in 1969. It wasn't until 1983, with the four-valve 308 model, that Ferrari showed him it

had taken full advantage of Fiat's capital, he said. "It took Ferrari a long time after Fiat to get a sorted-out vehicle. Whether the Diablo is or not, I don't know. The ideas behind the car are good. Whether they work or not, I don't know."

There's a certain seasoned wisdom coursing though these remarks—that assembly quality and user friendliness are now exoticar ideals; that developmental resources are essential to achieving them; that a mid-engine supercar is indeed a most appropriate standard bearer for the Italian automaker; that without driving a Diablo, there can be no final judgment. What Bob Wallace learned at Lamborghini may be matched only by what he taught.

Bob Wallace Cars, 2302 East Magnolia, Phoenix, AZ 85O34; (602) 275-2543

CHAPTER 6
"Ferruccio's Folly:" 350 GTV

*Lamborghini knew what he liked in
an automobile and asked stylist
Franco Scaglione to come up with a
design that satisfied his desires.
The result was an incoherent
collection of automotive cliches
around a basically sound shape
(above).*

An appearance at one of the world's premier auto salons is the flame of life for a fledgling exoticar maker. But showing up with an unfinished product can be the kiss of death. Ferruccio Lamborghini's debut at the Turin show in late October 1963 was mostly of the latter circumstance. His 350 GTV was unrefined in design and hastily built. It contained no engine. The debacle probably would have snuffed out the chances of anyone with smaller dreams...or thinner resources.

Lamborghini was as image-conscious as any automaker, so it's difficult to fathom just why he unveiled his first effort before it was complete—as he would do time and again in subsequent years. Perhaps he felt pressured to get income flowing. As Bob Wallace points out: "Your appearance at a major auto show is worth millions in publicity value." Maybe it was Ferruccio's innate naivete, simple open-heartedness, or perhaps the bursting enthusiasm of a bona fide "car guy."

Whatever the reason, the GTV's premature showing must have done some harm from a commercial standpoint. But it also reflected the fledgling firm's motivating spirit: It revealed the emotion of the adventure.

This farmer's son had gone into the automobile business to realize a dream: a GT "without faults," he had said, "a perfect car." It was hardly that, but the GTV ("V" for *veloce*: fast) oozed excitement, enthusiasm, and ambition. Lamborghini simply couldn't wait to show it off, a feeling car enthusiasts everywhere could understand.

And just how would you design a "perfect" GT in 1963? What was out there to improve on?

Actually, the opposition was not vast. The main players in this game were those two great Italian marques, Ferrari and Maserati. Each offered two-seaters and 2+2s that were spacious and plush enough to be comfortable on long trips, fast enough to shorten those trips significantly in a Europe still free of speed limits outside major cities, and costly enough to make one's arrival an event. Mid-year brought a new Aston Martin from England, the DB5, complete with lightweight *Superleggera* bodywork by Touring of Italy.

And that was about it. Alfa Romeo and Lancia, Jaguar with its curvaceous E-Type, Mercedes, Porsche, Chevrolet with its new '63 Corvette Sting Ray, and perhaps Carroll Shelby with his Cobra were

Only one 350 GTV prototype was built, and it was a show model with a crate of ceramic tiles in place of an engine (above). Displayed separately was its V-12, here seen in the square-tube chassis that succeeded the round-tube version used by the prototype (left). The vertical carburetor setup probably would not have fit under the hood and it wasn't used in the later production car.

all making worthy high-performance cars, but none had the blend of size, speed, and sex appeal that spoke to Ferruccio Lamborghini.

Ferrari was naturally his main target. Then 65, Enzo Ferrari had devoted much of his life to racing. He'd been a driver in the 1920s and manager of the great independent Scuderia Ferrari team that carried Alfa's banner in the '30s. Now, in nearby Maranello south of Modena, he headed a company that since the late Forties had been turning out a broad spectrum of pure racers, track-tuned sports cars and, more recently, roomier and more comfortable high-performance tourers designed to appeal to a maturing clientele.

And indeed, these newer Ferraris had their appeal. As Henry Manney noted in *Road & Track*, Ferrari had "a good racing name which gives vast publicity, there are parts and service in most civilized areas, and in recent years his cars have become quite fashionable to drive in spite of the stiff price tag."

So, all the *Cavaliere* had to do was beat the long-entrenched *Commendatore*, a formidable task but not impossible. As Lamborghini had found—or said he had—Ferrari didn't wholly subscribe to the "customer is king" philosophy of business, at least his non-racing business. Those wishing to trade at the Sign of the Prancing Horse often had to put up with distinctly, well, cavalier treatment.

And despite their impressive performance and undeniable mechanical spirit, roadgoing Ferraris were seldom at the forefront of automotive design. Engines, chassis, suspensions, brakes, body engineering—none were really state-of-the-art. The reason? Roadgoing Ferraris existed mainly to generate revenues for supporting the factory's various racing efforts. The imperious *Commendatore* considered his road-car buyers no more than a necessary evil and would take no more trouble over them than was strictly necessary.

Two obvious lines of attack lay open to Lamborghini, one human, the other mechanical. His own open, straightforward, friendly nature almost guaranteed success with the first. As for the second, how better to please a keen, knowledgeable, discriminating enthusiast like himself than by building a car to please...himself?

Ferruccio laid down definite guidelines for both the concept and layout of his ideal *gran turismo*. It would be basically a two-seater but, as sporting cars go, quite large and substantial so its wealthy owners could be comfortable and, it was hoped, comfortably accommodate more than one friend. It would be a closed coupe for quiet, refined, all-weather travel, and would have every motoring luxury of the day. And while it needn't be "a technical bomb," its specifications would be as advanced as Lamborghini's talented, experienced staff and large, ultramodern factory could achieve.

Oh, yes. Ferruccio also specified that his GT must undercut Ferrari pricing by at least a million lire, then equivalent to about $1600.

The heart of any car is its engine, and Lamborghini knew that whatever else it might be, his car must have its own powerplant. A proprietary engine just wouldn't be in keeping with the image he wanted to establish, and there were few suitable choices anyway. To be sure, Giotto Bizzarrini had settled on Chevy power for his own models, but that was more a practical than a marketing decision; Bizzarrini had the ability to design an all-new super-engine, but not the resources to build it. Ferruccio's situation was far different, of course. With an entire industrial empire at his command, he was bound to produce his own engine.

And it was bound to be a V-12, not only because Ferrari had built his reputation with them and not just because of its advantages in smoothness and flexibility, but for the prestige. Because Italy's motor-vehicle tax system put disproportionate levies on engines with more than four cylinders, only the wealthy could afford V-12s, so that's naturally what they wanted.

Bizzarrini's 12 cylinders were arrayed at the 60-degree angle that gives a natural dynamic balance to such engines (because of their 60-degree firing intervals). There were two valves per cylinder, each inclined at 35 degrees to the cylinder axis and fitted with double valve springs and inverted-bucket cam followers.

With bore and stroke of 77 x 62 millimeters (3.03 × 2.44 inches), total displacement was precisely 3464.5 cubic centimeters (211.4 cubic inches). The block was aluminum—cast, incidentally, by the small, struggling firm of ATS—with shrunk-in iron cylinder liners. Like other contemporary high-performance Italian powerplants, the liners were deliberately made over-long so as to stand slightly proud of the gaskets for improved sealing when the heads, also of aluminum, were bolted down.

The crankshaft, beautifully machined from nickel-chromium billet steel, ran in seven main bearings, each held firmly by four bolts. Very stout forged-steel connecting rods carried forged-aluminum pistons that were domed to give a compression ratio of 11.0:1 or better, according to Wallace. For quiet operation, the camshafts were driven not by gears but through a pair of chains, one for each cylinder bank. To avoid a narrow space between opposing camshafts, intake porting ran down into the centers of the heads,

alongside the spark plugs. Exhaust porting was conventional. Dry weight of this potent power package was said to be 232 kilograms, or 512 pounds.

Lamborghini's premier engine would retain this basic architecture for many years, but a few features were seen mainly on this original version: dry-sump oiling system, a pair of conventional spin-on filters standing at the front of the engine, and dual Marelli distributors, one for each bank, sticking out from the intake cams at the rear. For the first V-12 a total of six twin-barrel, 36-mm Weber racing carburetors were mounted in downdraft position.

In unveiling the GTV, Lamborghini stated that he'd considered fuel injection and had even experimented with various systems. Wallace, however, says this never went beyond the mockup stage, fuel injection being rejected due to its high cost and minimal benefit.

According to Lamborghini historian Rob de la Rive Box, the new V-12 first roared into life on May 15, 1963, on the company's Schenk dynamometer. It was a magic moment. Giuliano Pizzi was in charge. In a gentle first run-up to 4500 rpm he saw 226 horsepower on the European-standard DIN scale, about 235 bhp in today's SAE net measure. Sometime later he twisted it to 8000 revs and saw 360 DIN (374 SAE net). History records that as the official figure, although Wallace, as previously noted, says the ultimate numbers that determined Bizzarrini's payment were even higher.

No matter. The project was off to a good start. More castings were ordered from ATS and, with Bizzarrini out of the picture, Dallara was instructed to detune the V-12. His boss was happy with the aforementioned demonstration of its

potential, but for road use he wanted a smooth, quiet, tractable and relatively unstressed engine good for 40,000 hard miles between services. The dyno began humming to that end, with Stanzani and Wallace working under Dallara's direction. One of the many Lamborghini legends says they installed a development engine in one of Ferruccio's Ferraris for real-road testing, but Wallace debunks this as another bit of fanciful fabrication.

Mounted at the front of its chassis, the V-12 would drive through a Fichtel & Sachs clutch to an aluminum-cased ZF five-speed manual gearbox, both from Germany. Shocks were absorbed in the propeller shaft with a pair of rubber couplings rather than conventional U-joints. Behind that was a British-made Salisbury differential with limited-slip, the same final drive Jaguar used in its E-Type.

The chassis was equally worthy of the superb engine. Suspension was independent at each corner via coil springs and tubular wishbones, and both ends enjoyed the ministrations of an anti-roll bar. British Girling disc brakes with mild assist from a deliberately weak booster rode within 15-inch-diameter Borrani wire wheels. Tires were Pirelli Cinturato HS, plump for the day at 205 mm wide and rated for a top speed of up to 160 mph. Steering, also by ZF, was a worm-type mechanism that unfortunately had to have numerous jointed links to get around the bulky engine. The Modena fabrication firm of Georgio Neri and Lucciano Bonacini welded up the GTV's steel chassis, which was a round-tube racing-type structure designed by Bizzarrini. Wheelbase was given as 2450 mm, or 96.5 in. Front and rear track measured 1380 mm/54.3 in.

Cloaking these lovely components

Lamborghini's charging-bull badge made the leap from tractors to cars on the nose of the 350 GTV. It was accompanied by his signature rendered in metal (bottom, left). A businesslike but not uninviting cabin set the tone for Lamborghini GTs (below, right).

was a somewhat less-than-lovely body, though the styling seems to have reflected Ferruccio's tastes—and, it is understood, his considerable input. In general, Lamborghini wanted a coupe with aggressive aerodynamic lines and plenty of glass all-round. In particular, he is said to have asked for sleek frontal styling *a la* Jaguar E-Type and the tapering tail of an Aston Martin DB4.

As any commercial artist knows, a client with rigid insistence on his own ideas only makes a job tougher. Time was apparently very limited, too. These factors may explain some of the more unfortunate aspects of the GTV's styling. What puzzled many at the time was Ferruccio's choice of designer: Franco Scaglione, the former Bertone stylist whose previous high point had been the attention-getting, but bizarre, Alfa Romeo BAT show cars of the mid-Fifties.

The Lamborghini that emerged from his drawing board had similarly extreme flourishes and jutting angles, though the overall shape was essentially pleasing. What spoiled it was an unharmonious conglomeration of bold curves, sharp edges, odd proportions and awkward details.

For example, there was a gaping "mouth" grille with a vertical divider bar that ran up the hood, a heavy-handed rendition of the "nostril" effect that was something of a rage in Europe at the time but related to nothing else on the car. Also a little odd, if undeniably practical for outward vision, were the very tall rear window and generous rear quarter windows.

Hidden headlamps, still a novelty in '63, were housed in a giant front-hinged hood/fenders structure something like the E-Type's. A small but workable trunk lay across the rear between twin fuel tanks, while six under-bumper exhaust pipes, three per side, called attention to the mighty V-12 up front. Like many show cars, the GTV was without windshield wipers. On the hood, to the left of the central rib, was the Lamborghini "charging bull" emblem already familiar in the tractor world.

As published by Chris Harvey, the GTV measured 177.2 inches long overall, 64.2 inches wide and 48.0 inches high. Harvey listed weight as 1050 kg/2315 pounds, but other sources put it at 980/2160. Any such figures—including published performance data—have to be theoretical projections, because the car was never finished. "It was a non-runner," says Bob Wallace. "The engine was never installed. The car was put on display at the show with a crate of ceramic tiles in the engine compartment."

The car's skin was a handmade mixture of steel and aluminum paneling by Carrozzeria Sargiotto of Turin, which Scaglione was operating. Obviously done in haste to make the show date and, says Harvey, built by workers more used to making molds for a plastics factory than automobile bodies, the 350 GTV drew critical barbs for its careless build and poor finish. Comments ran along the lines of "Ferruccio's Folly," and there was no shortage of predictions of financial ruin for the ambitious millionaire automaker.

Still, the bold, metallic-blue GTV attracted attention. The world was evidently starved for such a car, for press coverage was extensive. Ferruccio made the most of it, eagerly welcoming reporters to his impressive new factory and cheerfully revealing the various ideas his team was working on. One them was apparently a competition version of the 350 GTV.

It's always been said that Ferruccio had an interest in racing but no interest in participating in it. There's hard evidence, though, that he was talking about a competition car based on his new roadgoing GT even at this early stage. Journalists who spoke with him reported as much. Griff Borgeson, for example, told readers in the February 1964 *Road & Track* that the original high-output engine and short-wheelbase design had "not been abandoned," but "moved to the back burner until the production-car program is far enough along to permit resurgence

of Lamborghini's desire to go racing."

Photos taken in the factory around that time often show two bare chassis. One, made entirely of round tubing, was identified by Borgeson as a *corsaiola* or competition chassis. Accompanying text referred to a race-tuned 3.5-liter V-12 with an estimated 350 bhp. Both car and engine were described as being planned for production. The impression was that the source of the information was Ferruccio Lamborghini himself.

Harvey had a somewhat different explanation. He said this lightweight tube frame was the very first chassis built, and that it had been designed by Bizzarrini at a stage when he still hoped to get Lamborghini to make a racer out of it. "But when it became apparent that the touring version had priority, Dallara had the frame reconstructed in heavier material."

Bob Wallace dismisses the *R&T* story with a wave of his gnarled hand. "Naw, that was just a

proposal." He recalls that the round-tube display frame was simply the first mockup of the GTV chassis; a duplicate rested under the GTV show car. Any plans for a *corsaiola* model went no further than that. Indeed, beyond a trio of experimental vehicles that Wallace built in his spare time years later, there never was anything that can be described as a racing Lamborghini automobile. If Ferruccio did harbor a competition itch, as many of his employees did, he managed to curb it. And them.

But was he deliberately holding up the possibility of a racing program as a carrot, perhaps to keep his youngsters motivated and bound to him? Perhaps to generate more press attention? Perhaps to needle Ferrari? No such Machiavellian streak has been ascribed to Ferruccio. Maybe at that stage he did think he might race—one day. Very likely he gave at least half an ear to all the people who were telling him he'd have to. Only Ferruccio knows for sure.

The GTV's specifications and theoretical performance may have been compelling, but when it became clear that the automotive establishment didn't think much of its appearance, the mockup quietly disappeared from view, and talk of its imminent production and eventual competition stopped. Ferruccio ordered that all work be directed toward the strictly roadgoing vehicle he'd envisioned from the beginning. Meanwhile, he began shopping around for someone to revise the styling.

History thus records the GTV as something of a failure, but that's an unkind appraisal. With the clarity of hindsight we can see that this awkward prototype was merely a first step toward a goal that was ultimately and successfully realized. Moreover, it was quite an ambitious effort, and much about it was good. Given the great Lamborghinis to come, perhaps the only thing that was really wrong about the GTV was that Ferruccio let us see it.

CHAPTER 7
Out of the Gate: 350/400 GT

Lamborghini was not deterred by the bad press and lukewarm public reaction to his GTV prototype. So the styling was a little off; that could be fixed easily enough. What mattered was that his vision of a Lamborghini *gran turismo* was no longer just a dream. He moved quickly, and within five months of the Turin show had in hand his first production car. It was a substantially new vehicle and was designated 350 GT, Ferruccio having apparently determined the *veloce* description unnecessary. The bull was about to charge.

The most obvious difference between the GTV and the 350 GT was the sheetmetal. One of Italy's most respected old-line coachbuilders landed the

Lamborghini body contract. It was Carrozzeria Touring of Milan, responsible for the handsome Aston Martin DB4 and the similar Maserati 3500 GT, as well as numerous other styling successes over the years. Its designers began working their magic on Ferruccio's unfortunate GTV in late 1963.

Meanwhile, the Lamborghini development team carried out an extensive under-skin revision. Engineering chief Giampaolo Dallara had Neri & Bonacini make up a completely different chassis (seen as a display piece in many early factory photos). Instead of the previous network of round-section members, it had a basic "floor" of square and rectangular steel tubing, plus a couple of round-tube

superstructures fore and aft to carry the suspension, a configuration that allowed easier fitting of a body with generous doors. Suspension was basically unchanged, though the arms at both ends were now steel pressings instead of welded tubes.

Though quite a few sources maintain that the GT rode the GTV wheelbase, this is certainly an error. For one thing, simply comparing profiles reveals that the GT has a much more open, expansive side window area and a less hunched roofline. More conclusive evidence is a Touring technical drawing that calls out 2550 millimeters/100.4 inches between wheel centers, not 2450/96.5. The same drawing, incidentally, indicates overall length of 181.5 inches, versus the GTV's

Lamborghini turned to an established coachbuilder, Carrozzeria Touring, to revamp the styling of his gran turismo for production. The result was a smoother, more coherent design on a wheelbase longer by 3.9 inches. The coupe retained just two seats, but its cockpit was enlarged and more neatly finished. The V in GTV stood for veloce, which meant ''fast.'' It was dropped for the production car, which was christened simply the 350 GT (both pages) for its 1964 debut.

published 177.2. To clinch the matter, actually measuring a 350 GT shows that, sure enough, wheelbase is 100.4, 3.9 in. longer than the GTV's.

Touring's schematic also shows a 2-plus-1 configuration, with a third bucket seat mounted behind the primary pair atop the driveline tunnel. At least one car with this layout (and small storage bins on either side of the third seat) was photographed, and Bob Wallace recalls that several early cars were indeed built this way. However, he believes they were all later converted to the final production configuration, in which the cramped little third seat was replaced by a simple bench. This was mainly intended as auxiliary luggage space (its flat portion had two chrome scuff rails), but as the rear bulkhead was trimmed in leather, the space could accommodate very small passengers on very short trips.

As for the exterior, Touring saved the best of what Scaglione had wrought and simplified the rest. Thus did the GTV's "prow" go away. So did the vents behind its four wheel arches and the full-length beltline trim above them. The six exhaust tips became four, and rear corners were rounded off to match the rest of the car. Wiping the windshield was a single large blade pivoted at the bottom center of the tall windscreen, which was raked at 65½ degrees from vertical according to the aforementioned Touring sketch.

So far so good, but what a pity that the GTV's unitized front sheetmetal and the generous engine access it provided were lost to a conventional hood. More disturbing was the decision to extend the

Stand-up Cibie headlamps recalled the original Austin-Healey Sprite, but ventless side windows and a single windshield wiper pointed the 350 GTV toward today (above). Badging itself is worthy of admiration (below).

headlights, powerful oval Cibies, from the nose in the fashion of a "bugeye" Austin-Healey Sprite. All in all, this wasn't the most beautiful example of Italian automotive design, but Lamborghini's GT was elegant and distinctive.

Touring was also contracted to build the bodies, for which it naturally employed its famous, patented *Superleggera* ("super-light") construction, which meant a framework of small steel tubes skinned with aluminum panels. Still, the 350 GT's official dry weight ended up at 1200 kilograms or 2646 pounds (various sources list several different weights, all lower), up from the higher numbers given for the GTV by a substantial 330 pounds.

Per Ferruccio's instructions, chief engineer Dallara detuned the Bizzarrini-designed V-12 and revised a number of details in the interest of a smoother, more pleasant, longer-lasting engine. The elaborate and costly racing-type dry-sump system was deemed unnecessary and gave way to a conventional oil pan. Because that raised engine position and because air cleaners had to be fitted, the expensive 36-mm vertical racing carbs were replaced by conventional sidedraft Webers, albeit with 40-mm bores. As recounted by Wallace, who did much of the hands-on work, compression was lowered from 11.0:1 or higher to 9.5. The exotic materials specified for the crankshaft and other components were cut back to reduce cost and cam profiles were softened.

Other changes to the original GTV engine included relocating the distributors to more accessible positions on the fronts of the exhaust camshafts, and adoption of a single, very tall Lamborghini-made oil filter. The production version also had expensive platinum-tipped spark plugs that could operate across a wider heat range and thus resist fouling in low-speed running.

After all this, the dyno showed "only" 270 DIN horsepower (280 bhp SAE net) at 6500 rpm. (As another example of the slippery nature of such figures, some Lamborghini information at the time quoted 280 bhp DIN.) Peak torque was listed as 239 pounds-feet at 4000 rpm.

Lamborghini's second shot at a "perfect" GT was shown to the world at the 1964 Geneva Salon in March. The world liked what it saw and orders began coming in. However, initial demand was dampened by another of Italy's periodic financial crises, while supply was limited by the factory's decision to take things slowly. As Wallace has remarked, there were various teething troubles to sort out on both car and assembly line, so only 13 units went out through the end of the year, which suggests that Lamborghini was making every effort to realize his "perfect car." Indeed, a year-end audit showed he lost approximately $1000 on each of those 1964 cars.

No wonder. Engine machine work was exquisite (crankshafts came out "smooth as a baby's bottom," said an admiring Griff Borgeson) and magnafluxing was used liberally to ensure top quality. Every engine was first run-in by an electric motor for 10-12 hours, then under its own power for a like period. By installation it was fully power-checked and backed by a complete pedigree of dyno sheets. On completion, each car was turned over to Wallace for a road test.

Over this frame of square and rectangular steel tubing (above), Touring stretched a hand-hammered skin of aluminum. The resulting bodywork was strong, but also light in weight, giving the method its **superleggera,** *or ''superlight'' name. Borrani wire wheels lent it all a classic air.*

Original factory brochures picture the 350 GT in its element of wealth and taste (above). With a suggested list price of $13,900 in the U.S., Lamborghini's first car was priced to compete with Ferraris of the day, though it was somewhat more mechanically advanced and offered greater creature comforts than the better-known Italian rivals.

carbs (versus Lamborghini's six), about 240 claimed bhp in the typical roadgoing form. In addition, the Ferraris had only four speeds (except for racers), a simple live rear axle, and mostly steel bodies instead of all-aluminum.

Ferrari also offered a 2+2 on the same 102.3-inch-wheelbase chassis, but this was a different sort of car. In addition, he was still turning out very small numbers of his 4.0- and 5.0- liter Superamerica and Superfast two-seaters. With an alleged 400 bhp, they were obviously more potent than the new Lamborghini but also less sophisticated.

In all, Ferruccio had pulled a decisive coup. As for price, the 350 GT listed in the U.S. at $13,900 in 1965, about the same or just a bit less than Ferrari was charging for cars that weren't directly comparable.

Journalist and sometime Ferrari owner Henry Manney tested an early 350 GT for *Road & Track* in 1965 and had many positive things to say. On climbing in, he appreciated how the tall windshield merging into the roof created a light, airy feeling. He found the driving position "outstandingly comfortable" despite pedals offset to the left and a seat that seemed rather low, which emphasized front-end width. He was impressed by the comprehensive instrumentation as well as overall finish that was "something you could be proud of."

On the road, Manney characterized the 350 GT as a "quickish, well-balanced car" with a "feeling of solidness." Admitting he was not one who quickly settled into a new car, he felt at home in the Lamborghini almost immediately. Its manual steering was especially nice: "Many high-performance cars require aiming rather than steering, but the Lamborghini's, in spite of strong self-centering action and not inconsiderable kickback from bumps at low speed, was extremely accurate." Manney judged the ride a bit stiff at low speeds and mentioned the heavy action of his car's early gearbox (but noted that "the synchro pressure has been reduced from 20 lb. to 5 on the later gearbox.") Engine behavior? Wonderful: flexible and smooth at the low end and strong at any rpm.

Strong, but not quite as strong as the speedometer suggested. On an *autostrada* run with factory test driver Bob Wallace at the wheel, Manney looked over to see an indicated 174 mph, with Wallace

And once buyers got to test it, they liked Lamborghini's new GT. Ferruccio had done what he'd set out to do: craft a quiet, smooth, sophisticated high-performer that was technically ahead of anything Ferrari had been offering, yet easier to drive and generally faster, too. Ferrari's latest, the 275 GTB, also introduced in '64, was very aerodynamic and boasted all-independent suspension, but its V-12 still wasn't advanced as Lamborghini's.

Ferruccio had definitely outpointed Enzo's long-established 250 GT series. Those Ferraris had a 3.0-liter V-12, but with only one camshaft per cylinder bank, three

One early proposal envisioned a 2+1 seating configuration, with a single, center rear bucket for the 350 GT (bottom). A few were built this way, but most were strictly two-place cars with a carpeted rear parcel shelf.

muttering that the engine was 500 rpm down. *R&T's* usual road-test data table showed the car geared for 152 mph at 7000 rpm, though Manney didn't claim it had reached that speed. Its final-drive ratio was 3.31:1, the taller (numerically lower) of two listed as available. Earlier reports, including original factory literature, quote a variety of other ratios. There's also a spread among reported top speeds. One that seems most likely has a 350 GT topping out at 149 mph (240 k/ph).

Whatever its true maximum, Manney was pleased to observe that "the Lamborghini seemed quite steady, even with a fair crosswind .... I wouldn't hesitate to do it myself."

Wallace ran the obligatory acceleration tests in demonstrating the car. It isn't clear whether *R&T*

used his results or its own, but a 0-60-mph time of 6.8 seconds and the standing quarter-mile in 14.9 seconds at 93 mph were the numbers printed on the page. (One presumes these are "corrected," as the data table included *R&T's* usual speedometer-error plot.) The magazine bought the quoted 2160-pound curb weight, which is frankly hard to believe. It got the wheelbase wrong, too, though the correct length was shown in an accompanying scale profile of the car.

During some twisty-road driving, the New Zealander who had described his as "the best job in the world" showed the American writer the value of the 350 GT's independent rear suspension—and at the same time provided an insight into the life of a factory road tester.

"Bob gave me heart failure for a while until I saw what he was about," Manney wrote, "hopping humpbacked bridges to show that it landed straight, clapping on the binders from full noise to burn in the new pads, and even braking furiously in Ginther's Corner near Nonantola to show how stable the car was even with everything locked up. I must say that I was impressed, as the i.r.s. removed all traces of hop or judder while refusing to do any of the horrid things that i.r.s. is supposed to do. Likewise, he went teeming around the bends at full chat without a wiggle...."

Good fun, that. "Purest joy," was Manney's verdict. "Driving a car like the Lamborghini is very good for the ego."

Other writers were similarly impressed. "Much less demanding

to drive than a Ferrari," said the March 1966 *Car and Driver*, "so smooth, and so quiet." Yet in steering, braking, acceleration and handling, the 350 GT scored as well as the magazine's test Ferrari 275 GTS. That same month, *Sports Car Graphic* editors enthused about the Lamborghini's excellent ride on all surfaces, and said its combination of "roadability," lack of noise, good engine idle, and other assets made it "the most enjoyable 150-mph-plus car" they'd tried.

Despite such praise, Sant'Agata didn't rest on its laurels, continuously making little refinements and improvements to the 350 GT as production continued. Among these were revised grille styling; the addition of cowl air intakes, a second windshield wiper, and a rear backup light; and substitution of leather dash trim for the early polished aluminum.

More important changes were made under the hood. The V-12 was enlarged to "four liters" via a bore stretch from 77 to 82 millimeters, bringing swept volume to 3929 cubic centimeters (239.8 cubic inches). That and a compression boost from 9.5 to 10.2:1 were said to add 50 horsepower for a new rating of 320 bhp DIN (332 SAE net), still at 6500 rpm. Torque improved, too, now 276 pounds-feet at 4500 rpm. In this form the V-12 would establish the tone and image of Lamborghini cars for the next decade.

This engine was made optionally available in '65, resulting in a new 400 GT model (not to be confused with the 400 GT 2 + 2, which had an altered body and is covered in the

Massive four-wheel-disc brakes helped the 350 GT stop while a well-sorted suspension gave it stability and a supple, controlled ride worthy of the thoroughbred it was (opposite, bottom). Lamborghini's gran turismo needed a true trunk to carry its owner's expensive bags on long, fast trips (top, right). What he didn't offer was a convertible body style, though Touring had a go at it with this graceful drop-top study (center and bottom right). Two examples were built and some owners converted their coupes similarly. Another extrapolation on the 350 GT was Zagato's one-off 3500 GTZ (opposite, top). Rakish and Ferrari-like, it was quite conventional in light of Zagato's usual flamboyance.

impressive and we've never been more impressed." Then again, this was before the age of strangling emission controls.

The editors also praised interior equipment and finish as "excellent" and fully in keeping with the $14,250 price tag. Incidentally, the U.S.-market 400 had four circular sealed-beam headlights, and the test car displayed modest bumper overriders and two windshield wipers.

Dynamically, *R&T's* testers were delighted with the 400's "remarkably light" steering, good handling and stability, and the lack of noise both mechanical and aerodynamic. They did complain about tiringly heavy clutch and throttle action, and remarked that gearshift throws seemed rather long. But these were nits. "One drive and everyone had a new favorite car."

Some Lamborghini historians mention higher-performance versions of the 400 GT. One has described a mysterious vertical-carburetor engine displayed at the 1965 New York show, another says a "400 GTV" unit was optionally available. Bob Wallace, who ought to know, says it wasn't so: "If a customer wanted to pay for it, we would fit things like polished connecting rods and maybe polish the ports a little. But all the engines were basically the same. There was never any such thing as a '400 GTV.' The only vertical-carburetor engine—except for the Miura, of course—was that first dyno test engine. There only was the one of those, and it was a balls-out racer. It never went into a car. Aw, we did have a second one, but that was just a mockup for display purposes."

There were, however, at least three 350/400-based specials. Zagato did a one-off fastback called the 3500 GTZ, rakish and, for this *carrozzeria*, handsomely conventional. It was first seen at the 1965 Earl's Court motor show in London. At the Turin show later that year, Touring

following chapter). After testing one for its October 1966 issue, *Road & Track* termed it "the finest GT car we've ever driven."

That assessment may seem a bit surprising, considering the 400 GT car was heavier and slower off the mark than the 350. Of course, there was reason. Experts generally agree that 131 original-type GTs were built between 1964 and '67. Just 23 had the 3.9 engine, and 20 of those were bodied not in "super-light" aluminum but in significantly heavier steel. Though *R&T* didn't mention it, its test 400 was obviously one of the steel-body cars, as curb weight was listed as 3200 pounds. That sounds believable, and

would account for the published 7.5-second 0-60-mph clocking and standing-quarter-mile time of 15.5 seconds at 92 mph. These numbers were noticeably inferior to those of the 350 GT tested the previous year, and came despite a shorter 4.08:1 final drive. *R&T* reported top speed as a marginally higher 156 mph.

Greater refinement was where the 3.9 engine scored over the 3.5. It was willing to run at any rpm, yet with a complete absence of fuss. It always started instantly and never oiled a plug, overheated or did anything else uncivilized. Yet it produced the highest flat-out speed *R&T* had ever recorded for a road car. "It couldn't have been more

displayed a convertible based on its production coupe styling. A second such car was also built.

There are those who still believe the 350/400 GT, with its smooth lines, light aluminum body and two-seat layout was the most appealing, most elegant car Lamborghini ever made. It was certainly the car Ferruccio Lamborghini had set out to make, the closest to his original concept. It could thus be argued that some of the later models—the high-style, hyper-energetic ones with the names taken from bullfighting—were less "true" Lamborghinis than these first ones.

There surely can't be too many souls who wouldn't like to have one of the early Lamborghinis in their stable—especially one of those three aluminum-bodied 400 GTs.

Just 23 of the original Lamborghini GT's were fitted with the 3.9-liter V-12. Three were skinned in lightweight aluminum; the rest had steel bodies. Some also got quad headlamps (above), but all retained the two-seat layout with its rear parcel shelf (left, and opposite top). To many purists, the 400 GT came closest to realizing Ferruccio Lamborghini's gran turismo ideal. **Road & Track** *in October 1966 called it "the finest GT car we've ever driven."*

CHAPTER 8
Refinement: 400 GT 2 + 2

Think "Lamborghini" today and the vision is of rakish, ultra-high-performance mid-engine two-seaters. To Ferruccio, however—and to a substantial number of aficionados of the marque—the quintessential Lamborghini is something quite different. It is, in fact, a rather maturely stated four-seat coupe. More practical and less emotional than a Countach or Miura, this Lamborghini more accurately expresses Ferruccio's original automotive impulse. And it's a damn fine car, to boot.

We're speaking of the 400 GT 2 + 2, which bowed at the ever-important Geneva Salon in March 1966. You need a very close look to see it, but the 2 + 2 bodies are really quite different from those of the 350/400 two-seaters. Primarily,

they're about 2½ inches taller, to accommodate the heads of "occasional" rear passengers, and all were made of steel rather than aluminum, which means they're heavier. So the sight of one is slightly less exciting.

But your chances of seeing a 2 + 2 are greater. During its production years, 1966-68, it outsold the two-seaters almost two-to-one.

It sold better because of greater practicality—the very impetus for the "+ 2" seats and steel construction, as well as the dual windshield wipers on some of the cars, and even the less-attractive quad headlights on all of them. Under the skin were more important changes that pleased the factory as much as customers. With the 400 GT 2 + 2, Lamborghini abandoned

the German ZF transmission and British Salisbury differential in favor of units made completely in-house, a step that underlined Lamborghini's emergence as a full-fledged automaker, not just an assembler of components.

An interesting feature of the new transmission was that its Porsche-patent baulk-ring synchronizer system was used not only for all five forward gears but reverse as well. The shift pattern

Small rear seats made the 2 + 2 version of Lamborghini's 1966 grand-touring coupe (above) more practical than the two-seaters it replaced, steel body panels made it more durable. A 3.9-liter V-12 offered more refinement.

Wheelbase and overall length were
unchanged from the 350/400 GT, but the
400 2 + 2's rear suspension was revised to
add back-seat footroom and its roof was
raised slightly for increased rear-seat
headroom. The backlight was smaller, but
the trunklid got larger.

was conventional, with fifth up and to the extreme right and reverse straight back from that. Lateral throws were rather wide, the mechanism noticeably spring-loaded so the lever would naturally stay in the middle (3-4) plane, and shift action was quite stiff, particularly when the gearbox oil was cold. The last made some wish for the old ZF, but everyone had to admit the new Lamborghini transmission was smoother and quieter. That was no accident. Each was put through a factory break-in regimen similar to that of every Lamborghini engine, with special pains taken to ensure quiet gear operation.

There have been some confusing reports over the years, but the 2+2 was in fact built on the same 100.4-inch wheelbase as the two-seat 350/400, its small extra seats being just properly upholstered replacements for their baggage shelf. To make a little more room in that area, upper and lower rear suspension arms were reversed back to front, so that what had been linkage leading forward from the axle centerline now went aft. For more headroom, Touring lowered the rear floorpan a trifle and, as noted, raised the roofline by 2.6 inches. The 2+2 thus stood 50.6 inches (1285 millimeters) tall instead of 48 inches (1220 mm).

Body panels were switched from aluminum to steel because the latter was easier to manufacture and more durable. The headlight system was changed to allow installation of U.S.-required circular sealed beams. Other departures from the two-seat models involved sharply reduced rear-window area (presumably so the Italian sun wouldn't bake back-seaters' heads so much) and a larger trunk and trunklid. A single fuel tank of 23 U.S. gallons (87 liters) replaced the previous pair of 10.5s—although some doubt exists as to whether any of these cars could actually carry that much.

Brochures touted the 400 GT 2+2 as the complete grand-touring machine (top and middle photos). Customers responded and Lamborghini produced 224 of the four-place cars against 143 350/400 GTs. More was changed to make the 2+2 than meets the eye. Not only was the roofline taller, the shape of the doors was different, and the body was mounted slightly higher: note the added metal between the front wheelarch and the accent crease.

frontale

Studiata nella parte anteriore per ottenere un'alta penetrazione all'aria per l'elevata velocità che può raggiungere, presenta una nuova sistemazione dei fari, ora doppi e affiancati con gli abbaglianti all'interno e gli anabbaglianti all'esterno, e con i fanalini di posizione collocati sui baffi dei paraurti realizzati in acciaio inossidabile.
Nella parte anteriore della carrozzeria, al limite della fiancata e appena sotto il parabrezza sono collocate due prese di aria protette da una grigliatura, che immettono direttamente un flusso d'aria nell'abitacolo, assicurando un facile e rapido ricambio ed una perfetta ventilazione.

LAMBORGHINI 400 GT 2+2

Quad headlamps are a 400 GT 2 + 2 hallmark, though they actually debuted on some 400 GTs. This allowed fitment of U.S.-required circular sealed beams. The "smile" around the front bumper also is slightly different on the four-place cars.

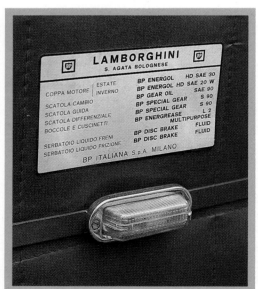

It was bulkier and heavier than the two-seaters, and didn't handle quite as well, but with elegant bodylines, durable coachwork, additional seating, and a powerful, refined powertrain, the 400 GT 2+2 is to many Lamborghini fans the quintessential **gran turismo** *from Sant'Agata (opposite page). To others, it was the foundation for flights of their own fancy. An American commissioned this coupe (right and below) on a 400 GT 2+2 chassis. It was dubbed the Monza 400. The one-off was built by the shop that had turned out the original 350 GTV and its styling was scarcely more pleasing, inside or out.*

Several histories allege that the 2+2 was longer overall than the two-seaters, and some add that the rake of its windshield and rear window were changed. Actual measurement shows that both the 350 and the 400 2+2 have 100.4-inch wheelbases, that their bodies (sans bumpers) are each 178 inches long, and that their overall lengths are identical at 182 inches. Windshields, moreover, have been proven by owners to be interchangeable.

Nevertheless, a close side-by-side examination reveals a number of subtle differences. For instance, the "smiles" beneath the front bumpers have slightly different curves, front fender shapes are not identical, and door dimensions vary slightly.

Chassis elements were virtually untouched, save the aforementioned rear suspension, where stiffer springs and shocks and slightly revised wishbones were also decreed, to handle a slight increase in overall weight. According to hard drivers familiar with the two-seater, these changes introduced a bit of tail-happiness into the 2+2's handling.

Of course, the 400 GT's 320-horsepower engine was retained, but the higher roofline and resulting greater frontal area meant that the 2+2 was only about as fast all-out as a 350 GT. Yet apart from the Lamborghini transmission's stiffer shift action, the 2+2 was at least as pleasant to drive as a two-seat 400.

In all, the 400 GT 2+2 was one of Lamborghini's more successful models, with 242 sold. Incidentally, its U.S. list price was $14,750, about $500 upstream of the 400 GT. That represented a surcharge of $250 for each of those new rear passengers.

Lamborghini was really rolling now, and the 2+2 generated sufficient orders that Ferruccio began talking about a full four-seater. With this as a goad, Touring used the 2+2 chassis as the basis for an avant-garde exercise that appeared at the annual Turin show in late '66. Named Flying Star II, after special bodywork the firm had done back in the 1930s, it was a small, sporty station wagon-style car—a smoother Italian version of Britisher Harold Radford's contemporary Aston-Martin DB5 "shooting brake" conversions.

Though it attracted attention, the Flying Star II was strictly a one-off and never a serious production prospect. It was also, unfortunately, a swan song of sorts for the grand old Touring works, then in the serious financial trouble that would force it to close in 1967.

Luckily, Lamborghini owned the tooling for its two-seat and 2+2 bodies. In their last production year they were supplied by a spin-off firm composed of former Touring employees working under one Mario Marazzi, who'd been in charge of Lamborghini body operations at Touring. (We'll have more to say about Marazzi in the next chapter.)

One other 2+2 chassis served as the basis for a one-off. On commission from an American customer, Neri & Bonacini, the shop that had built the original GTV chassis, did up a coupe (with a Ferrari windshield!) called Monza 400. It was a lean, rakish thing, much like a Le Mans or Mille Miglia racer of the previous decade, with lines both adept and awkward. It, too, led to nothing.

CHAPTER 9
Beauty Beneath the Skin: Islero

With supernovas like the Miura and Espada lighting up Lamborghini's skys, it's no wonder the Islero languished in the shadows. This follow-up to the 400 GT 2+2 bore Ferruccio's blessing in a way that neither the Miura nor Espada did. But that hardly helped. And slipshod workmanship only added to its burden.

Pretend for a moment, however, that the Islero was the only Lamborghini coming out of Sant'Agata's massive "Zeppelin-hanger" (as Griff Borgeson called it) during 1968-69. Now the car begins to come into perspective.

It helps to understand that men of maturity and wealth—men like Ferruccio Lamborghini himself—were supporting a healthy little market for true GTs with additional, "occasional" seats. These buyers insisted upon mechanical excellence. And the Islero delivered

Burdened by comparisons to the sleek four-place Espada, which debuted alongside it at the 1968 Geneva Auto Show, the Islero was the overlooked Lamborghini. Its name was drawn from that of a fighting bull—like the Miura—and its styling was directly influenced by Ferruccio himself. But the public had begun to expect something more fiery out of Sant'Agata than this staid-looking V-12 2+2.

Islero boasted the mechanical virtues that had established Lamborghini four years earlier: an aluminum quad-cam V-12, all-independent suspension, and disc brakes. The cockpit of the first-series cars (**right**) was functional and sumptuously appointed for a GT of the period, but like the poorly finished exterior, it suffered flaws in workmanship.

Brochure art illustrates the difference between the noses of the original Islero (top), which debuted in the spring of 1968, and the second-generation, or GTS, that arrived in late summer 1969. The chunky, slab-sided styling that chilled many critics is evident in this profile view (below), but demand was sufficient enough for Lamborghini to build 225 Isleros, virtually the same production as the 400 GT 2 + 2.

with an aluminum, quad-cam V-12; all-wheel independent suspension and disc brakes; comprehensive cockpit fittings and luxury appointments. These customers were men of business and industry and finance, not lotharios, and so their car's shape had to be refined, seasoned. And the Islero's lines certainly were restrained. In point of fact, Ferruccio himself had a strong hand in its styling. Indeed, the Islero was so much a reflection of *Il Cavaliere's* taste that whenever he wanted to go somewhere in one of his cars at the time, this is the one he generally chose. Now you see the Islero as Ferruccio did.

Lamborghini's task with the Islero was to update the 400 GT 2 + 2, to make the same sort of automobile, but one that was easier to build, with slightly more rear-seat room. With the basic 350/400 shape now approaching five years of age, the need for a reskin was obvious. So, as Mario Marazzi and his group of ex-Touring employees continued building the original two-seat and 2 + 2 bodies, Lamborghini sat down with them to work on a successor.

It's not clear just who came up with the name (pronounced "eez-LEHR-oh") but it continued the *corrida de toros* theme begun with the Miura (see Chapter 12). Although there is something ox-like in the Islero's blunt, straightforward body lines, the appellation was perhaps a trifle unfortunate, referring as it did to the bull that killed famed matador Manuel Rodriguez back in 1947. Still, it was much handier than "400 GT 2 + 2 Mark II," which was what the Islero really was.

Riding the original 350/400 square-tube chassis, the Islero employed steel body panels attached to the 400 2 + 2's inner structure. Wheelbase remained at 100.4 inches, but track dimensions were widened a bit as Lamborghini took advantage of new developments in tire science. Because the rubber was better, Bob

Wallace had to revise the suspension with stiffer anti-roll bars front and rear. Though the prototype appeared on Borrani wire wheels, production Isleros rolled on spiffy cast Campagnolos like those of the Miura and Espada.

The Islero was launched at the Geneva Salon in the spring of 1968. Unfortunately, it shared stand space with the Espada, Lamborghini's truly grand and slinky-sexy new four-seater (see Chapter 10), which was like a smartly dressed businesswoman standing next to a half-clothed starlet. Nothing against

the former, but you know the latter is going to get the eye.

Which was probably just as well, because early Isleros weren't up to close scrutiny. For reasons that must have seemed sound at the time, Ferruccio repeated the fundamental error he'd made with his very first car, the GTV. Thus, not only was the new Marazzi body not that pretty, it wasn't that well finished, the interior in particular.

"That was everyone's fault and no one's fault," says Wallace of this sorry situation. "Marazzi was just a bunch of ex-Touring people and they just didn't have the resources. There was never enough money or equipment available to do the job properly." And what of the finish on the Marazzi-built Touring-design cars? "They were better than the Isleros, but the Touring-built cars had better finish and craftsmanship than any of the others."

Still, the Islero's many good points overshadowed this bad one. Though no limo, it was indeed roomier than the 400 2+2, especially in back, and glass area was more generous. That glass, by the way, was bent in only one dimension as a cost-cutting

move (the previous Touring-design windows had all been compound-curve.) Soundproofing was said to be better, too.

Overall, the Islero was 4.5 inches shorter than the last 400 GT 2+2 and, although Lamborghini weights are always debatable, was believed to be considerably lighter. The notably high-set bumpers at both ends were an obvious benefit. But most important, the Islero had all the strong, silent performance of the original GTs that had made the world take note of Lamborghini, with the same marvelous, Bizzarrini-designed V-12 that was as content to trickle along in traffic as it was willing to rocket down the road.

After building 125 Isleros—and taking criticism of their problems to heart—Lamborghini began turning out a significantly improved model in late summer 1969. This Islero S, or GTS as some literature called it, had a mildly reworked exterior, a completely redesigned interior, several suspension improvements, and a much more potent engine.

Most noticeable among the body alterations were a "mailbox slot" air exhaust vent behind each front

wheel, a slight flare to all wheel arches, and the addition of fixed triangular panes on the front portion of each door window (previously one-piece). Closer inspection revealed a more prominent hood air intake as well as small inlets low down in front, flanking the main radiator opening. Fog lights hanging beneath the front bumper were newly standard, as was all-around tinted glass and an electrically heated rear window.

Inside, the Islero driver found improved seating, with higher front backrests and split rear seatbacks flanking a fold-down armrest. The original, somewhat haphazard gauge layout was more orderly, and safer non-protruding rocker switches replaced push-pull knobs in deference to new American regulations for such things. In place of the dash-mounted passenger grab bar was a proper glovebox, which had been missing before.

Rear suspension was revised in detail, with Espada-like components that improved stability under hard braking and acceleration. The changes were useful, as the brakes were larger and more powerful and

Islero basically mounted a new steel body on the square-tube 350/400 GT chassis frame. Shorter and a bit lighter than the 400 GT 2 + 2, it also was roomier, though the rear seats still were for "occasional" use only. The familiar Bizzarrini 3.9-liter V-12 was present also (left), making about 320 bhp and running much quieter than contemporary Ferrari twelves. The first-generation Islero pictured on both pages has been modified by its owner with functional side air outlets. These vents foreshadow a revision the factory would make on the succeeding version.

the V-12 was pumped up with the 10.8:1 compression and hotter cams from the Miura S. That gave a claimed 350 horsepower at 7500 rpm and a top speed of 161 mph, according to contemporary road tests. The Islero S was a real businessman's express.

Alas, all these improvements came a bit late. Time and reputation had turned most people against the basic car. Nor did the automotive press, all agog over its sexier sisters, devote much ink to the poor Islero.

One of the rare road tests that gives us a feel for the S appeared in Australia's *Sports Car World* magazine in May 1970. A sign that early quality problems had been solved was Graeme Harris' finding that the Islero now had "no mistakes" and embodied "perfection of

workmanship." He also appreciated that it was short enough to park easily yet offered ample front legroom. The low 4¼-inch ground clearance was a worry, and it's obvious from photos how items like mufflers, the front-mounted oil cooler and the rear anti-roll bar hung so close to the road.

Sports Car World found the Islero capable of 0-60 mph in 6.2 seconds and 160 mph at 6500 rpm all-out, yet "well tamed for city driving." Both clutch and throttle seemed heavy (shift action wasn't mentioned), but the power-assisted brakes were quite light. In all, Harris decided that "motoring in the Islero is ecstatically safe, with untouched power in hand to pull the car through any approaching danger...."

As we suggested earlier, had it

been the only Lamborghini of its time, the Islero might have been viewed more favorably, then and now. But it certainly lacked curbside presence next to the almighty Miura and exotic Espada, and the early workmanship flaws hurt, too. Price was another drawback: about $20,000 in the U.S., on the same order as the Miura's. Thus was the Islero put to rest before its time. The last one left Sant'Agata in early 1970—appropriately, perhaps, on tax day, April 15.

With just 225 built, including a mere 100 S-models, the Islero cannot be described as an overwhelming success. Yet in some ways, the S is arguably the best of the front-engine Lamborghinis GTs, which makes it the kind of success anyone with automotive soul will value.

Functional air-exhaust slots in the front fenders identify the second-generation Islero, called the S or GTS (above left). Slightly flared wheel arches, fixed vent windows, and fog lamps also are clues. More extensively revised was the cabin (right). A new dashboard brought a rearranged instrument cluster, safer rocker switches in place of toggles, and a proper glovebox. Though the rear seat of the GTS gained a fold-down center armrest, it really was no bigger than the first-generation back seat (top right). Under the skin were larger brakes, rear-suspension tweaks that improved stability, and a 30-bhp boost—to 350 bhp—for the V-12. Top speed was 161 mph.

CHAPTER 10
Supersedan: Espada

The uncharitable might have suggested that it was the answer to a question that hadn't been asked. But Lamborghini knew better when he blended four-seat luxury, lusty V-12 power, and true exotic-car lines. The Espada (above) bowed in 1968, was in production 10 years, and became the second-best-selling model ever to wear the charging bull.

It's been the goal of many automakers to synthesize authentic four-seat luxury with genuine grand-touring muscle. Ferruccio Lamborghini was different only in that he succeeded.

It was his Espada that showed the others how it could be done. When it burst upon the scene in 1968, nothing on the road could rival its medley of four-place comfort, sports-car moves, and exotic-car looks. And nothing really has

matched it since. In production a full decade, it remains one the most admired and commercially successful of Lamborghinis. It was also among the few that should have survived even longer than it did. Even so, the Espada was the one car fully embodying Ferruccio's own tastes to live on after he left the company.

In Spain, *espada* ("eh-SPAH-duh") is a matador's sword. Italy's Espada had its roots in a pair of 1967

Espada's inspiration was the 1967 Marzal show car by Bertone (this page). It used a stretched Miura chassis and split the mid-engine two-seater's V-12 to form a 2.0 liter inline six, which was then mounted in the tail (left). The show-car's glassy gull-wing doors opened to a futuristic cabin (above). Marzal was a bit too radical for Lamborghini, but its profile proved quite right.

Bertone show cars. One was the oddly named Marzal ("mar-TSAHL"), which was an attempt to meet Ferruccio's desire for a genuine four-seater in the lineup. The other was just an oddity: a rebodied Jaguar E-Type commissioned by a British newspaper. Both appeared when the front-engine 400 GT 2+2 was current and the amazing mid-engine Miura two-seater was making its mark. Given these existing models, the big questions about a new and roomier Lamborghini were: What would it look like, and where would its engine be?

Bertone's Espada prototype (**this page**) *retained Marzal's gull-wing door design, but substituted steel for glass below the beltline. Instead of a rear-mounted six, Bizzarrini's 3.9-liter V-12 was placed in front and ran longitudinally. A semi-monocoque of sheet steel replaced the tube frame. Inset windows foreshadowed the Countach's side glass by three years, but were dropped in favor of conventional roll-downs and wing windows on the production Espada. Front-fender ducts, however, survived in smaller dimension.*

One could easily imagine the Miura as the basis for a full four-seater. For the Marzal it was. Adding 4.4 inches to the Miura's 97.7-inch wheelbase, all ahead of its compact, transverse-midships V-12 power package, made room for the required second set of seats. But in working out the details, chief engineer Giampaolo Dallara decided that the V-12 was too big and split it right down the middle to form a twincam slant-six of 1965 cubic centimeters (120 cubic inches). Meantime, Bertone's Marcello Gandini drew up a radical body with a huge gullwing door on each side that was virtually all glass. The marriage of this body and engine, built in 1966 and publicly displayed at the annual Geneva Salon early the next year, was undeniably striking. But it just wasn't what Ferruccio wanted.

Gandini's Pirana was more like it. Financed by London's *Daily Telegraph*

as a publicity vehicle for a new weekend magazine, this daring and dramatic restyle of Jaguar's sports car premiered at the October 1967 London Motor Show. Of course, few people felt that the two-seat E-Type needed restyling. But the longer, rather dumpier 2 + 2 model was perhaps another matter, and this was the Pirana's basis.

In English that groped a little, a Bertone press release explained the thinking behind the Pirana design: "The car should have represented the ideal means for a certain type of man: high social level, love for sport driving, but no more spartan driving. A desire, then, to provide the car with all those technical contrivances granting to the passengers the best comfort, safety, relax [sic] and pleasure in driving." Sporty but not spartan: Wasn't that

The Espada prototype was fashioned around the body buck of the Pirana (above), a 1966 show car by Bertone's Marcello Gandini. Pirana was a front-engine four seater built on the platform of a Jaguar E-type 2 + 2. Espada's first production interior (left) was an inviting blend of low-slung sports car and four-seat sedan—precisely what Lamborghini sought.

In the Espada, stylist Carrozzeria Bertone created a vehicle distinctive from every angle. It was European grand touring at its innovative best, with lines that are fresh even today.

precisely what Ferruccio had been talking about?

The Pirana's actual wooden body buck was used to shape Bertone's second stab at a four-seat Lamborghini, the prototype for what ultimately became the Espada. This retained the Marzal's general shape, gullwing doors (albeit less glassy ones) and four seats, but put the engine up front. There was still some discussion about motive force, for Ferruccio had an itch to offer a smaller, less exotic engine—like Dallara's slant-six, for instance—while Dallara himself was proposing a V-12 enlarged to 4.5 liters. But there was no time for either, so the familiar 3.9-liter engine it would be.

Slotting it in front provided more luggage room at the back of Gandini's egg-like body design than a midships layout would— desirable, as four people could be expected to take a few bags along on their grand tours. The V-12 would sit "north-south" as in the 350/400 GTs, not sideways as in the Miura, but it would be set 7.9 inches farther forward to open up more cabin space. The old separate tube frame would be abandoned for what amounted to a semi-monocoque of sheet steel, as on the Miura, with tubular structures at each end to carry an improved version of the now-familiar all-independent Lamborghini suspension.

Though this attempt was still a bit ungainly, its essential lines were right. Further refinements (including

replacement of the gullwings with conventional doors) were made for the final production prototype, which was painted a spectacular metallic gold. Dubbed Espada, it went on show at Geneva in the spring of 1968 alongside the new Islero and S-version Miura—and promptly caused a sensation. Lamborghini had scored another coup, one almost as great as the original Miura two years earlier.

The Espada was a compelling blend of contrasts. It wasn't exactly beautiful to some eyes, but its daring distinctiveness captured every eye. A sedan on the inside, it was a low-slung sports car outside. It looked large but really wasn't. Its 104.3- inch wheelbase, for example, was 3.6 inches longer than the 2+2 Islero's but four inches shorter than that of the typical late-'60s American ponycar. Drivers discovered that the Espada felt like a small car when in motion, while two adults found adequate room in its sumptuous aft cabin. Ten cubic feet of luggage would fit under its racy, near-flat rear hatch without blocking vision. And as with all Lamborghinis, its engine was masterful at both ends of the speed spectrum. Though ever so docile in traffic, this "family sports car" was not only the fastest four-seater on the market but one of the fastest automobiles in the world.

Dimensions gave the Espada much of its considerable visual impact. At 186.5 inches stem to stern it was about as long as a contemporary U.S. compact but broader of beam than most any car of the day, 73.3 inches wide. Height was perhaps most striking of all: a squat 46.7 inches, making the Espada 4.5 inches lower than its new Islero sister.

Nevertheless, a wheelbase 1.9

inches longer than the Marzal's allowed doors of sufficient length to grant passengers the same ease of entry that had been Gandini's intent with the gullwings. As in the Miura, left- and right-side seats were well separated, here by a full-length center console that served as a route for ventilation ducts to the rear and increased chassis beam strength as well. Air ducts surrounding the engine bay were designed to add stiffness in that area, too. A 24.6-gallon fuel supply was carried in Jaguar-style twin tanks, one in each rear fender (fillers were hidden inside little grilles back there), thus lowering the luggage floor.

A number of reports credited the Espada with having aluminum body panels (some even warned they could be dented with a thumbnail), thus its fairly low curb weight. Not so. The Espada's only aluminum panel was its hood; the rest was steel. It had to be, in order to weld to the steel floorpan. (Writers in rust-belt areas seem to avoid this mistake; one Englishman remarked that his test car showed signs of rust by the 10,000-mile mark.) Besides, the factory's quoted dry weight was 3583 pounds, a reasonably accurate figure for once, but hardly svelte.

Rack-and-pinion steering had been specified for the Miura, but the Espada retained a ZF worm-gear mechanism, with no power assistance available at first. Suspension was like the Islero's except for improved geometry and softer spring, shock and anti-roll-bar rates. Brakes were discs at all four corners, of course. Top speed was said to be a rousing 155 mph—again, close to reality.

Several Espada details were, in the vernacular of the day, as far out as its overall styling. Atop a notably low, flat hood were a pair of bold NACA-pattern air ducts that fed not the carbs, as some thought, but an elaborate cabin ventilation system. Engine-compartment air exited the front fenders via a pair of "mail slots" flanking each wheel arch, a developed version of an idea that had appeared on the gullwing prototype (and would resurface on the Islero S). Rear side windows were hinged to swing out from the top. The nearly horizontal roofline and mostly glass rear hatch were worthy of frequent comment in 1968. As the resulting profile was better for aerodynamics than visibility, Bertone added a distinctive secondary vertical rear window below the hatch opening and above the taillights. (This feature was revived for the Bertone-styled

Maserati Khamsin of 1974, and more recently was employed by Honda on its second-generation CRX.) The "hexagonitis" that had afflicted Gandini on the Marzal flared up again on the Espada instrument panel, though the symptoms were far less severe.

With bodywork mounted by Bertone at Grugliasco near Turin, what the factory called the 400 GT Espada began coming out of Sant'Agata Bolognese in the summer of '68. It would continue to do so into 1978—the longest production run for any Lamborghini to date save the Countach.

Those 10 years produced three distinct Espada "series." What is now known as the "Series 1" were the cars built through 1969, a brief period that nevertheless brought numerous running changes. For example, a subtle but significant floorpan alteration increased rear headroom by 20 millimeters (about $^4/_5$ of an inch); the original opening front quarter-vents were fixed; and grillwork on the rear lower window was deleted at some point. Unlike the haughty Enzo Ferrari, *Il Cavaliere* was always open to granting special customer favors, so one early Espada was built with a large fixed glass roof panel. At least one other example, a Bertone show project called V.I.P., was equipped with a TV and rudimentary dry bar in the rear seat.

More meaningful experiments in this period included something called "Lancomatic" suspension, unveiled at Turin '68. A hydropneumatic rear self-leveling system, it was developed in cooperation with its German manufacturer, Langen, a subsidiary of the large Ehrenreich suspension-component company. Ferrari's lush 365 GT 2 + 2 had arrived the previous year with something similar, and Lamborghini evidently felt compelled to compete. But Lancomatic never found favor and quietly disappeared.

Bob Wallace explains why: "The idea was exceptionally good, but unfortunately it was a little ahead of its time. The technology available was such that they couldn't solve heat and friction problems with the seals, and the ride frequency was too harsh. And it was expensive. I did a lot of testing on it. It was extremely promising, and would have given a fairly substantial technical advantage to Lamborghini."

Another Detroit-style luxury touch was also floated for the Espada. According to marque historian

Early Espada dash showed the hexagonal influence of the Marzal (below). Later, AC vents were added to the rear of the console (middle, right). Back windows were hinged at the top; padded handles released them (middle, left). Brochure was in Italian, French, German, and English (bottom).

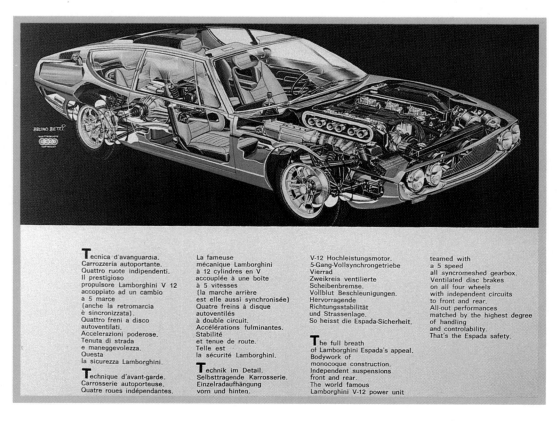

Tecnica d'avanguardia.
Carrozzeria autoportante.
Quattro ruote indipendenti.
Il prestigioso propulsore Lamborghini V 12 accoppiato ad un cambio a 5 marce (anche la retromarcia è sincronizzata). Quattro freni a disco autoventilati. Accelerazioni poderose. Tenuta di strada e maneggevolezza. Questa la sicurezza Lamborghini.

Technique d'avant-garde. Carrosserie autoporteuse. Quatre roues indépendantes.

La fameuse mécanique Lamborghini à 12 cylindres en V accouplée à une boîte à 5 vitesses (la marche arrière est elle aussi synchronisée) Quatre freins à disque autoventilés à double circuit. Accélérations fulminantes. Stabilité et tenue de route. Telle est la sécurité Lamborghini.

Technik im Detail. Selbsttragende Karrosserie. Einzelradaufhängung vorn und hinten.

V-12 Hochleistungsmotor. 5-Gang-Vollsynchrongetriebe Vierrad Zweikreis ventilierte Scheibenbremse. Vollblut Beschleunigungen. Hervorragende Richtungsstabilität und Strassenlage. So heisst die Espada-Sicherheit.

The full breath of Lamborghini Espada's appeal. Bodywork of monocoque construction. Independent suspensions front and rear. The world famous Lamborghini V-12 power unit

teamed with a 5 speed all syncromeshed gearbox. Ventilated disc brakes on all four wheels with independent circuits to front and rear. All-out performances matched by the highest degree of handling and controlability. That's the Espada safety.

The Espada (below) actually was an inch shorter than a 1969 Ford Mustang fastback, but the Lamborghini looked incredibly long and sleek, an impression fostered by the fact that it was just 46.7 inches tall and 73.3 inches wide, four inches lower and two inches wider than the American pony car.

Espada's rear-cabin space fell somewhere between that of a 2 + 2 and a true sedan, though no car could offer back-seat riders passage that was at once more sumptuous, stylish, and swift (left). Design details included a grille on each sail panel (below) that hid filler doors for the 12-gallon fuel tank beneath each rear fender. The triangular NACA inlets on the hood (bottom) fed not the V-12's carburetors, but the cockpit's comprehensive ventilation system.

Jean-Francois Marchet, "Ferruccio Lamborghini, a self-confessed woman's man, had even asked for servo assistance on the clutch...." But this was something he didn't get.

An early-1970 Brussels show was the stage for unveiling a "Series 2" model, though it wasn't called that but rather "400 GTE Espada." Though its most visible alteration was an all-new instrument panel, rear passengers benefited from additional ventilation and a new illuminated center armrest.

Technical improvements were more extensive: vented brakes all-round (replacing solid rotors); Lobro CV joints for the rear halfshafts; and newly optional power steering. The big event was adoption of the high-compression Islero/Miura "S" engine (sans identifying letter) with 350 bhp at 7500 rpm on a 10.7:1 squeeze (previously 325 bhp @ 6500 rpm and 9.8:1). A later running change brought five-bolt wheels of

more subdued design to replace the dramatic Miura-style centerlocks originally used.

Under normal circumstances, the Espada would have been ready for retirement by 1973. But Lamborghini's circumstances weren't exactly normal at that point, not least because of growing labor and economic troubles. Besides, Bertone and Lamborghini couldn't come up with anything better, so they decided to simply improve Espada.

The result, introduced at the 1973 Turin show, was the retrospectively named "Series 3," identifiable by a mildly restyled nose and taillamps. Power steering (an improved ZF system) and air conditioning were newly standard, spring and shock rates rejiggered, rear suspension arms slightly altered, and brakes made more powerful. The dash was revised yet again, newly wrapped around toward the driver from the middle and matched by a more upright kickup from the front of the

center console. Options expanded to include a sunroof and, beginning in March '74, automatic transmission.

That latter item may seem curious for a thoroughbred Italian GT, but some customers with more money than driving ability apparently wanted one. To avoid the expense and bother of making its own, Lamborghini adopted Chrysler's excellent three-speed TorqueFlite (already familiar to Europeans in recent Chrysler-powered Bristols and the Jensen Interceptor from Britain), tightening a few tolerances but not altering its basic design. (This option was extended to the Espada's 2 + 2 derivative, the Jarama, at the same time.) Unfortunately, full-throttle upshifts were set at 4800 rpm—fine for typical Detroit iron but not the Lamborghini V-12. With the automatic, the V-12 couldn't turn within 700 rpm of its torque peak, let alone reach the meatiest part of its power band some 2000 rpm above. The slushbox also absorbed

89

an inordinate amount of the power available at low revs, so step-off was truly disappointing. Then again, maybe the kind of buyer who craved an automatic Lamborghini didn't care.

High demand in Europe had been leaving only a very few Espadas for American customers each year, though Lamborghini still hoped to sell more. U.S. regulations insisted that all cars be desmogged more completely than ever. Accordingly, the factory devised a smog pump that cut out at high revs, leaving peak power unaffected; special carburetors and ignition settings completed the engine cleanup. The U.S. also required five-mph "impact" bumpers, so Sant'Agata drew up "safety" bumpers for the Espada. Though not as dreadful as some of that era, they hardly enhanced Gandini's lines. (European cars got them, too, beginning in 1976.) Some Lamborghini specialists took to calling the later U.S.-spec models "Series 4."

Like many Lamborghini chassis, the Espada's was used to support non-standard coachcraft—though

Espada retained Lamborghini's lauded all-independent suspension, but marked the company's first use of "unibody" construction. It's body was made of steel, though the hood was aluminum. "Mail-slots" in the front fenders helped vent under-hood air.

only once, and very late in the model's life. At Turin '78, when the Espada story was all but over, Carrozzeria Frua presented a one-off four-door built on an early chassis with Miura-style wheels. Called Faena, it had Espada-like proportions and a similar "flatback" roof and vertical rear sub-window, but its hard, heavy lines lacked the grace of the Bertone design. Wheelbase was nearly seven inches longer—and looked it. Curb weight was several hundred pounds greater—and you could see that, too. The Faena may well have been a

fine, big over-the-road sedan, but the streets were full of those.

Historian Rob de la Rive Box tallies a total of 1217 Espadas built in the decade-long production run, making this the most "common" Lamborghini to date.

In other respects, of course, the Espada was quite uncommon— eye-catching, exotic, and fast—so it naturally attracted much press attention. Indeed, the amount of published material is so large as to give us a very clear idea of what it's like to drive.

First, it was the largest

Lamborghini, though not nearly the size of a "Yank Tank" of that era. The American magazine *Road Test* made the valid point that the low-slung Espada looked longer than it really was. Still, even in lands with wide-open spaces, you knew you were "covering a lot of square feet on the road surface," to quote Australia's *Sports Car World*. Ray Hutton, who drove an Espada from Sant'Agata to the *Autocar* offices in crowded London, found it "too big a car to throw around on narrow mountain roads." But fellow countryman Simon Taylor, reporting on a weekend of *Autosport* business in southern England, said it was "very manoeuverable and seems to shrink around the driver as he gets used to it." With that, Taylor found that "the Espada could be booted through roundabouts and tight corners like a car of half its size, weight and power."

That sensation of bulk diminishing with experience also was noted by *Motor Sport's* Denis Jenkinson, who went on to remark about how cleverly all the machinery was packaged—the "incredibly compact" engine nestling between the front wheels, and all four wheels being "very much at the corners." He also was delighted by the "incredible" turning circle: "Just when you think you have turned the wheel to its maximum, you find there is more to come....That helps to reduce the apparent size of the car when manoeuvering and at first glance gives the impression of low-geared steering, which is entirely false, for on the open road the gearing is perfect for all speeds."

Jenkinson thought the suspension equally impressive. You could feel the wheels undulating with surface changes, but the motions were well damped, the ride comfortable. "Comfort is easy to obtain," he wrote, "but directional stability coupled to good cornering, minimum roll or pitch and effectiveness at all speeds is another matter, and the Espada has all these and more."

Echoing this view was Australian Mel Nichols, a well-known Lamborghini admirer: "Offering handling, roadholding and stability that gives the car a natural cruising speed of 115 mph, it also offers one of the most supple rides in existence," he said in *Wheels*. "Many a limousine could learn a commendable lesson from it." The overall effect, he continued, was that "the ride blends with the thoughtful and sumptuous interior appointments to give the Espada its excellent ultra-Grand Touring capabilities, swooping down the road with the kid-gloves and silence of a big jet."

Hutton was a bit less lyrical. He agreed that the ride was good on bumpy roads, although an unanticipated sharp brow would occasionally bottom the suspension.

The backlight was hinged to open like a hatch and was supported by struts, but its near-horizontal position made for poor rear visibility. The vertical glass panel in the tail improved the view aft (above).

Across The Pond, *Road & Track* admired a "soft and quiet freeway ride," but discovered its Espada would hit the bump stops too easily with four persons aboard. Conversely, the rear brakes tended to lock up early sans passengers and luggage. The American magazine thought Lamborghini should adopt some sort of automatic load leveling system, as Ferrari had for its 365 GT 2+2. Well, Lamborghini was working on it, as noted.

On the subject of brakes locking, detailed study of this literature reveals a variety of observations on certain points like this. Some testers agreed with *R&T*, others reported front brakes locking first, and at least one found the brakes so perfectly balanced that they wouldn't lock at all. Such differences evidently reflect the different vehicles tested.

Similar discrepancies crop up about steering effort, but this was probably more a matter of differences in personal taste. Reporting on the early non-power-assisted Espada, some drivers spoke of how much muscle

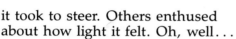

it took to steer. Others enthused about how light it felt. Oh, well....

What most everyone agreed on was the handling: superb. We let the experienced and eloquent Mr. Nichols speak for all: "Left to itself (that is, with a light or trailing throttle) the Espada is an understeerer. Coming through long bends, the front end wants to run out in a very wide line, away from the apex. This can be disconcerting and rather disappointing until you learn to squeeze on more throttle (the pedal, incidentally, has an extraordinarily long travel, but is sponge-soft), progressively increasing power as the car goes

through the bend. The response is immediate—the car just runs around neutrally.

"If you experiment, going much harder into tight bends, you find backing off sharply brings the tail around in progressive oversteer that can be halted precisely to the inch where the driver wishes by bringing on the power once more. In other words, ideal handling for fast, responsive motoring in the hands of someone who knows how. Taken one step further, with all the power (and those 350 bhp suddenly become very real indeed) booted on hard in a low gear the tail will come snaking 'round in full-bore power

oversteer.

"The point here is that the Espada offers every handling condition from Mr. Average's quiet-driving understeer to the red-blooded expert, with the ability to satisfy both types of driver, and all those in between."

Fine, Mel, but how do you like the car? "It is," he answers firmly, "a superb blend of most of the things that are eminently desirable in a motor car; the epitome of an Italian GT."

So why was it killed? Well, sales had tailed off by 1978, and the Espada was hardly the fresh face it had been a decade earlier. But the

Revisions to the Espada in 1973 brought a new instrument panel that had its center section canted toward the driver (top, right). It was actually the car's third dashboard design. The revamp also included Espada's first automatic transmission, the three-speed Chrysler TorqueFlite (top, left). With full-throttle upshifts set for 4800 rpm, it wasn't a great match for the high-revving 3.9-liter Lamborghini V-12 (right), which reached its peak 350 bhp at a thrilling 7500 rpm.

main reason was adverse circumstances affecting Lamborghini as a whole rather than any real deficiencies in the product. Remember that 1978 was the year the Italian courts took control of the company, whose financial health had deteriorated to the point that suppliers demanded cash-on-delivery. Its body builder, Bertone, was its major supplier and its major creditor and, as Marchet records, "relations between Bertone and Lamborghini were at their coldest point." As the money-spinning Countach could be made completely in-house, it just didn't seem worth the struggle to keep the Espada

going. Some years later, Giulio Alfieri confessed sorrow at the car's cancellation to writer Rob de la Rive Box, saying he believed the Espada could have been profitable even at that late date.

But as with the Miura five years before, time had run out for one of the most interesting and appealing cars ever offered by an outfit renowned for interesting and appealing cars. The Espada would hardly be forgotten, though—too unusual, too good, too exciting for that. So don't be embarrassed if your head automatically whirls in its direction on the rare sight of one today. Lamborghinis are like that.

Contemporary reports liken the sensations imparted by the 3583-pound, 155 mph Espada to those of a big jet. "Offering handling, roadholding and stability that gives the car a natural cruising speed of 115 mph, it also offers one of the most supple rides in existence," was the assessment of Australian journalist Mel Nichols. "It is," he said, "a superb blend of most of the things that are eminently desirable in a motor car; the epitome of an Italian GT." The last of the breed were fitted with U.S.-spec bumpers (this page), but were no less lusty.

CHAPTER 11
The Boss's Heavyweight: Jarama

I t had become clear in Sant'Agata by late 1969 that the Islero had to go. In the showroom, the 2 + 2, with its blunt bodywork by Marazzi, looked distinctly boring beside the sleek Espada supersedan and the sultry Miura sports car, both Bertone designs. Also, Islero's 350-era separate chassis was now low-tech *chez* Lamborghini. So, after just two years, the powers-that-were decided it was time for a replacement. They called it Jarama.

Urged by technical director and plant manager Paolo Stanzani, Ferruccio Lamborghini decided to abandon his second fling with a comparatively unknown designer and give all the firm's body business to Bertone. Marazzi's little company might still assemble the shells, but Bertone would press their panels at its Grugliasco facility, not just style them.

This arrangement was economically as well as aesthetically sensible because the Islero's successor would ride a shortened version of the Espada chassis that Bertone was already making. Both ends of this sheet-steel platform, including drivetrain and suspension mounts, were left alone, but 10.6 inches lopped off the middle gave the new 2 + 2 the shortest wheelbase in Lamborghini history: 93.7 inches—6.7 inches down on the Islero's and 2.75 inches briefer than that of the 350 GTV.

So the Jarama was also the lightest Lamborghini ever, right? Sorry. It was one of the heaviest. Not, as some state, because it was bodied in steel instead of the aluminum panels used for the Espada; both cars were steel. No, the real reason was that tiny Marazzi didn't have facilities anywhere near as specialized as Bertone's. According to Bob Wallace, this meant that the structure had to be built up in layers, one panel over another— inefficient construction that partly explains why the Jarama ended up "a good 600 pounds

overweight," as Wallace growls now. And compared with previous Lamborghinis, the Jarama carried more of its total weight on the front wheels, as the engine was planted squarely between them. Shifting the battery to the trunk didn't do much to counterbalance that.

The Jarama looked so different from both the Espada and the Miura that it's hard to believe Marcello Gandini had a hand in it, but he did. True, he was a genius, but one working to a particular constraint. Like the Islero, the Jarama was the "businessman's Lamborghini," the sensible, deliberately unspectacular one—the one for people like the boss.

So Gandini drew an envelope that managed to harmonize a wide "bullet" nose with a boxy tail and trapezoidal side-window openings (the last, perhaps, a vestige of his "Hexagon Period" with the Marzal). The result was a roomy, glassy coupe with suppressed excitement in its sharp creases and muscular wheels—a taut GT looking at once practical and powerful, though perhaps more bold than beautiful. Its most distinctive styling feature was the headlamp treatment: fixed round quads semi-concealed via

Jarama bowed at the Geneva show in 1970 as Lamborghini's 2 + 2 successor to the Islero. It was built on a shortened Espada platform and retained the front-engine V-12 layout. Bertone drew the brawny body around a cabin flawed by poor ergonomics and sloppy assembly. The driving position was typical arms-out-knees-up Italian (above).

body-color covers that pivoted down, like a snake's eyelids, when the lights were switched on.

The letter J is pronounced as Y in Italian, so Jarama is "Yah-RAH-mah." The name was taken from the district in Spain that breeds fighting bulls—and also, one presumes, the like-named racetrack outside Madrid that often hosted the Spanish Grand Prix in those days. The public first saw the Lamborghini Jarama at the Geneva show in the spring of 1970.

Reaction was decidedly mixed. Contemporary reports say some folks appreciated the audaciously innovative styling. Others, in the word of Italian writer Stefano Pasini, found it "disturbing." Most everyone, he went on, was bothered by the "mediocre" interior finish, "incomprehensible" controls, and "irrational" driver's seat. These "and other defects combined to give a rather negative picture of the Jarama."

Then there was all that weight. Despite the slippery nature of poundage figures quoted for various Lamborghinis, the Jarama was certainly much chubbier than the Islero and perhaps as weighty as the

four-seat Espada. Still, the Lamborghini V-12 was as magnificent as ever, and there were wider and stickier new Michelin tires, so the Jarama's performance was still plenty high. Trouble was, it didn't seem quite as high as it should have been. Again, exact numbers differ, but many thought Lamborghini's latest 2 + 2 incapable of its claimed 162-mph maximum, and most everyone believed fuel consumption was excessive.

But don't dismiss the Jarama as either disappointment or failure. To be sure, purists didn't find it as thrilling as its two sisters, but it wasn't meant to be. Like the Islero before it and the Touring-bodied GTs before that, the Jarama was supposed to be relatively conservative. Again, the driver Ferruccio Lamborghini had in mind was one much like himself—a prosperous, more mature enthusiast who needed a genuinely fast yet easy-to-drive car for long-distance business travel. As ever, *Il Cavaliere* was not one of those at Sant'Agata pressuring for show-off hot rods.

And there was evidently much to like about the Jarama. Even those who didn't much care for the styling

appreciated the airy thin-pillar roofline and the adequate rear headroom it conferred, though rear legroom in early models was next to nil. Equally practical were fold-down rear seatbacks for extra cargo space.

Although naturally as wide as the Espada, the Jarama was trimmer in length and thus felt more compact on the road, yet offered the same combination of fine road manners and ride—the latter more comfortable, in Pasini's opinion, than any rival's. "On the road it was a very nice car," agreed Jean-Francois Marchet, "with truly excellent suspension behavior, both comfortable and efficient in cornering and without noticeable roll."

Britain's *Motor* tempered its praise with a list of unfortunate first impressions, citing "poor driving position, heavy steering and indifferently-planned cockpit" as well as poor interior finish. But the editors found that "soon these things are overshadowed, if never eliminated, by other more agreeable qualities like the superb ride, which puts to shame that of many luxury saloons, let alone other sports cars. The roadholding is also outstanding

Critics charged that the Jarama was overweight at 3600 pounds, but its stellar open-road performance belied its heft. After 177 first-generation cars, Lamborghini introduced the improved "S" or "GTS" version (both pages). Front-fender vents helped distinguish it externally, and the cockpit was revamped with better switchgear, additional sound insulation, and more rear legroom (left). The V-12 remained at 3.9 liters (above), but gained 15 bhp, to 365. Top speed increased from 152 mph to 161. It would be Lamborghini's last front-engine sports car.

....The performance is exciting, the noise exhilarating, the brakes and stability at speed superb."

Perhaps because of that noticeably short wheelbase, *Motor's* report returned to matters of roadability and ride: "At speed the Jarama is impressively stable, maintaining an arrow-straight course at its natural cruising gait of 130 mph....The suspension combines those desirable but usually incompatible qualities of resilience for soaking up the bumps, and firmness to minimize wallow and roll."

England's *CAR* also lauded the Jarama's dynamic qualities. Ride was termed "absorbent yet responsive,"

handling as "beautifully balanced" despite the evident nose-heavy weight distribution. "Indeed, the latest car is as precise in its handling as the original 350 GT, which is saying something, as the original model was superior to each of its successors in this respect...."

Observing how well the rear wheels maintained contact on bumpy roads, *CAR* credited the efficient suspension design, calling the Espada/Jarama geometry "a considerable advance" on that of previous Lamborghinis. "The wide-based double wishbones...are arranged to give more or less constant wheel alignment from

bump to rebound," aided by the constant-velocity rear-halfshaft joints. This sophistication helped the "monster" 215-section tires (wider than the Espada's) stick to the road like lint on velvet, making it "surprisingly difficult to get the tail out even in the lower gears."

We repeat such glowing reports to ensure the Jarama receives fair historical due, but it would be wrong to gloss over its shortcomings. Indeed, many road tests agreed with *Motor's*: The Jarama was plenty flawed.

For instance, those wide treads and the lack of power steering made parking an arm-wrestle. Everyone

Just as the stodgy Islero had played a supporting role to the spellbinding Miura and the scintillating Espada, so too was the Jarama sandwiched between Lamborghini's superstars, as a page from the brochure attests (right). Note how this profile view exposes its 93.7-inch wheelbase, the shortest ever turned out by Sant'Agata. Still, the Jarama was a more stimulating car than the Islero and was better able to stake out its own turf betwixt the racer-like Miura and the space-age Espada.

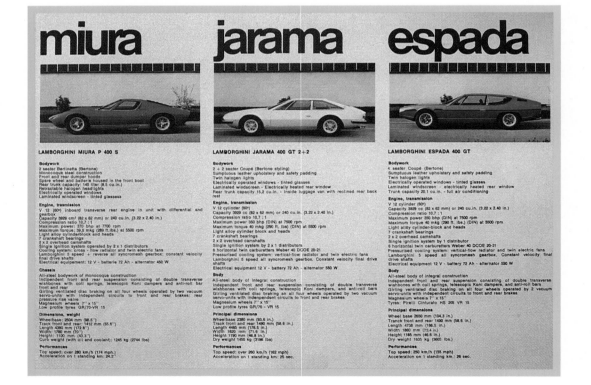

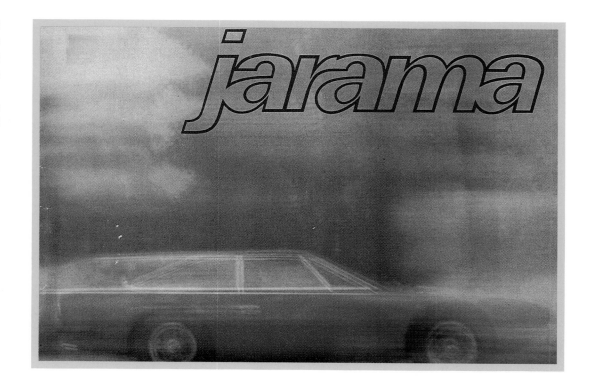

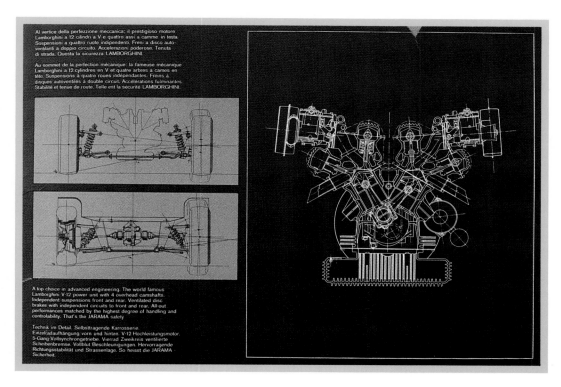

mentioned it, although some added that steering effort and feel were just fine at speed. As *CAR* said, steering that grows lighter with speed is "an incentive to get a move on if ever there was one."

Move off the straight-and-narrow and the higher cornering forces generated by the better tires and suspension revealed inadequate lateral location in the Jarama's seats. Some drivers complained they couldn't see the widely spaced tach and speedometer with both hands on the steering wheel, and the low, centrally mounted clock was hidden by the shifter. Marchet found the dash-mounted wipe/wash controls "nearly invisible at night, requiring much memory and the touch of a blind man."

The Jarama's climate control was something of a contradiction in terms. The system wouldn't give you cool and warm air simultaneously, and its levers sometimes didn't seem to control anything, including the defroster. Also, the fixed rear side glass dictated opening a door window for ventilation—hardly conducive to serene 130-mph cruising.

Like the Espada, the Jarama also suffered a low "bathtub" driving position, so despite narrower pillars and a "vast" windshield, some felt its outward vision was just as difficult. One tester complained that the parked wipers actually obscured his view. He also said the rounded front fenders dropping away from sight made it hard to judge lateral clearances in this wide car. Maybe that was tester-talk for "I scratched it."

The list of liabilities seemed endless: ill-fitting carpets and poorly finished dash wood, seats that would jump their tracks if adjusted too far forward, sluggish cold starting on one car, overheating in traffic because one or the other of the electric radiator fans didn't work, complete failure of all lights on one test run, doors that wouldn't stay open and were hard to close, a curious under-dash handle marked "start" that actually released the hood. Of the awkward pedal and steering wheel arrangement *CAR*

said, "it is sad to see that Lamborghini's development staff have...caught the malignant Italian disease which causes the legs to shrink." The wheel was adjustable, but only with wrenchwork.

Almost as numerous as the gripes were references to the Jarama's weight—and the figures published for it. Again, it's hard to pin down the accuracy and relevance of such numbers, but various reports show a range of 3219 to 3898 pounds. That last was a "test weight," presumably meaning the vehicle with driver, fuel, and test equipment aboard.

And how did it test? Try 0-60 mph in 6.8 seconds and a standing quarter-mile of 14.9 seconds at an estimated 95 mph. That was for a European model, but *Road & Track*'s

U.S.-spec sample wasn't far adrift. Purportedly weighing 3600 pounds at the curb and 3865 pounds as tested (apportioned 53/47 percent front/rear, incidentally) it clocked 0-60 in 7.2 seconds and ran the standing-quarter in 15.6 at 97 mph. This was with the lower, 4.5:1 axle ratio (vs. 4.09), which kept top speed to "only" 152 mph at 7050 rpm. By the way, *R&T*'s Jarama made the skidpad tour at 0.81 g.

Boy, what lousy numbers. See how far sports-car technology has come in 15 years?

You're right. We're making a point. The Jarama of the early Seventies had the specs and speed to match any number of 1990-era "supercars." And though a 3600-pound curb weight may have seemed excessive

99

A hood scoop, new wheels, and more prominent parking lamps helped identify the second-generation Jarama (this page). Unchanged were the NACA hood ducts, which delivered fresh air to the cabin, and the headlamp hoods, which did not retract upward, but instead pivoted down when the lights were switched on. The "S" bowed at Geneva in 1972. The 2+2's U.S. price was $22,625, compared to $23,750 for a Ferrari Daytona and $22,525 for a Maserati Ghibli.

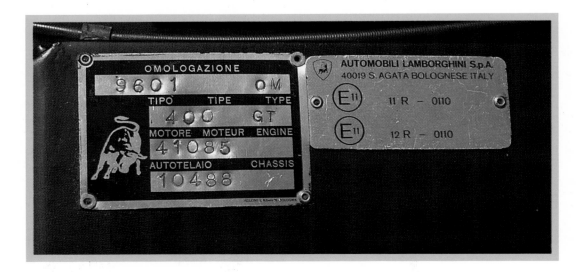

Though 53 percent of its weight was on the front wheels, the Jarama was an extremely capable handler on the open road. Tractable from 1000 rpm, it could scramble to 60 mph in under seven seconds and cover the quarter-mile in less than 15.

then, it doesn't now. Of course, the Jarama wasn't burdened by federal bumpers and other safety equipment, so it obviously was built stout. But let's also not forget that more than a few newer cars return gas mileage on the same order: 10.9 mpg.

For all its faults, the Jarama was redeemed, as *Motor* noted, by its open-road performance. Stroke that long, silky-smooth gas pedal and all the quibbles were drowned in the V-12's howl—a howl that could reach 100 decibels on a sound meter, according to *R&T*, which makes you wonder what happened to the "quiet GT" Ferruccio envisioned. But to anyone with "Blood of the Miura" in the arteries, the sound was glorious.

Jarama production spanned a period of economic turmoil and inflation, so price figures are problematic. However, *R&T* put the Jarama's 1972 U.S. list at $22,625, including dealer prep. That compared to $23,750 for a Ferrari Daytona and $22,515 for Maserati's Ghibli. All, incidentally, are about four times what a Chevy Corvette cost in those days.

As with the Islero, Lamborghini eventually found it necessary to revise the Jarama quite heavily. Thus, after 177 first-generation cars came the "S" or "GTS" model, which saw 150 copies (both figures from Rob de la Rive Box).

Presented at Geneva in 1972, the Jarama S predictably claimed more horsepower: a total of 365, up by 15 bhp, thanks mainly to a more efficient exhaust system, according to Wallace. Heads, cams, and carburetion also were revised. Some published data indicates that the S was substantially lighter than the first-series Jarama without

explaining why, but Wallace says it's not true. In any case, the extra power supposedly lifted top speed to a genuine 161 mph.

Probably more important from the customer's viewpoint was a revised interior featuring slimmer front seatbacks that left more leg space behind, plus a reworked instrument panel with better switchgear labelling and trim of aluminum instead of wood. Heat and noise insulation was said to be improved, too. Power steering became standard equipment a little after launch. It made parking easier, but some felt it detracted from high-speed stability. Later still, one could specify Chrysler TorqueFlite automatic and a pair of narrow, removable roof panels, but neither option garnered many orders.

Lamborghiniphiles could spot a Jarama S by its prominent hood scoop between the existing NACA ducts, and new outlets on the front-fender sides, one behind each wheel arch. Both helped move more air through the engine compartment to keep it cooler. Closer examination revealed parallel-action windshield wipers that parked to starboard, replacing the Espada-style "clap-hands" arrangement where the left blade rested above the right one. Completing "S" exterior changes were slightly revised bumpers and new five-bolt wheels borrowed from the Espada.

Bob Wallace was becoming unhappy about the direction Lamborghini was taking with cars of this nature, and during 1972, to show what he was talking about, he turned one Jarama into a literal hot rod. "We had a lack of things to do, I guess," he explains facetiously.

Wallace first went through the bodyshell with a welding torch to

add stiffness and remounted the engine a few inches rearward to improve weight distribution. The cabin was stripped of all unnecessary equipment, a rollover bar was installed and the back-seat area was turned over to fuel tankage. Outside, he attached lighter body panels, including aluminum doors, and substituted plastic for glass in the side and rear windows. Bumpers were scrapped, a racing-type chin spoiler went up front, the stock hood was swapped for a special item with radiator air extractors, headlights were moved down and lost their snake-eye lids, and a quick-fill fuel cap was stuck out the rear window. Wheels were Miura-type Campagnolos, with wider rear rims as on the Miura SV.

Bob doesn't recall the exact numbers, but this Jarama "was quite a bit lighter" than stock. Quite a bit faster, too. A racer's grin twists his lips as he remembers: "The thing was quicker than stink off the line!"

That, he was trying to say, was what a Lamborghini should be. History bears him out. With all due respect to the company founder and his preference for a certain low-key refinement, it is for their glorious, even raucous highway performance that his cars will always be remembered.

"For it is only, I promise you," said the writer for *CAR*, "when you start to thrash a car like this, to belt it and boot it and cane the living daylights out of the poor inanimate thing, that it really comes alive and demonstrates what it is to have so much investment, so much skill and so much faith built in with every loving twist of every nut and bolt." The Jarama had all that and more. Wheelbase notwithstanding, it was every inch a Lamborghini.

CHAPTER 12
Dreaming the Dream: Miura

It was loud, sexy, and very, very fast. It was born in secrecy, unveiled to wild acclaim not once but twice, and secured Lamborghini's name forever among the supercar elite. With its howling V-12 set amidships, it was the first production automobile to express racetrack technology in strictly highway terms. Some otherwise sober auto historians swear it is the most beautiful car ever built. It's the Miura.

The debut of Lamborghini's first mid-engine supercar is one of but a handful of automotive events that has justifiably taken on legendary stature. In fact, the car was actually unveiled twice, and each was, in the vernacular of the day, a happening. It was only fitting that the car should enjoy such a beginning, for it would go on to prove itself one of the few automobiles worthy of its myth.

So great was this Lamborghini's impact that when it first stunned the world at the Turin Show in November 1965, it was no more than a prototype chassis, the product of a year's worth of secret development work. The new car was unnamed, and work had not even begun on a design for its body. Given the GTV's premature showing, you'd think Ferruccio wouldn't have presented his new sports car until it was completely ready. But again, he couldn't wait. Only this time his impatience didn't hurt.

Aboard the chassis was a V-12 displacing 3929 cubic centimeters and bristling with four camshafts and a dozen intake stacks. That the engine sat both amidships *and* side-saddle only enhanced the mystery and surprise. The monocoque was festooned with lightening holes for all to see—the ultimate in automotive "high tech." Like art that leaves much to the imagination and thus fascinates the most, this chassis started wild daydreams—and caused would-be owners to start waving fat checkbooks. No question: even

without a body, it had more sex appeal than anything else on show.

Yet up to this point, the new supercar had not really been an important project at Lamborghini. Oh, the company's cadre of hotbloods were quite serious about it and Ferruccio himself was enthusiastic. But in terms of funding and corporate priorities it was essentially a promotional exercise, just something to attract buyers to the "bread-and-butter" Lamborghinis. Production? Sure, it was feasible, but nobody at Sant'Agata thought it would amount to more than a handful.

But now, at Turin, Ferruccio found himself besieged by eager buyers, and the promoter in him couldn't resist taking a stack of firm orders—for a car that wasn't even a fully finished prototype, let alone ready for production.

Three of those four deficits were made up in a mere four months. The main one, body design, was paradoxically the easiest of all. Perhaps remembering the aesthetic disaster the GTV had been, Ferruccio wanted this one to be right the first time. Touring, which had been responsible for the production 350/400 GTs, was going out of business and thus unavailable. No problem. Every coachbuilder in Italy was clamoring to clothe the spectacular new chassis, so Lamborghini had his pick. He settled on Carrozzeria Nuccio Bertone.

Styling is one thing, melding appearance with function quite

another. Yet here, too, the project was a success. Bertone worked closely with Lamborghini, each clearly understanding the other's problems and sharing the same ambitions. No surprise, then, that the automobile they created was as lovely in motion as it was at rest.

It was completed, or at least assembled, just in time for the March 1966 Geneva Salon and a second debut, this one a "full-dress" affair. Done in a startling orange-red set off by black trim, the production prototype caused the same stir its bare chassis had in Turin the previous fall. Thus did Ferruccio Lamborghini suddenly find his name on the lips of beautiful and important people everywhere not three years after establishing himself as a boutique automaker to the wealthy.

The car had a model designation by the time it reached Switzerland: P400. The number represented the now-familiar 4.0-liter displacement (in deciliters). P denoted *posteriore*, though here it meant a midships engine, not a true "posterior" one behind the rear-axle centerline. But Ferruccio thought his latest should also have a proper name, and a dandy one came to him. It not only related to his birthsign, Taurus, but referred to one of the most respected of Spanish fighting bulls: the ferocious breed of Don Eduardo Miura.

Technically advanced, astonishingly beautiful, and unbelievably rapid, the Miura was a dream come true: a road car in the

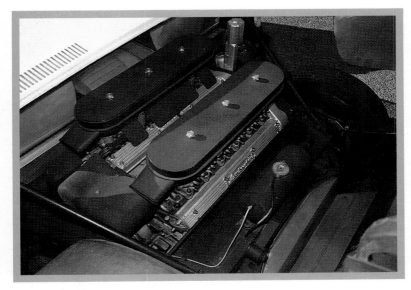

image of the latest mid-engine racing machines. It shook up the sports-car establishment like nothing else before and put "Lamborghini" right up there with "Ferrari" in the hearts and minds of enthusiasts everywhere.

In many senses, the seed for the Miura (MYUR-ah) was planted in 1964. Lamborghini's first production model, the 350 GT, had been well received upon its launch the year before and had settled into steady production. Refining it was all Lamborghini need do to cement his reputation as an automaker. But though it was solid and speedy, the 350 was conventional and not very exciting. Automobili Ferruccio Lamborghini was in danger of becoming just another purveyor of GT cars in a Europe already filled with them.

In the autumn of '64, as one story goes, Sant'Agata's key triumvirate— Giampaolo Dallara, Paolo Stanzani,

and Bob Wallace— found they had a little time for daydreaming. Mainly, they daydreamed about going racing under the Lamborghini flag. "Here we have this fine new factory and this fabulous new V-12," they likely mused. "Wouldn't it be great if the boss let us build a race car?"

Much folklore, some reasonably accurate, has grown up around the Miura's gestation, but Wallace was there: "You've got to remember that back then we three were just part of a whole very good design crew there...a whole bunch of young but very gifted designers and draftsmen— very, very enthusiastic young kids. Initially there was no one in the technical office over the age of 25. We'd sit down in the evenings, probably eight or 10 of us, and kick it over about building a rear-engine car, because we felt that everything that was on the market, including the 350, design-wise, was antiquated."

So the story that the Miura sprang from just "three musketeers" is an oversimplification. What about the allegation that it was supposed to a race car?

"I've always been a firm believer in racing," Wallace answers. "Stanzani was very enthusiastic about racing. How deep his involvement would have been, I don't know, but he was always very enthusiastic about it. Dallara was crazy about it, and so were most of the other kids. So in our minds, we had hoped to make a race car as well. But Lamborghini was adamant. In fact, he was the only person there with enough common sense to not divide up the factory's efforts."

As a self-made man from a hard-eyed farming family—a man whose only race outing (with the little Fiat Topo in the '48 Mille Miglia) had ended in disappointment— Ferruccio Lamborghini, at age 48, was too careful to risk capital on the uncertainties of the track. True, archrival Enzo Ferrari had built much of his reputation on racing, but he'd been in the game for decades. Then too, Ferruccio was concerned (as he revealed years later) that son Tonino might take his involvement as a green flag for a competition driving career of his own. No, thanks: Ferruccio would not go down Racer Road.

Wallace justifies the decision by pointing to the sad case of ATS, the tiny Italian maker of racing and road cars. ATS was formed by some of those who broke from Ferrari in 1961. "They started out with gobs of money and some very good designers [with] very good ideas," he recalls. "Then they divided everything up into two abortive programs and ended up with no money and not doing anything anyway."

So though Ferruccio's youngsters

LAMBORGHINI MIURA P 400

This chassis mockup electrified Turin showgoers in 1965 **(right)**. Up to then, setups like this had been the province of pure racing machines. The road car it would carry had no name and had not yet even been designed. But it's soul was intact: Lamborghini's thunderous 3.9-liter V-12 with an integral transaxle mounted in unit with the crankcase **(above)**. It fit neatly sideways behind the cockpit in the finished auto **(opposite, top right)**, though linking it with the five-speed shifter **(opposite, top left)** taxed the engineers. Don Eduardo Miura, breeder of fighting bulls, a P for **posteriore**, and a rounded-off 400 to denote engine displacement provided the name. Say, MYUR-ah.

Giampaolo Dallara, Lamborghini's chief engineer, was impressed by Ford's mid-engine GT40 sports-racing car of 1964 (top). Major changes beneath the skin were necessary to transfer the idea to a road car. But the GT40's influence upon the Miura styled by Bertone's Marcello Gandini less than two years later is evident (above and opposite).

might have dreamed of building a racer, they knew that they'd have to build a street machine first and that it would necessarily be the basis for a racing Lamborghini—should the boss ever approve one. And, of course, for the racer to have any chance for success, its road-car parent would have to be outstanding.

As for the oft-told tale of enthusiastic young conspirators working on this supercar in secret, Bob replies that the boss knew what they were up to all along. "Basically, he was involved pretty much right from the beginning. We'd actually ask him, 'Can we pursue something like this?' and he'd say, 'Yup.' We'd go back to him when we had some concrete proposals, something pretty much 90-percent clear as what was going to be done. And he was all for

it right from the start."

What's significant here is that Ferruccio had clearly changed his mind about not building "a technical bomb." And far from discouraging his spirited crew, he gave them free reign of his sparkling new factory to realize something very close to their dream.

"Okay," he might have said, tapping their drawings, "I won't authorize a race car, but I'll let you build a car as much like a race car as it can be and still be a good street car. I'll let you build the most technically advanced sports car in the world." He might not have admitted it aloud, but he'd surely concluded that such a no-holds-barred machine would enhance his firm's performance image without risking a thing.

So the "musketeers"—however

many they were—refocused their sights and set about applying their knowledge of racing design to create the fastest, most advanced, most exciting road car they could imagine. And that meant joining the mid-engine revolution.

Putting power behind the people was an idea as old as the automobile itself, and a small number of designers had revived it from time to time for both racing and road use. But it never really took hold despite the likes of the all-conquering Auto Union Grand Prix cars of the 1930s and the giant-killing Porsche 356s and 550 Spyders of the '50s that were their spiritual descendants.

The early '50s also saw Cooper of England start to make its mark on the racetracks of Europe with small-displacement, mid-engine single-seaters. The tiny specialist

107

firm relentlessly kept fitting ever-larger engines, step by step, until its 2.5-liter, 180-mph GP car won the Formula 1 World Championship in 1959. Cooper repeated as champion the following year.

That was the breakthrough. The news that a race car worked better with its engine behind the cockpit and ahead of the rear axle spread

rapidly, and most everyone designing racers of any type or size were soon doing "middies." The reasons were as compelling as a checkered flag. The layout enabled a more compact power package to be situated more closely to the vehicle's dynamic centers of roll and gravity for flatter, faster cornering. It also allowed a more compact, aerodynamic vehicle that was

accordingly more agile and better able to put its power to the road.

In 1959, Cooper also built an open-cockpit sports-racer, the "Monaco," along the lines of its winning F1 design. British rival Lotus followed the next year with its similar "Monte Carlo." Then, in 1961, Italy's venerated Maserati unleashed its Tipo 63, a curvaceous, open sports-racer carrying a massive

The Miura employed a GT40-like monocoque hull in which the roof was integral with the structure. Front and rear body sections were separate, unstressed panels—in effect, just hinged covers (above). Miura's cabin (right) was far more accommodating than the Ford racer's, however. Mounting the engine transversely instead of longitudinally allowed the seats to be set well behind the front wheels and comfortably apart. It was still a noisy, hot place, but with the potential to exceed 170 mph on tap, some compromises were necessary.

3.0-liter V-12 amidships. It was bold but unsuccessful. Wallace, who worked on it, terms the 63 "the most abominable thing you've ever seen in your life."

But it was also in seminal '61 that neighboring Ferrari unveiled its mid-engine 246SP. Powered by a healthy little 2.4-liter V-6, it worked well enough to win races, prompting Ferrari to design a similar chassis around its classic 3.0-liter Testa Rossa V-12. The resulting 250P of 1963 worked even better, becoming the first mid-engine machine to win the prestigious 24 Hours of Le Mans. An evolutionary successor claimed outright victory in '64, and a coupe version, the 250 LM, would do the same in '65.

Meantime, very early in 1963, the tiny English firm of Lola had unwrapped a sleek little GT coupe designed around American "small-block" V-8 engines (which seemed quite large in Europe). This Lola GT caught the eye of Ford Motor Company, then charging ahead with its "Total Performance" assault on most every form of motorsports worldwide. With Lola's help, the U.S. giant developed this basic car into the Ford GT40, a landmark design that first raced in May 1964 and, in later forms, would win Le Mans four years running

(1966-69).

The GT40's true stature was not yet apparent in late '64, but its design had impressed Lamborghini's Dallara, who began drawing up a similar layout. Of course, he was no amateur sketching a dream car but a professional designer.

The car he and his two "co-conspirators" wanted to build would have been primarily a competition machine like the 250 LM and GT40. As the state of the racing art hadn't yet seen sports-racers entirely removed from the old dual-purpose, "race-and-ride" ideal, both the Ferrari and Ford could also be—and were—driven on the road. But neither was at all roomy, comfortable, or easy to live with—in short, not very practical. And while the look of these "GT Prototypes" had enthusiasts drooling, no one had yet come up with an honest, powerful mid-engine road car in the same mold. Lamborghini would be the first.

Dallara worked from the inside out. His 350 GT chassis was a steel-tube structure (like the Ferrari LM's), but race-car builders were turning to a more advanced type of construction inspired by aircraft practice. This naturally appealed to Dallara, who'd trained as an aeronautical engineer, remember.

The new mid-engine Lamborghini would thus employ a GT40-like unitized or monocoque hull, light but enormously strong and fabricated of sheet steel, which was then more practical for this purpose than aluminum. As on the Ford, the roof would be integral with the structure and front and rear body sections would be separate, unstressed panels—in effect, just hinged covers; radiator and spare wheel would nestle under the front one. Suspension would be all-independent, of course, and Lamborghini would naturally use its "stock-block" engine.

At this point, we can imagine Giampaolo sitting back and chewing his pencil. It was time to strike out on his own. The GT40 was magnificent for its mission, but the Lamborghini was to be a very different animal: not meant to lap a track quickly but to carry people happily. And people don't like being cramped.

Designers of single-seat race cars had found that mid-engine positioning facilitated driver positioning, because drivetrain components didn't intrude on cockpit space, and the driver's legs fit naturally into the space between the front wheels. But laying out a two-seat middie was more of a

Miura was more than beautiful, it was efficient inside and out. The radiator, battery, and spare tire filled the forward compartment **(right and opposite, top).** *Cooling air routed through the nose, then out the front-hatch ducting, where it created downforce. Rear louvers and a small ducktail spoiler* **(opposite, bottom)** *also helped reduce aerodynamic lift.*

challenge because the cockpit would have to be wider to accommodate an extra set of legs.

There were two obvious ways around this: an extra-long wheelbase, to put the front wheels farther ahead of the cockpit; the other was to mount the seats very close together. The latter was preferable for a racer, but the traveling companion of a rich person (the new Lamborghini wouldn't be cheap) would not take kindly to crawling across a foot of chassis structure, rubbing shoulders with the driver, or squeezing legs into a narrow, angled tunnel. GT40 passengers endured all of this.

A longer wheelbase wasn't the way to go, either. The new Lamborghini was supposed to be at least as agile as the GT40, which spanned 95 inches between wheel centers. Yet the Lamborghini V-12 was long: some 43 inches with

clutch and other accessories—almost twice the length of the GT40's longitudinally sited 90-degree V-8. If Dallara weren't careful with packaging, his mid-engine sports car would end up having the looks, handling, and mass of a limo.

New approaches were clearly needed. Wallace says that the first considered was a three-seat arrangement: "Our car initially was pretty well drawn up as a central-seater, three-seater car." The one-off

Ferrari 365P of 1966 showed how it might have worked. Driver's seat, steering wheel and pedals would have been in the middle. Given sufficient cockpit width, this would have left room for two flanking seats near enough to the doors that passengers wouldn't have to clamber in very far. And once installed, they'd have adequate foot room despite wheel-arch intrusion.

Such "1+2" seating might have been acceptable given reasonably

Ponder these numbers from a **Road & Track** *test of a 1967 Miura: Curb weight, 2840 pounds; 325 bhp at 7500 rpm; 0-60 mph, 5.5 seconds; quarter-mile, 13.9 seconds at 107.5 mph; top speed, 180 mph.* **Magnifico!**

athletic owner/drivers; it certainly would have attracted the desired attention to the new Lamborghini. But the idea just didn't seem right somehow, and it never even reached Ferruccio's desk. "We'd seen ourselves that it was impractical," Wallace recalls. "I think we had someone make a one-to-five scale model of the body, or something like that. But that was all. It was a real wild-looking thing, but it was scrapped as being completely impractical as a road car."

Besides, Ferruccio's charges had stumbled on a much better idea. In pushing some spare parts around on a big, sturdy tabletop, they suddenly realized that their V-12 measured only 21 inches across its widest point. It could go in sideways! "Just kicking things around, moving all the units around on a chassis table, keeping it within a certain wheelbase and a certain cockpit size that we wanted and so forth, the transverse engine came up and sort of snowballed from there."

With that, everything else literally fell into place. And such an elegant solution: The sideways engine made for a more compact powertrain that allowed the entire cockpit to be behind the front wheel wells, so foot room was no problem and occupants could ride comfortably apart within a manageable 97-inch wheelbase (on the prototype). That was two inches longer than the GT40 span but three inches shorter than that of the 350 GT.

There was still the puzzle of how to get the drive to the rear wheels, but that was a problem for everybody in those pioneering mid-engine days. Lamborghini would have to build its own transaxle anyway, so it might as well be a specialized one, mounted at the "rear" of the engine—in unit with the crankcase, in fact, just like a motorcycle gearbox. "That was to make the whole thing much more compact," Wallace observes, "to keep the whole engine and transmission within a certain size and therefore have room for the driver and also fit everything in a certain wheelbase."

A radical new concept? Some people hailed it as such, but Wallace doesn't view the Miura that way: "Just an overgrown Morris Mini-Minor," he says with a grin. The Mini, of course, was a tiny front-drive econobox with a small inline four, but midships-transverse positioning was a perfectly logical layout with numerous precedents. In fact, that same year—1964—Honda campaigned its first Formula 1 car, a

1.5-liter V-12 job of exactly this configuration.

Wallace had already seen something quite like this during his time at Maserati: "It was done by Giulio Alfieri on a shoestring, when there was a dollar or two to spare. He put [the engine] on a dyno occasionally. It never went into a car, and Maserati was very secretive about it. When the Honda transverse V-12 came out, it was virtually identical, so much so it seems strange. But it's not that unusual for different design teams to come up with very similar designs."

The Austin/Morris Mini appeared in 1959, but transverse engines weren't news even then. Bugatti's last racer had run four years before with a rear-mounted crosswise straight eight, and early Coopers wore their motorcycle engines the same way. Among road cars, at least one, the little French-built de Dion Bouton, had an "east-west" engine as early as the turn of the century.

That the Miura's layout was merely a refinement of existing technology clearly didn't diminish its wondrousness. And that other stylists had created swoopy bodywork certainly couldn't dim the drama of its shape.

Bertone broke with the team-design tradition for the Miura

and instead assigned one main creative spark, a young man about the same age as Dallara, Stanzani and Wallace. Marcello Gandini was 25 in 1965, and what sprang from his drawing board was a young man's sports car: lithe, energetic and sensuous. Overall, it was somewhat reminiscent of the GT40 that had so impressed Dallara. But instead of the Ford's rather utilitarian lines, the car Gandini drew was so sweetly harmonious, so boldly imaginative, so exquisitely alive that it remains fresh decades later. Indeed, this automobile has long since gone down as a design tour de force.

No man is an island, however, and at least two elements of the eventual production Miura could well have been inspired by the work of an equally talented Gandini colleague. This was none other than Giorgio Giugiaro, already winning fame with designs like the neat little Sprint coupe body that Bertone was starting to build for Alfa, and destined to move on to Ghia (where he'd pen masterworks like the Maserati Ghibli) before setting up his own firm, Ital Design.

In his earlier Bertone days Giugiaro had styled the Testudo, a striking one-off fastback based on Chevrolet Corvair running gear that toured the international show circuit in 1963. The name roughly

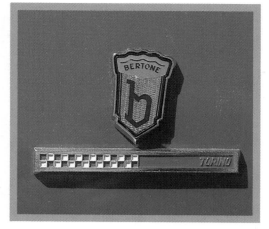

translated as "turtle," but no turtle ever looked like this: sleek, low and rather wide, with a very long, shapely snout and a rounded, substantial rump (which may have prompted the name). Its most radical feature was a huge front-hinged canopy-cum-doors with side windows fully wrapped from B-pillar to B-pillar and no windshield posts. The side glass swept up at the canopy's trailing edges inboard of vertical slots that fed air to the rear-mounted Corvair flat six. The Miura's midships V-12 would be served in almost exactly the same way.

The Testudo headlamp treatment was equally predictive: dual round units that "reclined" flush with the nose when switched off and

snapped to attention when switched on. This idea also resurfaced on the Miura—to such striking effect, in fact, that Porsche was likely moved to copy it for the 928, initiated in the early 1970s.

The first Miura was completed, or at least assembled, just in time for the March 1966 Geneva Salon and a second debut, this one a "full-dress" affair. Done in a startling orange-red set off by black trim, the production prototype caused the same stir its bare chassis had in Turin the previous fall. Thus did Ferruccio Lamborghini suddenly find his name on the lips of beautiful and important people everywhere not three years after establishing himself as a boutique automaker to the wealthy.

Locating a V-8 engine lengthwise was fine for the Ford GT40 **(opposite),** *where simplicity took precedence over passenger comfort. But mounting the Miura's V-12 that way would have necessitated an extremely long wheelbase or a very cramped cabin. Setting it sideways was more complicated* **(above left),** *but allowed for a relatively roomy cockpit within a compact 98.6-inch wheelbase. The house of Bertone won the coveted task of clothing Miura's ground-breaking chassis. The P400 prototype was completed just in time for the March 1966 Geneva Salon, where the car's second coming out was no less sensational than its first.*

CHAPTER 13
Building the Dream: Miura

On the stand at Geneva in 1966, Ferruccio Lamborghini basked in the glow of his luscious new P400 prototype. The Miura legend pictures wealthy enthusiasts pressing in on him. They are breathlessly waving deposits. Ferruccio is cheerfully taking orders. Meanwhile, frantic Lamborghini staffers can barely contain their horror. They know the prototype is but the outline of a dream. They realize that the first production Miura is at least a year away. But they are too timid to burst the boss's bubble.

Bob Wallace grins at the image. "Naw, it wasn't quite that bad, but not far from it. It did take us a while to get it into production, and even then it was hurried—lack of experience on our part, and a bit of everything, really. Working on development there were probably two or three of us. We used to work all sorts of hours, and you just sort of did what you could. . . ."

The reality is that the Lamborghini camp set off on the Miura adventure with little notion of what it was building or how many it should make. "Lamborghini, at first, didn't really see it as a production car," Wallace explains. "It was going to be a car that, if we were lucky, we'd make 25 a year—maybe we'd find 25 people to buy 'em." Even the Geneva showing, where Wallace remembers that "people went stark raving mad over it," didn't foretell the magnitude of demand. "No, we never thought we'd get that sort of reception." So it's hardly surprising that neither the car nor its tooling were designed for a long production run, let alone anything like significant volume.

Take the engine/transaxle package, extremely complex to make. To a draftsman it was mere artwork, just a matter of lines on paper. But to the people running Lamborghini's foundry it presented a three-dimensional problem of major

It's said the Miura concept was hatched by a trio of Lamborghini hotbloods with designs on racing; the prototype engine (right) even had a racing clutch. Ferruccio wouldn't race, but he soon fell under the car's spell. Seen initially as a high-image, low-volume toy, the Miura turned out to be one of his best-sellers. Taking the bare hull (above) to finished product (left), however, proved an ambitious, problem-plagued undertaking for the little company.

proportions. "Back then, doing a one-piece casting of that size was difficult," says Wallace. "There were a lot of bugs to iron out."

Then there was the method chosen for making the bodyshells, especially the aluminum front and rear hinged sections. "All that panel work was done with locally reinforced resin dies. They won't do a production run of more than 200, 240 units." Eventually, the Miura would sell nearly that many copies in a single year.

Lamborghini wasn't the first outfit to underestimate demand for a complex automobile, and the consequences of this fundamental error would dog Miura production from start to finish. As Wallace observes: "The car was costing a fortune to build because of the inadequate tooling for it, and that's why the cost of reproducing body parts for them today is enormous."

One final factor complicated the "what are we building?" stage: As with the 350 GTV three years before, there were early thoughts of a competition Miura. While Wallace and his colleagues probably knew this was just a pipe dream, others in the organization were openly and officially predicting it. For instance, a June 24, 1966, press release from Lamborghini's eastern U.S. distributor promised that the new Miura "will be in production this fall in two models, one for the road and one for the track." That "fall" timetable was equally optimistic—by no less than six months.

Further, though less direct, evidence that a racing Miura was at least contemplated is seen in the first four-color Miura brochure put out by Lamborghini's *Ufficio Stampa e Propaganda* (Office of Press and Public Relations). On the back cover was a spec chart in four languages listing "Maximum speed: 300 Km/h road version." Granted, "road version" appeared only in the English section, so Italian, French and German readers who couldn't read English missed this clear implication that there was something else. But inside, over a photo of the original Miura engine with multi-plate clutch, is a statement that "the house" offers two models—*"La casa ne offre due versioni: normale (350 cavalli DIN); spinto ["pushed"] (430 cavalli DIN)."*

On that last point, Wallace says nothing so grand as 430 horsepower was ever extracted from a 4.0-liter Lamborghini V-12 (not even the one in his Jota hot rod, more of which in Chapter 15). Even 350 bhp was very optimistic for an early Miura; 320

was more like it. In any case, however strong the impulse to build a racing P400, it weakened, and all efforts duly concentrated on readying the production car.

Not counting the bare chassis shown at Turin '65—which was just a mockup, that was never bodied and was ultimately scrapped—the orange Geneva car was Miura No. 1. This hand-built prototype was soon subjected to exhaustive tests on the roads and tracks of Italy to exterminate the inevitable bugs in its basic design.

Hard work, but also a little fun.

Two months after its triumphant splash in Switzerland, the orange Miura was guest of honor in Monaco, serving as the ceremonial circuit-opener at the single most important race on the Grand Prix calendar. It was another Lamborghini front-page production. Wallace drove the car over from Italy the day before the race and in the evening parked it in the absolute center of rich-and-famous activity, Casino Square in front of the grand Hotel de Paris.

Thus began another Lamborghini legend. As Pete Coltrin related the

story, within seconds there were Beautiful People gathered five deep around the lovely, exotic piece of rolling sculpture. Ferruccio himself, watching from the outskirts, waited for the strategic moment; then, on the pretext of showing the car to one of his industry friends, made his way through the throng, opened the door, climbed in and fired the engine. The crowd instantly swelled to 10 deep.

"Lamborghini himself was pretty much a showman," remembers Wallace with a smile. "He'd get in it and rev the hell out of the thing,

scream it around the block. We also gave it to one of the Italian drivers, I think it was [Lodovico] Scarfiotti, to do some hot night laps around the track.

"Yeah, Monte Carlo was when it really woke Ferraris up to something, because Agnelli [Gianni, chairman of Fiat] had one of the Ferrari engineers with him, and just pulled him out of the hotel and showed it to him. 'You people better wake up!' he says. Yeah, it caused quite a sensation."

But there wasn't much time for crowd-stopping, because the test

Light, but enormously strong, Miura's unitized central shell was fabricated of sheet steel. The non-load-bearing front and rear panels were made of aluminum. In the back of the tail was a small, carpeted luggage compartment accessible from outside via a hinged trunk lid.

schedule was grueling for a single "mule." Actually, a second prototype was completed, a mustard-yellow car, but test-driver Wallace says it was used more for show. That one, Miura No. 2, survives today. No. 1, the first complete P400, unfortunately does not. It was destroyed—crushed. No, not by the factory. By a truck.

Wallace recounts the sad tale. "Someone drove it up to Bertone's one day, on business, and was on his way back when he stopped at a stoplight. He was sitting there when he saw the wheels of this truck climbing up the back bodywork. All he could do was bail out and watch it happen."

Some historians believe a third prototype was built to the original configuration, but Wallace says no. The third car built was to final production specs, and getting to that point involved important changes to both body and powertrain.

The engine/transaxle package was altered in two ways. First, the original clutch was an exposed three-plate design mounted on the input end of the gearbox, much like a typical motorcycle clutch. This gave way to a more conventional, single-plate enclosed unit at the end of the crankshaft (on the car's left). However, the clutch was still cantilevered out, or overhung, to

extend beyond the geartrain that took drive to the transaxle. The flywheel and clutch pressure-plate were overhung extensions of the crank and were moving elements.

A second change concerned the direction of crank rotation. In the Lamborghini V-12, like most auto engines, the shaft turned clockwise as seen from the front. With the engine situated 90 degrees, clutch-end to the car's left, the crank thus revolved in the same direction as the road wheels. This was reversed on all production Miuras so that the crank rotated "backwards."

Wallace explains that these two changes were intimately related: "The first engine had an external, race-type clutch, and it was completely impractical for a road car. There were a lot of ideas that were impractical. We had a chain drive in there at one stage, like an Olds Toronado. When we had a train of gears, we had lubrication problems, you name it. We had just a whole bunch of problems. We tried different things, and none of them worked."

Other sources speak of early harmonic vibration problems severe enough to shatter gearwheels. The final solution was to send power from the clutch to the transmission through an intermediate idler gear. That gave the powertrain four basic

geared shafts—crank/clutch, idler, transmission mainshaft, and final drive—and meant that crankshaft rotation had to be reversed to make the rear wheels turn in the desired direction. Otherwise, the car would have had one speed forward and five reverse! Wallace says there was no need for fundamental engine alterations, just details like cam timing.

More second thoughts involved the alternator and shift linkage. The former was originally gear-driven from the output end of the crankshaft, but this was changed to a more conventional belt drive in the interest of reduced noise, which in turn dictated grouping the alternator with other ancillaries at the "far" end of the engine.

The linkage problem was a lot more complicated: How to transfer gearshift motion from the middle of the car all the way around to the back of the engine where the transmission was. One early scheme employed a complex system of hydraulic lines. Wallace says this actually worked quite well—when it worked. Problems with heat and seals proved so annoying that the team scrapped the idea and evolved a straight mechanical linkage. Engine-block castings were changed to bring a tubular shifting rod straight through the crankcase from

Miura's knotted exhaust (opposite) robbed it of the mellow tones associated with the front-engine Lamborghinis, but its war cry at full throttle was glorious nonetheless. The V-12 in this installation was very compact, but since it didn't need to clear the lower hoodline of the 350/400 GT, it could wear its four triple-throat Webers vertically, though they looked less imposing with air cleaners on (left). It made an estimated 325 bhp. The command post for all this rocketry is itself an essay in high-performance sports cockpits (above).

119

front to rear below the crankshaft; a system of cranks and rods then transferred motion up to the transverse gearshafts. The dauntingly elaborate, necessarily stiff-shifting mechanism that resulted is the single flaw in an otherwise brilliant powertrain.

Important detail revisions occurred in the body/chassis design. Let's start with the radiator. On the bare show chassis it mounted in an odd lay-down position atop the front structure; this was changed to a more conventional position. As Wallace cautions: "That first chassis mockup—don't even call it a chassis—was done pretty much by hand and pretty much in a hurry. You can see it utilizes pretty much the 350 suspension stampings and bits and pieces like that. It was just something to make a mockup of the ideas and to start looking around for someone to put a body on the thing. It's a lot better with a mockup of a chassis like that. You can sit down back at the factory and take a second look at things, and then start putting the whole thing on paper in a fairly rational manner."

The first running car was the second step in the debugging process, and a cooling problem surfaced quickly once Wallace got it out on the road. He remembers the solution mainly involved attention to radiator air-outlet ducting, but better airflow through the engine compartment was also needed.

Like the GT40, the original Miura body had a transparent exterior rear window—actually just a plastic sheet. Trouble was, it kept a lot of heat from escaping the engine compartment (and probably gathered a lot of oily dirt that quickly rendered it opaque). Adding vent holes provided only partial relief. Happily, replacing the window with a bank of open louvers provided the practical (if noisy) solution—and a distinctive styling feature that would be later imitated by other automakers and numerous accessory houses (in bolt-on backlight "blinds" that rarely looked all that good).

Of course, the Miura had a second rear window—in the bulkhead separating cockpit from engine compartment. It had to. With the engine just inches behind the cockpit, noise and heat levels in there would have otherwise been unbearable. After an early trial with an elaborate double-walled, gas-filled glass pane, simpler construction in a special plastic called Visarm was found to provide adequate insulation.

Cockpit ventilation dictated another "aerodynamic" refinement. According to chronicler Chris Harvey, the first Miura had a small, driver-operable hatch in the roof at a point where low air pressure at speed would pull air out from inside. But it didn't work all that well and ultimately gave way to a rank of small, fixed extractor vents like those on the original GT40.

Much less easily remedied was a cockpit that was simply too small. That's why the roofline was raised a little and the cabin lengthened beginning with Miura No. 3. Some historians believe the cockpit was stretched to improve handling; others state that it was to make room for thicker heat and sound insulation in the firewall. Of the latter, Wallace says, "No, that was never changed. It was always inadequate! No, that [insulation thickness] dimension never changed at all. It was just to get a little more room. The first two cars, the first two hand-built prototypes, were a little cramped. The additional length went into more foot room."

It amounted to 1.4 inches, leaving wheelbase on production Miuras at 98.4 inches. The height increase was much less—a mere 10 millimeters (call it 3/8 inches)—but lowering the seats an equal amount gave a useful overall gain in headroom.

All these improvements were built

into operational car No. 3, the first Miura built to final production specs, though both the design and manufacturing details were further refined even after this. Aggravated by delays in gathering all needed components, the assembly line didn't really began to stir until late 1966. The first customer car finally went out the door early the next year—some 12 seemingly interminable months after Geneva.

Was it worth the wait? The verdict of those who drove the Miura and wrote about it was a resounding yes. Here's a sample of contemporary comment: "...one of the more memorable high points in the history of automotive architecture... furious performance and terrific roadholding...the most glamorous, exciting and prestigious sports car in the world...an absolute blast to drive on a winding road...a long surge of power and a beautiful noise that could best be described as ecstasy...this car is the ultimate."

So even after all those months, the Miura was still fresh and exciting, not least because it was the only big mid-engine sports car on the market (for all the time that had passed, it wasn't enough for competitors to have issued replies). Even better, its radical design really worked, and Lamborghini could claim the fastest and most capable production car on earth.

Posing on the factory floor is a production P400 engine (above). Compare its clutch position, inside the large "dome" on the extreme left, with the prototype's exposed clutch on page 115. Beneath the spare tire (left) nestled the 24-gallon fuel tank, but only $^2/_5$ of the car's weight was up front.

CHAPTER 14
Driving the Dream: Miura

It's parked beneath a canopy of tree branches on the graveled driveway of your estate. It is a somewhat frivolous two-seat coupe. It makes a lot of noise, has fragile aluminum fenders, no real bumpers, and wants a skilled mechanic living nearby. But none of that matters. For it is a wild-looking thing, an obvious product of impulse and passion, a car with a florid, hothouse appearance. One of the sexiest shapes ever drawn around four wheels, its combination of smooth, sensuous flesh and rock-hard muscle stirs your soul.

It is the summer of 1967 and you're about to climb into your new

Lamborghini Miura. It set you back about $20,000, half again as much as any other Lamborghini and some $5,000 more than Ferrari's fastest, the front-engine 275GTB/4. The same money would have bought you five Chevrolet Corvettes.

But none of those cars stimulates your intellect with avant garde thinking the way the Miura does. The 1960s are witnessing revolutionary changes in racing (as in society) and the mid-engine Lamborghini incorporates much of this new technology.

With approval, you note how the flowing body of your car works with the atmosphere instead of against it.

The designers clearly learned from track experience how to exhaust radiator air into the region of low aerodynamic pressure atop the nose, and how a small spoiler at the rear helps manage the spill of high-speed airflow off the tail. Instead of simply tolerating today's wider, flat-treaded tires, fenderlines are harmoniously shaped to accommodate them. Overall, the Miura's curvaceous sculpturing boldly celebrates its competition-inspired midships layout and high performance potential, while the low, efficient-looking nose implies a most intimate relationship between driver and road.

The Miura could be vicious in the wrong hands; driven with the proper combination of respect and authority, it was the ride of a lifetime. Visibility forward was excellent (**opposite**). It was poor to the rear, but what could be gaining on you? Twist the key, ignite the twin-cam V-12 (**left**) and WHOOOM! Feeding time at the lion house. Pedals and steering wheel (**below**) were straight ahead, not angled as in some cars, and the footwells were as wide as in many front-engine autos. The lucky passenger got a comfy foot rest, but grab bars on the console and dash hinted at what was really in store.

Of course, racing has taught you to appreciate the mid-engine layout's dynamic benefits, including that "low polar moment of inertia" you've been reading so much about. The rear-driven wheels carry nearly three-fifths of the car's total weight, which ought to improve acceleration, braking, and cornering while making for more agile handling and responsive steering. With all-independent suspension and four-wheel disc brakes, the Miura should manage with perfect aplomb the bumpiest, twistiest road you can find.

You had already made up your mind to accept certain practical drawbacks inherent in the midships configuration as the price of this enhanced performance. Happily, the Miura's imaginative design keeps that price low. The transverse engine positioning contributes to a cabin entirely free of front wheel-arch intrusion. That means ample foot room: 18 inches across the pedal area on each side, more than in many orthodox sports cars. Pedals and steering wheel are die-straight ahead of you, not awkwardly angled as in so many cars—mid-, front-, and rear-engine alike. Also, the two shapely seats are set comfortably far apart, so occupants don't *have* to rub shoulders.

Though the Miura rises to barely above your waist (overall height is a rakishly low 41.3 inches), getting in and out is relatively easy. Doors are long and front-hinged, and you need negotiate a sill only seven inches across and six tall. Unlike the

Ford GT40's wider, deeper sills, the Miura's don't double as fuel tanks; a single 24-gallon reservoir mounts snugly in the forward part of the chassis beneath the spare wheel.

Another area where your car's designers thought for themselves is behind the engine. Where the GT40 has a bulky racing exhaust system and a jutting transaxle, the Miura's transmission hardly protrudes at all, and pipes tucked down and under leave room for a full-width trunk in the tail.

That hold is reasonably generous, too, though at 41 inches wide by 20 "long" and about a foot deep, it helps to have sausage-shaped luggage. A small bin is provided on each trunk sidewall for storing tools and the jack. But a word of warning to enthusiastic pilots: Be sure everything is well secured back there, because there's nothing to protect the soft aluminum bodywork from dings caused by flying cargo within.

Whatever you carry pretty well has to go in the trunk because, as in other midships two-seaters, the Miura's cabin has little room to spare. Your passenger, for instance, won't be able to recline the seatback for a snooze (the insulating bulkhead separating cockpit from engine bay precludes it), so your driving had better be entertaining!

No fear of that: This automobile was built for pure driving pleasure. And should any nagging doubts about the wisdom of your purchase still linger, they'll flee the instant you fire up that superb V-12 right

behind your ears.

First, turn the switch and wait a moment for the electric fuel pump to fill the quartet of big, three-barrel Weber carbs (this may take a bit if the car hasn't been driven in a few days). There's no choke, so stab the throttle a couple of times to squirt raw gas into the intakes. Then just turn the key. WHOOOMM!

You'd think it was feeding time in the lion house back there. Such a cacophony: roars, rumbles, growls, whines and shrieks. But what else from four whirling camshafts, a dozen throbbing pistons, two-dozen popping valves, and well over 300 rampaging horses? And you can hear every single one of them all. This may be a street motor, but it's every bit as exciting as a Formula 1 engine to listen to.

And it's almost as entertaining to drive. Lamborghini makes a fabulous high-performance powerplant, one of the best yet. On wide-open throttle it simply hurls the Miura up the road like a springing wildcat. Yet this highly tuned jewel is no one-dimensional rough and rumbly lump of heated-up Detroit iron. It has a sweet, civilized side that allows it to endure the tedium of city traffic with utter grace. And the transition from chore to full-bore is so smooth, so free of temperament, the power curve unmarred by lumps, dips, or steps.

Yes, the carburetors (the same type Porsche uses on the 911) must be in perfect tune, all four of them—which may take some time for even a good mechanic. But it's time well spent. Driving a Miura with maladjusted carbs is a disappointing experience.

Even when all is not quite well, this engine is complemented by a chassis in which everything works smoothly and honestly, though it, too, must be set-up properly. This is a machine that does not mute its machinery—hardly surprising in a roadgoing GT from people who'd really have rather built a race car.

Consider pedal effort. Step on the gas and you know you're opening 12 throttles. The clutch isn't heavy or abrupt, yet you sense that it's completely up to the task of taming

that herd of horses. You will need real muscle to get the best from the brakes because there's no servo, but race cars don't have one either.

Rack-and-pinion steering is also expected in a modern sports car, and the Miura has it. Like the brakes, there's no power assist, though you may not miss it. Medium-fast gearing gives 3.25 turns lock-to-lock, and only 42 percent of the car's 2800 pounds is on the front tires. Still, helm control is far from a fingertip business.

That aside, the steering could be called light and lively despite a very slight stickiness, perhaps caused by the hydraulic vibration damper. The gearing makes it seem a trifle slow at first, but you soon grow used to this and come to appreciate the extra precision it confers at high speed.

Even better, the direct, purely mechanical linkage allows your hands to sense exactly what's happening at the road. As the tires encounter little ripples, they "talk" to you through the wheel. When the front end loads up under braking, the steering becomes palpably heavier and dartier. Come out of a curve, get back on the power—of which there is plenty—and you will feel the front end lighten up and maybe start to drift across the road.

Such clear and honest communication characterizes the Miura's entire dynamic repertoire. To be sure, some find the new mid-engine Lamborghini tricky, even vicious—ready to bite any unskilled hands that try to lead it. Labeling it treacherous would be wrong, but it's certainly up-front about being difficult. Then again, anyone who gets into a Miura—let alone buys one—should always remember that this is a sophisticated high-performance thoroughbred built much like a championship competition car.

Which means that the Miura is neither forgiving nor facile in hard and fast driving. It is demanding. It will keep you busy. You must keep bringing it back to course on straight stretches, and a brisk run down a curvy, bumpy road will exercise you more than the car.

Moderate understeer is its basic attitude in steady-state cornering.

Go in too hot, let up on the gas, and the back end will step out, but it happens so decisively that you can't miss the implication: Go fast enough, lift off abruptly enough, and you'll spin. "Drive me with a tender touch," the Miura insists, a message it constantly telegraphs loud and clear. But it rewards caressing hands and smooth footwork with equal authority. It is a driver's car in the literal sense of the term.

It is, of course, not perfect. No automobile has been, or ever will be. Still, one finds more awkward details and even outright problems than maybe there ought to be in a car of this performance, panache, and price.

One deficit stems from the lack of a limited-slip differential even as an option; it couldn't be fitted because engine and transaxle share the same supply of relatively lightweight oil. The Miura thus doesn't put its power to the pavement the way cars of this caliber should.

Worse, that shapely nose

apparently generates severe front-end lift from about 100 mph on up—enough to make the steering alarmingly light.

Ergonomics leave much to be desired. Though your car has 20 millimeters (³/₄-inch) more headroom and a 1.4-inch longer wheelbase than the original Miura prototype, the cockpit is still a bit cramped for anyone over about 5'10".

Yet despite what you may think from the outside, the Miura is surprisingly light and airy inside, though occupants are constantly aware of how close their foreheads are to the windshield. Most hot-shot cars still have long hoods, and even the daring Maestro Gandini apparently couldn't tear himself away from this style, which partly explains why the glass is so near. It's also large and steeply angled, and as air conditioning isn't available, either, the cabin becomes a real hothouse on sunny days. You can, of course, lower the door windows (which go down all the way, unlike those on most exotics)

depending on velocity and how much wind buffeting you can tolerate.

At least the A-pillars are quite slim and, being so close, practically disappear, so your view over the short, ground-sniffing snout is panoramic. That's all that really matters when you're able to use this car the way it was meant to be. But in all too many situations, what's behind and around you also matters, especially in a car that attracts attention the way this one does.

Here appearances do not deceive, and vision directly astern can be poor. Not because the carburetors get in the way (they don't) but because of sun glare from the distinctive louvers above the engine bay. Over-the-shoulder vision is nonexistent. The side mirrors are apt to show more of the car than its surroundings; even craning your neck for a look out the left window is more awkward than usual. And in this very low-slung beast your eyes are at a level that's perfect for

studying other cars' trunklids and doors. In all, threading a Miura through rush-hour traffic is an object lesson in defensive driving.

A host of irksome little cockpit details don't make things any easier. The gas pedal rises so straight from the floor that you almost have to tilt your foot backwards, which may be fine for foot-to-the-floor European driving but quickly causes ankle-ache in speed-limited American conditions.

The dash layout is just as unfriendly. A large, impressive 10,000-rpm tachometer and matching 200-mph speedometer (320-km on European cars) flank the steering column low down in front of you, but there's a bit of wasted space between and around them that forces the minor gauges over to the top of a central binnacle, where they're hard to read at a glance. Switches for lights and fans are overhead, aircraft-style. Each connects to an annunciator light on the binnacle, but nothing is labeled. The turn-signal telltale is frankly

Pure athlete, the Miura was created not to take one to work, but to work for one's pleasure. Its speedometer read to 200 mph, the tachometer to 10,000 rpm (opposite). It had its delicate touches, like the exquisite door handles and the gossamer strakes of the air intakes. But the heavy plate of the shift gate—with its flip-up reverse lockout—told the truth about this car. So did nearly 100 mph in second gear.

ridiculous—a tiny little green thing that's hard to see even when you're looking for it—and if there's an associated noisemaker, you'll never hear it.

There's more. The seat adjusters are way under the cushions and thus very hard to reach. Cranking the windows down takes more than seven turns, and the winders are so deeply recessed that you can scuff your knuckles on the door panels.

Such aggravations don't end with the interior. To release the huge rear-hinged engine cover (roughly the back third of the body) requires opening both doors and pulling a T-handle behind each seat. And you must remember to push them back in before closing the doors or else the handles might break off. Pit stops seem to take an age because the fuel-filler neck, sharply angled so as to come up beneath the nose-top grillwork, only lets the vital fluid trickle in. A rainstorm means getting water inside whenever you open the door, because the Miura's stylist refused to provide rain gutters, while the most insignificant parking-lot shunt guarantees a nasty mar on the beautiful body, because the stylist rejected serious bumpers.

On the move you'll find the gearshift rather stiff and heavy, and first gear is occasionally hard to engage even at standstill. One design problem in most mid-engine cars is the long, tortured path the shift linkage must take around the engine—complicated here by the transmission's transverse orientation, which required that shift motions be turned through 90 degrees before reaching the gears. Lamborghini's solution—running the linkage straight through the engine—is

practical and effective, but there's still a rather elaborate train of rods and bellcranks behind that. Of course, the gears are pretty beefy (to handle all that torque), and the odd clutch design and Porsche synchronizers add drag of their own. With all this, shifting is real work.

More worrisome is what happens to engine lubrication in hard cornering. Your new Miura whips around a skidpad with torso-tugging lateral acceleration of 0.85 g or better, but as the sump is wide and has only a single pickup in the middle, such shenanigans can induce oil starvation. Sustained, hard counterclockwise cornering will result in a major oily mess as the engine loses its lifeblood out the right-side breather.

On a happier note, the Miura's ride is a good compromise for a car with such high potential speed and cornering. Springing is as firm as you'd expect—as firm as it needs to be, really—but the car is quite comfortable over most surfaces. Some rougher patches will jar you mercilessly, though, and that can be tiring.

So can talking, because of all the noise. Cockpit decibel levels do drop some with the windows up, but why should such an expensive high-flyer of such advanced design force a choice between baking in relative quiet or breezing along bathed in mechanical noise? That noise is undeniably beautiful—a symphony of finely machined, high-strung mechanisms—and listening is no hardship for enthusiasts. But it is loud enough that, if you insist on extended conversations with your passenger,

you'll find yourself shouting—and a little hoarse after awhile.

All this strain, physical and mental, results in a buildup of nervous fatigue. After a couple of hundred miles in a Miura, you may feel as drained as if you'd covered the distance on a sports motorcycle.

But life with any exotic demands commitment, and this particular exotic is no car for casual cruising. The fiercest of the fighting bulls from the Lamborghini farm, this is an all-out sports car, a hardcore play-partner for those who relish driving as sport and participate in it with passion, skill, and decision.

For them, the main impression is still positive. That's largely due to the engine: so strong and rich in personality that it dominates every other sensation. You may have fallen in love with the Miura for its body, but it's this great mechanical soul that will have you enthralled after just one drive. In fact, the Lamborghini V-12 casts such a powerful magic spell that you scarcely notice the Miura's many shortcomings, things that would seem unforgivable in lesser machines.

Flat-out, the Miura is probably the world's fastest road car in this year of 1967. It will cover 0-60 in about 5.5 seconds, a quarter-mile in under 14 seconds at over 100 mph, and will sail on to upwards of 170 mph! And when you're hanging onto all that, who has time to notice the niggles?

Still, those annoyances do exist, and Ferruccio Lamborghini set out to build cars free of annoyances. The plain fact is that the dream in your driveway has not fully come true—at least not yet.

CHAPTER 15
Perfecting the Dream: Miura

I t didn't escape Ferruccio Lamborghini that his most sensational car ran counter to the philosophy on which he had founded his automobile company. Lamborghini's goal was to manufacture premium cars with a standard of refinement that was higher than those of rival makers. He sought comfortable, quiet grand tourers without mechanical troubles. The Miura wasn't that sort of car at all, at least not in 1967. While it was undeniably splendid—fast, fun and, if pushed hard, quite a challenge—it wasn't much of a tourer.

So the little firm deserves credit for making a serious attempt to

improve the P400, for though the car's initial flaws were many and obvious, sensational styling and thrilling performance virtually guaranteed that every Miura built would be sold. Wallace and Co. got right down to work and ultimately made many refinements, probably more than on any other Lamborghini model. Some were put into production as soon as they were ready. Others were part of two formal upgrades: the S-model, introduced in 1969, and the still-better SV that succeeded it two years later.

Incidentally, many of these modifications can be—and have

been—made to early examples, P400 owners apparently being less reluctant to individualize their cars this way than is usually the case with high-performance exotics. Of course, this tends to make model identification tricky, but that's more a problem for concours judges and automotive historians.

The single most major revision—so fundamental as to make retrofitting entirely impractical—was heavier-gauge sheet steel for the chassis. Effective with Miura No. 125, according to factory records, it brought metal thickness from 0.9-millimeter to an even 1.0 mm (0.039-inch). Dallara's original design

The Miura that bowed in 1967 likely went into production before it was ready. But gradually, over hundreds of cars, the roughest edges were honed from the initial design and the first formal upgrade was introduced in 1969. Called the Miura S (both pages), it got a stronger engine, subtle rear suspension revisions, and optional air conditioning. Though useful, the wide rear wheels and tires on the yellow car were not part of the original S specification.

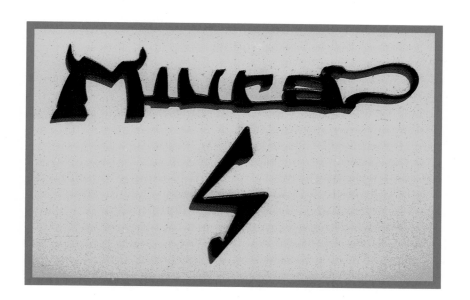

Reshaped combustion chambers, higher-lift cams, and bigger carburetors increased output of the S version (both pages) to 370 bhp, up at least 20 from the last of the original Miuras. Styling was unchanged and the car, in overall shape and in every detail, remained modern sculpture.

calculations perhaps didn't fully anticipate the sheer ferocity of the final production car's performance, especially with the ever-grippier tires that became available after production commenced. As Bob Wallace admits, sensitive drivers could detect distinct chassis flex in hard work, and some early Miuras apparently suffered actual structural failure.

But Wallace notes that stouter steel wasn't the total cure, so various gussets were added at various times for further structural strengthening, particularly where the front and rear extensions joined the central tub. These reinforcements can be retrofitted, and Wallace recommends just that. By the time production ended, both measures had rendered the chassis flex "very, very minimal," he says, though it was still noticeable if you were looking (and driving) hard enough.

Rear suspension was the second-most important area of change, and it was changed twice: for the S and again for the SV, each accompanied by upgraded tires. The former gained subtly altered mounting points that reduced squat under hard acceleration. The SV's suspension was completely redesigned front and rear, supplemented by much wider aft tires and rims that dictated bulging the rear fenders. Wallace says these revisions, together with the strengthened chassis, were enough

to make the SV "pretty well completely a different car" compared to earlier Miuras. "The handling difference is an enormous improvement."

Wallace observes that two other problems were finally corrected with the SV. The solutions were linked. One was a new sump with sufficient added depth that the oil pickup no longer unported in hard cornering, thus eliminating the tendency of previous cars (most Miuras built, in fact) to bear damage in sustained hard cornering.

Why didn't the factory correct this sooner? "They could have," Wallace allows, "but there was also a question of money. Lamborghini never wanted to throw anything away. There wasn't a great deal of money to change anything once things started going. Plus, the philosophy was, 'Oh, the customers will never drive that hard.' Which was bull, because they did."

The deeper sump coincided with the redesigned suspension to raise static rear ride height on the SV, and that, plus a slight lowering at the front, altered its aerodynamic "angle of attack" so that the nose no longer lifted at very high speeds. Some earlier Miuras were fitted with various crude sheetmetal front spoilers toward the same end, but Wallace says none were effective.

Other interim improvements were less drastic but quite worthwhile. Vented brake rotors, an S running

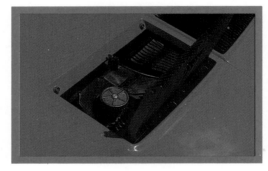

Hinged body sections exposed Miura's main mechanical components (above), but access to the fuel-filler neck was somewhat simpler (right). Originally, the ribbed bezels around the headlamps rose with the lights and looked like eyelashes. They had been detached and remained flat by the time of the S model (far right).

change, markedly reduced fade in severe use, and later SVs gained a partition twixt crankcase and transmission, thus providing separate oil supplies at last. The latter had the dual benefits of allowing lubricants suited to the specific needs of each mechanism, and of keeping contaminants generated by one from harming the other. But the real reason for this belated change was to provide for the equally belated installation of limited-slip differential (supplied by ZF), which couldn't work properly in the comparatively light engine oil of the previous shared sump. This may have contributed to an improvement in the shifting feel. Whereas some of the earlier Miuras had required the strength of a bull to get a gear, the SV's transmission mechanism had been massaged to the point where, while shifting effort was not exactly light, it was at least reasonable.

The Miura's brilliant 3.9-liter V-12

was also improved in stages. As ever, published horsepower figures are various and thus debatable (especially those in factory ads), but it's likely that the earliest Miuras packed no more than some 320 DIN horsepower at about 6500 rpm (though that was hardly chicken feed). Later P400s seem to have had nearer the advertised 350 bhp at 7000 rpm.

For the S, reshaped combustion chambers, higher-lift cams and bigger carburetors on fatter manifolds brought output to 370 bhp at 7500 (one source says 7700 rpm). The SV had the most Miura muscle—a claimed 385 bhp at 7850 rpm—thanks to still-different cam timing, bigger valves and altered carbs. As this increased fuel consumption, Lamborghini offered a larger fuel tank (110 liters/29 U.S. gallons) as a new option. Of course, the SV's greater structural mass and wider tires pretty much negated its extra power, so top speed wasn't up

by much (if at all) compared to that of previous Miuras.

Running changes during the Miura's 5½ years of production also embraced numerous comfort and convenience details. Power windows ultimately ousted the original knuckle-scuffing manual window-winders to remove a source of real annoyance to many while making the Miura a little more like other Lamborghinis, and the two engine-cover latch handles gave way to one, a much handier arrangement. Beginning with the S, a locking glovebox was installed, factory-fitted air conditioning and radio came at extra cost, and the original wood-rim steering wheel was exchanged for a leather-wrapped item. SVs added real leather interior trim, replacing the previous leather-look vinyl. (One early Miura had already been retrimmed—in wild boar-hide, no less—by its owner, a certain Frank Sinatra.)

134

Other interim cabin changes involved passenger grab handles and, to comply with U.S. "secondary collision" rules, rocker switches to replace toggle types. For some reason, the original 200-mph speedometer on cars sent to nonmetricated countries was later replaced by one calibrated to "only" 190.

There was no need to tamper much with the Miura's styling—and, wisely, Lamborghini didn't—but a few minor adjustments were made. The most visible involved the lay-back headlights, or rather the high-style grillwork that initially surrounded them. On the earliest Miuras this took the form of black-painted fins attached to the lights so that they, too, lifted up into the airstream—where they looked for all the world like eyelashes. The fins were soon separated to remain flush with the nose when the "eyes" were up, which stopped the laughing. The SV arrived with no eyelashes at all, and it is these "plucked" headlights as well as the noticeably more muscular rear flanks that most easily identify this final Miura evolution.

Ascertaining correct production for any Lamborghini is often as difficult as pegging precise power numbers. The Miura is no exception. An exhaustive study by Pete Coltrin and Jean-Francois Marchet has put the total run at 762 units. Obviously, the factory's initial sales forecast for its wild new car was wildly off. Author Rob de la Rive Box breaks out the three versions as follows: 475 P400s, 140 S-models, and 150 SVs. That makes 765 in all, three more than the Coltrin/Marchet total, but Box's P400 figure undoubtedly includes the mock-up show chassis and the two running prototypes. We hasten to add that other sources put SV volume at only 120.

The "last" Miura was built in late 1972 and wasn't delivered until the following January. We qualify "last" because a final, brand-new one was put together from leftover parts in 1975 to the order of Lamborghini superfan Walter Wolf.

Every Miura but one was a coupe. The sole exception, not counting several cars later converted by individual owners, was an open-top proposal built by Bertone in 1968 and officially designated P400 Roadster, though some Europeans insisted on calling it Spider. While it never had any form of top or side windows, numerous detail alterations to cockpit and rear bodywork made it a serious study that attracted much favorable

Along with more power, S-model Miuras got slightly altered mounting points for the rear suspension to reduce squat under hard acceleration. Inside, a leather-wrapped steering wheel was added, but the awkward pedal mounting wasn't changed (above).

The ultimate Miura bowed in 1971 as the SV (both pages). The bloodthirsty V-12 stayed at 3.9 liters, but new cam timing, bigger valves, and altered carbs gave it 385 bhp at 7850 rpm. A redesigned suspension was supplemented by wider rear tires that dictated the bulging rear fenders. Handling was vastly improved, but the SV's weight increased, too, so all-out acceleration and top speed were pretty much unchanged from earlier Miuras.

attention. But, as Bob Wallace says, there was no money for this or any other additional production model, and the Roadster was soon sold to the International Lead Zinc Research Organization. With Bertone's help, ILZRO turned it into the "Zn 75," a rolling exhibit of possible automotive applications for those metals.

Likewise not an "official" Lamborghini, though built at Sant'Agata, was an even more special Miura called Jota (YAW-ta). Another one-off custom, it was the most ambitious of Bob Wallace's personal Lamborghinis.

Jota is the letter "J" in Italian. Here it referred to Appendix J, a section of the international auto-racing rules in force around early 1970. Yes, racing. No more fooling around for Wallace. He wanted to go racing, he wanted

Lamborghini to go racing, and this "J-car" was conceived as a flat-out P400 racer. But he never actually proposed that it be raced. "No. I knew that was a waste of time," Wallace rues.

It would be logical to assume, as some have, that the Jota was a test bed for the changes to come on the following year's Miura SV, but Wallace denies this: "It was useful for tire testing, and it also acted as a, call it stimulation, for the design office, but it had no real practical bearing on any of the production cars. It was basically just a toy of mine.

"I built it on my own initiative with two of the people who worked for me and only for me, so I could do anything I liked. I had a little department of my own, so to say the 'hot-rod shop,' there at the

factory. Ferruccio didn't mind. He just told me, 'You're stark raving mad, and the weekends and evenings you can do anything you want.'"

This particular "toy" was recognizably Miura-based, but few elements were left untouched. The basic steel chassis was given a new floor made of aircraft aluminum, and more of the lightweight stuff was used in the body, whose fender profiles were distinctly more aggressive than stock. The pop-up headlights were discarded for fixed units under plastic fairings; a "moustache" type front spoiler was added; large air vents were cut in behind the front wheels; the normal dual windshield wipers gave way to a single large blade with racing-type parallelogram action; and side windows changed from glass to

fixed lightweight plastic sheeting incorporating small sliding hatches for ventilation. The interior was naturally stripped to the bone, bereft of central console and all normal trim. And where the Miura's brake and clutch pedals grew up from the floor, the Jota's hung from competition-style master cylinders above the footwell.

The Miura's suspension geometry was reworked for the Jota to accommodate very broad-shouldered tires on lightweight non-standard wheels measuring nine inches wide fore and 12 inches aft. To improve weight distribution, Wallace replaced the front-mounted fuel tank with a smaller one in each door sill (shades of GT40) and moved the spare wheel to just behind the engine. In all, the Jota ended up some 800 pounds lighter than the stock

Miura—about 1950 pounds empty.

Wallace also hopped up the engine, of course, boosting compression to 11.5:1, fitting wilder cams and electronic ignition, separating the crankcase and transmission oil supplies, rigging a dry-sump lubrication system, and adding a competition exhaust system that terminated in a quartet of megaphones. Some very elevated horsepower figures have been printed for the Jota, but honest dyno testing, according to Bob himself, showed about 418 bhp at 8000 rpm.

This racy red confection must have sounded glorious and given a ride to remember. Unfortunately, memories are all we have. The Jota was not Wallace's personal property, and once cash began running low, Lamborghini management saw it as a disposable asset. "It had a fairly

A deeper sump cured oil-starvation problems in hard cornering, the SV's nose was slightly lower to combat lift at high speeds (top), and the "eyelashes" around the headlamps were plucked (above). Genuine leather swathed the cabin, which got a bigger center grab bar. Note the 190-mph speedometer that for some reason replaced the original 200-mph unit.

short life," says the man who put so much of himself into it. "The factory had financial problems, and it ended up being sold to a rich industrialist up in Brescia. His mechanic took it out with his girlfriend on a Saturday night and ripped out the side fuel cell against a freeway bridge. The car caught fire, burnt to the ground, and that's it."

The loss was a sad one for Lamborghini enthusiasts, and a few rushed to make up for it by turning their cars into Jota replicas. Of course, none of these cosmetic

"wannabes" could approach the performance and roadability of the One True Jota.

On the other hand, a handful of enterprising craftsmen went Wallace one better by building pure racing chassis from scratch to take the splendid Miura powerplant. Among the constructors were a Bolognese shop called AMS, a Frenchman named Edmond Ciclet, and an Italian émigré to Brazil, Ottorino Bianco, who titled his creation the "Furia." Giotto Bizzarrini returned to the Lamborghini fold in this way,

albeit briefly, when he finally put the engine he'd designed back in '63 into a car of his own: an open sports-racer that was one of a short series otherwise powered by Chevrolet.

All these ventures are historical sidelights, of course, and Lamborghini had little to do with them other than providing hardware and, in some cases, a bit of expertise. The roadgoing production coupe was always the main focus of the factory's Miura business. After all, there was no commercial need

whatsoever to enhance the image of the spectacular, sensual, and sensational P400 that had so stunned the automotive world in 1966 and continued to draw eyes and capture hearts well into the following decade.

In 1981, some eight years after the Miura had breathed its last, journalist Mel Nichols, who'd logged a lot of miles in the successor Countach but very few in a Miura, borrowed a privately owned SV for a get-acquainted gallop over remote British roads. Recalling the

Though some owners had their Miuras transformed into convertibles, the factory never offered one for sale. Bertone, however, built an open-top proposal from a coupe in 1968 (above). It later was sold to the International Lead Zinc Research Organization, which had it turned into the "ZN 75" (top) a rolling showcase for zinc and lead.

139

experience for *Automobile* magazine in 1986, he was surprised that this trendsetting machine "really felt nice and not as dated as I thought it would. I played a couple of times, taking second for some of the tighter bends and booting out really hard to see if the rear Pirellis would let go. They did, where current tires on today's good automobiles would not. The breakaway was lightning fast, too...."

As always, the engine was magnificent: "The rumble of sounds from the V-12 at tickover began to blend together on the way to that glorious midrange bellow. I was

pushed back into the little racelike bucket. With less lifting of the nose and dipping of the tail than I expected, the SV rocketed ahead—hard, sharp, and truly potent, if not quite savage."

At steady speeds around 160 mph, Nichols found the Miura "gave the impression of needing more road" than other cars of its type. The same was true when decelerating: "On the faster stretches, I found that the SV needed room to romp, weaving slightly under braking. And the brakes, good though they might have seemed a decade or two ago, were barely all right by today's

standards. If you're playing with a Miura, play cautiously."

But play by all means: "The Miura was devastatingly fast for its time, and is still among the very quickest of cars, with the purpose and spirit of a sports-racer but produced for the road." Nichols then quoted another writer who'd been just as bewitched by this magical motorcar. "'He said the Miura was the twentieth century's answer to the razor-taloned falcon, the favored suit of Swabian armor, the private bodyguard of Prussian mercenaries, a fine pair of dueling pistols, or any of the other virility symbols of

Bob Wallace built one Miura to racing specs, but the Jota (opposite) never raced. Much of its chassis and body structure was of lightweight aircraft aluminum and magnesium. It had reworked suspension geometry and wider tires and wheels. The stock fuel tank in the nose was replaced by dual tanks in the door sills, the cabin was gutted, and the 3.9 V-12 was massaged to about 418 bhp at 8800 rpm. To the exterior, Wallace added an aggressive chin spoiler, set fixed headlamps behind plexiglass, and opened various vents for better air flow. Miura's engine did see sanctioned competition in the AMS (this page).

bygone eras.'"

Stefano Pasini records that *Il Cavaliere* himself saw the Miura as "a splendid paramour: very costly and unforgettable." How true: The P400 remains, above all else, an object of passion, a matter of purest emotion. Conceived in fervor and made in heat, it met a premature death with the same eerie sense of a love gone bitterly wrong that characterizes so many classic operas.

Automotive journalist Pete Lyons confessed that he, too, was unable to regard the Miura objectively. Of all cars, he said he holds the Miura to be one of the half-dozen most beautiful, exciting, and desirable. Lyons said that after spending two days with a Miura on late-'80s American roads, he found himself with the bittersweet feeling that though something bright and beautiful had once danced across the world and was still visible, it had somehow been lost behind a hazy veil.

In setting down the experience for *Car and Driver*, he wrote: "She is old, but she has not aged. Having reached her 21st birthday, she is still one of the most youthful automobiles ever designed. Her achingly lovely body can haunt your dreams. As, in another way, her voice haunts the air. A full mile distant, you can hear her engine clearly. Strapped inside, you can hear nothing else. With your foot to the floor and all twelve bores pulling hard, the interior decibel reading is 99. In most circumstances, so much noise would brush your pain threshold. But in this circumstance, just this once, 99 dBA is a measure of exquisite delight. . . .

"Behind your ears looms the very

definition of motorsport. The Lamborghini engine is magnificent, delightful, perfect, an uncanny blend of savagery with civility. It trickles along sweetly in traffic at idle rpm, yet it responds to the throttle with the instant whining of a superbike engine and its power builds like the long, smooth slope of a volcano. The Lamborghini V-12 is an engine to live for.

"No, it's not quiet. If it were quiet, how would you be able to enjoy that gorgeous, splendid, strong, raspy, raucous, metallic, hollow, whining, moaning, roaring, shrieking, wonderful noise? . . .

"The Miura is not a car for everyday use. It is fragile. It is finicky. It is expensive. It can be driven gently, even reasonably quietly, but driving such a car in such a way seems immoral. They didn't build the Miura to race, but

they built a lot of racer into it. Like a high-performance motorcycle, this car requires concentration. It demands your whole attention. You don't jump in for a restful cruise, listening to the radio as you go. The only sound system is connected to your right foot.

"Nor is it a car for today. Look at it: It's naked. No bumpers. No door beams. (No rain gutters, either.) No shoulder belts. No emissions controls. No cruise control. In its innocence it is charming, but it is also wearing. Alas, the Miura was born in a distant time, and for another place.

"Ah, but watch as the liquid light pours over her, so pretty it actually hurts. What sweet contrasts it reveals: her sensual, soft skin, her muscled wheels. *Contrappunti!* How lovely she is. How young.

"In such a light, she is perfection."

CHAPTER 16
Intemperance: Countach

Taking the supercar to a higher plane was the goal of the Lamborghini crew when it began to map out a Miura successor in the early 1970s. That alone was a formidable challenge, one that would by definition demand an expedition into uncharted realms of performance and styling. But who could have predicted a result that would so shock the senses? Who could have anticipated such a brazen, outrageous affront to normalcy? What seer could have foretold the epochal Countach?

A "gunslinger of a motor car," was the assessment of auto writer Pete Lyons. "This is a bad boy's car and everybody knows it," wrote Car and Driver's Larry Griffin. If such

metaphors seem too dark, too melodramatic, you have never driven a Countach.

It is an automobile that "treats velocity with the same casual contempt it does society," Lyons said. "In this car, a hundred miles in an hour is nothing. Such a rate is but an inadvertence, an abstract instant of position on a dial, an unnoticed gate through which one passes, effortlessly, into a realm where speed seems to have no taint of risk—and only barely of vice.

"It hardly seems to be moving at 60. At 120 it is as steady as an everyday car at 60. For the first time you feel 120 is not fast; it is merely twice 60. Your thoughts extrapolate: 180 would be merely half-again

faster. This stupefying road machine, you well know, can easily reach 180, and at that speed, you are quite sure, would leave the driver as utterly without qualm as it does at 90."

If the Miura made Lamborghini's name famous, the Countach made it immortal. It's no accident that both cars were conceived very much in the same spirit. Unlike other Lamborghinis, which had to be at least somewhat practical and civilized, the Countach-to-be had no purpose other than flat-out performance—a competition-inspired bullet train for two. At least that was the vision of those who designed and built it. To Ferruccio Lamborghini it was merely the latest

The Countach followed the Miura as
Lamborghini's pure-performance car. It
was as close in concept and construction
to a competition machine as was driveable
on the highway. The original LP500
prototype (both pages) was a little
smaller, a bit lighter, and a lot more
powerful than the P400 Miura.

From Bertone's 1968 Carabo show car **(top)** *came much of the inspiration for the Countach* **(above),** *which debuted in prototype form in early 1971. As with the Miura, Lamborghini saw the Countach as an extremely low-volume image builder. It turned out to be its best-selling car ever.*

flagship of his fleet.

The Countach was primarily the brainchild of Paolo Stanzani, the assistant to Lamborghini's first chief engineer, Giampaolo Dallara, who'd taken over the job in 1968. It was under Stanzani and his assistant, methodical testing specialist Massimo Parenti, that the factory development team had refined

Dallara's initially flawed Miura to its ultimate near-perfection in the 1971 SV model. With that, their thoughts quickly turned to a still-better land-bound missile—an all-new car of all-Stanzani design.

There was no specific name at first, the effort being known simply as "Project 112." As Dallara had done with the Miura, Stanzani—

Countach prototype No. 1 **(above)** *originally had a 5.0-liter V-12, but the engine blew and was replaced with a 3.9. Unlike the Miura, its layout* **(right)** *put the gear lever at the driver's hand. Its digital gauges* **(bottom)** *were high-tech for 1971.*

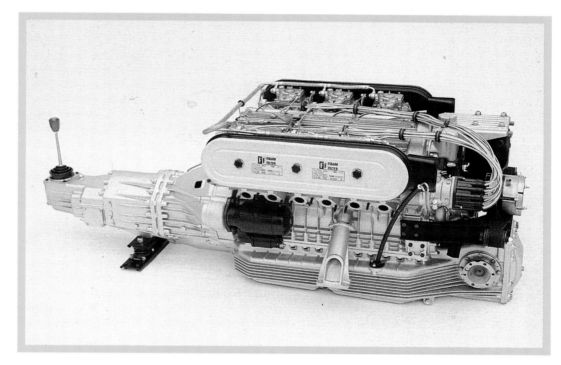

with Bob Wallace right at his elbow, no doubt—went back to first principles and began drawing on clean paper.

Despite the suspension improvements wrought for the SV, the rapid advances in the sciences of tires and high-speed dynamics were beginning to expose deficiencies in the basic Miura chassis. Specifically, the team wanted to correct the high-speed front-end lift, the tendency to snap oversteer on corners entered too quickly, the stiff gearshift action, and the excessive cockpit heat and noise.

Initial design and testing proceeded around an experimental tire that Pirelli had shown to Lamborghini, one that promised to give Sant'Agata's new supercar much higher cornering power than anything else on the road. But as Bob Wallace attests, "That tire was never released, [so] we had to put the Countach into production on some older Michelins, which weren't really right for it. In fact, they were terrible on the car. It took years before Pirelli came back with the P7, which was something like the tire the car had originally been designed to accept."

Since he was starting anew,

The Countach would retain its scissor doors throughout its life, but the clean lines of the original prototype (bottom) couldn't last; more ducts would be need to cool the V-12 furnace that toiled amidships. Prototype No. 2 (right) shows the solution: big air scoops atop the back fenders and NACA-type inlets in the rear flanks. It would take yet another prototype stage and much more development work before production Countachs were ready for painstaking assembly at Sant'Agata in 1974 (left).

Stanzani decided to rethink engine/transmission packaging, though a midships configuration would be retained. (Lamborghini could hardly abandon for the 1970s what it so thrillingly realized in the '60s.) What he evolved was as fresh and imaginative and at least as elegantly practical as the Miura layout.

After putting the gearbox back on the end of the crankshaft, Stanzani turned the entire drivetrain 90 degrees so that it was longitudinal again—only *backwards* from the usual orientation. This meant a "south-north" engine driving to a transmission mounted ahead of it; power then went back to the differential (still behind the engine) through a simple step-down gearset and a shaft running through a sealed tunnel in the sump under the bottom of the engine.

The in-sump driveshaft had two theoretical disadvantages: It forced the engine weight to be carried a few inches higher than in the Miura, thus raising the center of gravity; and it added a bit of overall weight.

But against these were numerous practical benefits.

First, though drivetrain mass was higher, it was also farther forward than in the Miura. This offered the possibility of putting more of the Countach's total weight on its front wheels, thus counteracting both nose-lift and tail-snap tendencies (though aerodynamics and suspension geometry would also enter the equation). In fact, production Countachs, which were heavier than the prototype concept, had almost exactly the same 42/58 percent front/rear weight distribution as the Miura.

Second, the forward clutch mounting left the differential and rear-wheel centerline as close behind the engine as they could be, so the engine occupied the minimum

possible amount of the wheelbase (short of placing it *over* the axle line, as Ferrari did in its Berlinetta Boxer).

Third, the reversed inline drivetrain put the gearlever right under the driver's hand for improved shift action—aided by a switch from Porsche synchronizers to a lower-effort ZF system. Finally, much less of the engine's bulk was close to the cockpit, so insulation was easier. Granted, the hot transmission now sat between driver and passenger, but that was the case in most any car of the time.

Of course, in situating the long V-12 lengthwise, Stanzani was abandoning one of the chief benefits of the Miura's transverse layout: its wide, unencumbered footwells. In the new car, driver and passenger sat between wide sills, each containing a fuel tank, and had to cram their feet into comparatively narrow, angled tunnels between the front wheels. A pity, that though

it's hard to imagine many sales being lost just because seating in this new ultracar was more like that of a race car! And Lamborghini sales people could always answer any such objections by pointing out that wheelbase was a mere 96.5 inches, almost two inches shorter than the Miura's and identical with that of the first-ever Lamborghini, the 350 GTV.

Stanzani departed from Miura practice in most every other area of the Countach design. For example, instead of being of all sheet-steel construction, the prototype chassis was a space-frame of square-section steel tubes and sheetmetal stiffeners welded together with a handmade steel bodyshell. Production models would delete the sheet and have a more elaborate structure welded up from round tubes, as well as a non-stressed aluminum body.

Though a slow and costly type of chassis to fabricate, the space frame

was adopted partly because Lamborghini again did not envision building many examples of its new supercar, and partly because welded-tube construction was relatively easy for a low-volume builder. But where the Miura chassis suffered persistent stiffness problems, the final Countach design was enormously strong. Wallace also notes that corrosion had proven a significant problem with the Miura tub; a tubular frame was considered easier to rust-proof.

Another major difference was engine displacement, which in the Countach prototype was more than 25 percent greater. The now-familiar 3929-cubic-centimeter (239.7-cubic-inch) quad-cam V-12 was treated to a Detroit-style bore-and-stroke job, ending up at 4971 cc (303.35 cid) on bore stretched from 82 to 85 mm (3.23 to 3.35 inches) and stroke extended from 62 to 73 mm (2.44 to 2.87 inches). According to Wallace,

the basic block casting couldn't be stretched this far without some makeshift steel spacers, but it was just an experiment anyway. The result was a factory-claimed 440 DIN horsepower at 7400 rpm and 366 pounds/feet of torque peaking at 5000 rpm. These were substantial improvements over the 3.9's outputs.

This 5.0-liter engine, located longitudinally but still "posterior," gave Project 112 its official designation: LP500. To differentiate it from the Miura then still in production, the P400 became known as the TP400, the "T" for *trasversale* ("transverse").

For styling, Lamborghini turned once more to Bertone. The talented Marcello Gandini did not disappoint, rendering another breakthrough design. Though obviously inspired by contemporary GT endurance racers, such as the Porsche 917, as well as by Bertone's own 1968 Carabo ("Beetle"), a one-off built on an Alfa Romeo Tipo 33 racing chassis, Gandini's Countach was like no other road car in history. It fearlessly took up the wedge profile that was becoming *de*

rigueur for competition cars in those early days of downforce aerodynamics, tempered by one of the geometric forms with which Gandini was experimenting at time—not the hexagon, as on the Marzal, but the trapezoid. The result was much less sensuous than the Miura, yet graceful in its way, and the maestro managed to retain enough animal curvature to give the LP500 an alive, "crouched-cat" look.

By now, some five years after working on the Miura, Gandini was obviously quite comfortable with the fundamentally different proportions dictated by mid-engine positioning, and the sketches that multiplied on his drawing board had no hint of the "long-hood syndrome." Indeed, the LP500 emerged with practically no hood at all. Instead, an expansive, steeply sloped windshield plunged almost straight forward into a knife-edge nose with little apparent break at the windshield base. A small hinged nose panel flipped up to reveal the spare tire and a few ancillaries. From the windshield back was a pronounced "mound" profile

appropriate for the huge engine lurking within. Bold vertical slats were cut in behind the doors to feed a high, sidemount radiator on each side.

The LP500 body was just as startling and dramatic everywhere else. The near-horizontal "tunnelback" roof made scant concession to rearward vision, so a central rear-facing periscope was faired-in on top just aft of the windshield crown. As on the "beetle-winged" Carabo, there were long doors hinged to lift straight up in modified gullwing style. Roll-down windows were precluded by the marked difference in curvature between the greenhouse and bodysides, but a separate opening "windowlette" was provided for ventilation as well as access to tollbooths and the like. Engine access was via a front-hinged lid immediately aft of the cockpit. Behind that was a second panel covering a small trunk. Retracting headlights were incorporated near the tops of the front fenders; immediately below were recessed parking/turn-signal lights styled to

148

Countach's original designed called for a space-frame of steel tubes and sheetmetal welded to a steel body. The production space-frame (left) dispensed with the sheetmetal, and aluminum was used for the body (bottom). Interim version (below) has early lowline nose.

Nearly in final production, the third prototype—the second LP400—shows its bolder, higher bumper, semi-roll-down side windows, and non-recessed front luggage lid. The cockpit is no longer space-age, just good sports car, though the gauges are sited a bit low. Note the narrow, angled, footwells. Compared to the Miura, access to the Countach's engine was difficult (left). The aft luggage compartment could get quite hot.

look like faired-in headlights. Asymmetric rear wheel arches were another daring departure from conventionality.

Lifting the doors (a sight in itself) revealed a similarly unusual two-place cockpit—very clean and futuristic—dominated by a high center tunnel bearing a hefty, resolutely vertical gearlever. Digital instruments were a new and highly experimental development in the early '70s, and these were intended for a production LP500. The same go-for-broke approach was seen in the extensive (and expensive) use of magnesium castings for components like suspension uprights, steering rack, engine mounts, oil-system housings and sump—but not the engine block itself, as has been reported.

Inevitably, it took a last-minute rush to get the LP500 finished in time for its world premiere at the 1971 Geneva show. Reportedly, it was very late on the very night work was being completed at Bertone's Grugliasco plant—perhaps even as the menacing wedge slinked out of the paint booth in its bright lemon yellow—that someone stood back, took a look, and exclaimed, "*Countach!*"

"COON-tahsh" or "CUN-touch" (Italians use both pronunciations) is an expression in the local Piemontese dialect that seems difficult to render in English without offending someone. Even the hard-bitten Bob Wallace squirms and comes close to blushing when asked to explain it: "Aw, well, it can mean one of about 10 different things. It depends on how it's used more than anything else. It, uh, can be an obscenity or it can be sort of, 'Oh, you wondrous, sensuous thing,' or, ah....'' Let us relieve the good Mr. Wallace from his discomfiture by saying that "*Countach!*" is the sort of thing a northern Italian male might utter to express appreciation for a particularly attractive female.

As noted, the Countach, like the Miura before it, was envisioned as a *very* limited edition—not so much a money-maker as a low-volume showcase for the manufacturer's technical and artistic prowess, with a "let-'em-eat-cake" regard for practicality and a price to match. Again, however, the public had other ideas, and it's likely that the first offers to buy came within minutes of the Geneva show's opening. But like the Miura that wowed the crowds in early '66, the Countach of early 1971 was nowhere near ready for sale.

That first yellow car was just a

prototype, little more than a hasty mockup, though it was fully roadworthy. With a laugh, Wallace quashes the often-repeated story that he drove it straight from the Bertone plant to Geneva over the Alps in winter. "Naw, it was about 2 a.m. We sent it up there by truck!" But he soon did begin to cover the first of thousands of hard test miles in it. Reason: In almost every detail, the LP500 needed substantial revision before Lamborghini could think of beginning even limited production.

First of all, the big-bore engine blew up almost immediately. In Chapter 5, we heard the laconic Wallace recount the incident. The car was saved from complete immolation, but the 5.0-liter was never replaced. All subsequent testing was done with a 3.9 motor, although the LP500 type designation was left unchanged.

Paralleling the Miura experience, overheating surfaced as the next immediate problem. Even the 3.9 furnace within the belly of the beast was way too much for the twin sidemount radiators buried in its flanks. Exhaustive work (pun intended) brought about a completely changed cooling system. Retained were the side radiators, but the lean, clean louvers had to be exchanged for a pair of grotesque scoops atop the rear fenders. Also added were NACA inlets behind the doors.

Another problem was also aerodynamic in nature. In their zeal to avoid the well-known nose-lift tendency of early Miuras, Lamborghini and Bertone gave the LP500 a very wedgy schnoz that proved *too* effective. "There was excessive downforce on the nose of the first car," Wallace reports. "Under weight transfer under braking, the car was a little scary." And you can imagine how much tail-wobble a car must have for the likes of Bob Wallace to call it "scary." In any case, it was cured by reducing the nose slope—actually by raising the "bumper point" a little—a change first seen on the last of the three Countach prototypes built before production began.

On the subject of aerodynamic instability, some critics have claimed that aft body shaping disposes the Countach to *rear* lift. Wallace denies this, and snorts his derision at the optional inverted rear airfoil that was adopted to counteract it after he left the firm: "I think all the wing on the car does is make it look racy and slow it down. There were no real tests done on the efficiency of

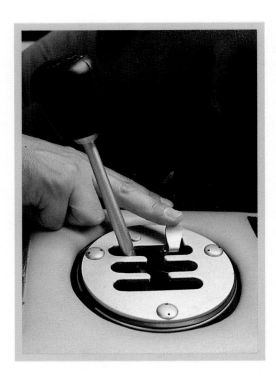

the wing on the car. It was just tacked on."

Despite that initial instability under hard braking, Wallace was agreeably surprised by the generally good behavior of the yellow LP500. Right away, he says, he could feel that even this raw prototype was a better machine than the finely honed Miura SV: "The car was very, very quick, and far more stable than the Miura was. It had substantially more wheel travel on bump and rebound....And due to its suspension geometry, it was a far more stable, far more forgiving car, a far superior-handling car right from the start."

In mid-May 1972, Wallace took this very first Countach to Monaco

for the same kind of public airing the first Miura prototype had enjoyed six years earlier. It proved so fast, competent and reliable that he and Stanzani ran it down to Sicily the following week to view the classic Targa Florio open-road race. By the time they returned to Sant'Agata, they knew they had a real car. It was at this point that Lamborghini actually decided to proceed with production.

Two more Countach prototypes were built, both key steps toward the ultimate production design. Because the 5.0-liter engine had proven unreliable, the trusty 3.9 was standardized and the model designation switched to LP400.

Onto the all-new, all-tube chassis

was hung an all-new suspension built with the steel tubes of a pure race car to substitute for the modified production-car pressings of the LP500 prototype. That car had used metal-to-metal suspension pivots, however, and they made things just too harsh and noisy. Instead of reverting to conventional rubber bushings, as on the Miura, the development team adopted nylon pivots to give the production Countach the best of both worlds.

As they were working on what was still intended to be the world's ultimate exotic, they chose to craft the bodyshell of aluminum a scant 1 mm thick; specified light-but-strong and very costly Belgian-made glass for windshield and side windows;

152

used even more magnesium throughout; and added expensive racing-type Koni shocks and Girling disc brakes all-round. But the digital gauges and periscope were abandoned as impractical, and there were numerous detail changes inside and out. Why, there was even a proper windshield wiper system now (like many prototypes, the LP500 didn't have one, until Wallace himself installed a single blade so he could drive it).

Painted a hot red, the first LP400 appeared at Geneva '72. The day the show closed, Wallace took it over for a second round of hard road and track testing. Lessons learned there were applied to prototype No. 3, the second "totally tubular" Countach, which had the aforementioned modified nose. This car, painted green, appeared at Paris in '73. Meanwhile, the short, hard life of the yellow No. 1 car ended with a barrier crash-test at the Motor Industry Research Association in England.

Wallace had never so much as sat in the red prototype until he picked it up for the drive home after Geneva '72, and he remembers its seating position was completely different from No. 1's: "Stylists are smaller than normal people," he remarks with a wry smile. "Or they think of things as being smaller. When I first got that first tubular prototype chassis, the red one, my knees were level with my eyes...." He even had to throw out the oh-so-stylish multi-block upholstery in favor of "just a padded sheet of aluminum" so he could fit.

Such matters would ultimately be fixed on production cars, of course. Meanwhile, Wallace set off across southern Europe on long days of high-speed testing. He found No. 2 excellent for that kind of driving and raves about its performance to this day. (Indeed, he keeps a photo of it in a place of honor behind his desk in Phoenix.)

At last, the Countach was ready for production—very limited production. Successful though it

In overreaction to the front-end lift that dogged the Miura, Countach got a door-stop prow that produced too much downforce. Contrast the corrected nose (top) with the yellow prototype No. 1 on page 145. Final engine (middle) also shows detail differences; turn back to page 145 to compare ignition distributors and transmission casings.

Countach's trademark scissor doors look unwieldy, but they're weighted to open quite easily (opposite, top). Entering the cockpit still requires negotiation of the wide door sills (above). Various rear wings were fitted over the years; below is a look at a 1975 experiment. The Countach started out as a show car, then it became an item to be sold only to the "right" people. It was not seen at first as a seriously viable enterprise, but in the end, it kept the company alive. Sadly, Ferruccio had already sold his auto factory by the time the Countach debuted in 1974.

was, the Miura had opened a commercial can of worms by being too much car for too many of its buyers. Accordingly, the initial plan was to restrict the Countach to those who could prove themselves not just keen but capable—skilled drivers who really knew what to do with an ultra-fast road car that acted more like a racer. *Poseurs* need not apply. In fact, Lamborghini was reluctant to offer air conditioning not only because it sapped performance but because it might render the car just civilized enough for such pretenders. This decision would be overturned once the company changed hands but, in the beginning, the Countach had a soul

as pure as that of any Le Mans racer.

Alas, the times were a-changin' and the tide of events seemed to move against the Countach. It had taken the little development team three long years to make a saleable product of it—three long, difficult years that saw the rise in labor unrest that hastened the decline of *Cavaliere* Lamborghini's fortunes. By the time the first production LP400 bravely greeted its public at the 1974 Geneva show, Ferruccio had sold out to Swiss partners Georges-Henri Rossetti and Rene Leimer. For Automobili Ferruccio Lamborghini, the future looked far less bright than that vivid yellow Countach.

CHAPTER 17
Excessive Force: Countach

Serious drivers can be forgiven for sometimes dismissing the importance of a car's appearance. Design—how layout and shape contribute to the machine's function—is one thing. "Styling"—the manner in which it wows the easily impressed—is quite another. Not that an automobile shouldn't look good. It's just that in such matters, hard-core enthusiasts prefer a stage whisper to a war cry.

That makes the automotive community's reaction to the first production Countachs all the more remarkable. Remember, the Countach had become somewhat of a familiar face between the debut of its prototype in 1971 and the launch of the roadgoing model in mid-1974. But it was such an alien face, one still so clearly from some distant future, that it mesmerized even the most jaded observers, especially motor journalists, for writer after writer was moved to measure the car by its impact on non-enthusiasts.

"The people who live in the outskirts of Modena are used to seeing exotic cars 'on test,'" said Ray Hutton in Britain's *Autocar*. "But this one still makes them stop in their tracks, stare, smile and wave in encouragement." *Road & Track's* Tom Bryant concluded that the evocative name was appropriate, "as the Countach inspires exclamations from nearly everyone who sees it. It is the first sports car I've driven that

Aluminum, magnesium, and steel never looked so menacing. Lamborghini's new high-velocity projectile stunned the motoring world when it finally surfaced in production form in 1974.

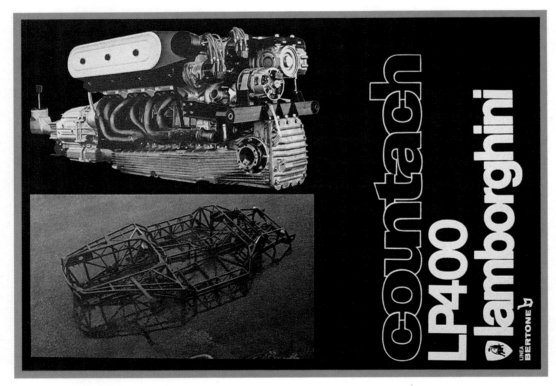

unpleasant automobile to live with. Take the large "beetle-wing" doors. They pivoted up and well forward, but were nonetheless clumsy despite assistance from gas-filled struts, and it wasn't easy clambering over those wide sills. Once seated, occupants usually felt as if they'd entered a race car—which in a sense they had, because things were just as snug here, even if you fit.

Straight ahead, where the bodywork all but vanished, your view was excellent; in any other direction there seemed to be nothing *but* bodywork. Even the right door mirror was cunningly located so the A-pillar blocked most of it.

Owing to the sharp upper-body tumblehome, each door window was split in two (three counting the fixed front ventpanes): a non-opening upper and a drop-down lower, separated by a horizontal bar. Trouble was, the lower part was too small for sticking one's head through for a look-see when backing up. The rear-quarter windows should have helped, but didn't: too small, laid almost flat and thus perfect for viewing...the radiator scoops. No, the only safe way to reverse a Countach was to open the door, sit on the sill and look back over the roof while somehow manipulating the pedals. Hopefully, it wasn't raining.

Back to those "beetle-wing" doors, which were fine as long as the car was on its wheels. Trouble was, badly driven Countachs sometimes wound up on their roofs. A steel roll cage provided sturdy support in that event, but some occupants got out of an inverted Countach only with great difficulty. This problem was recognized from the start, and there was much talk of using a kick-out windshield and even explosive emergency bolts in the door hinges. Neither idea was adopted, though. By the way, it's been taken as gospel that the door hinges on production Countachs had special pull-out "linchpins." While this perfectly good idea has been applied to certain aerobatic aircraft, this Lamborghini legend is another of the false ones. Prudent Countach drivers simply strive to keep the rubber side down.

These and other design irritations made the Countach wildly impractical for everyday use. Which raises the question of why the Countach has always been such a huge hit with the public. Could the root of its appeal be that very outrageousness, that wild impracticality? Does the adulation that has attended the ultimate

brought older ladies out of campers to look it over while parked at a coffee shop."

Doug Blain told readers of Britain's *CAR* magazine that "in town, the Countach creates as much of a sensation as would a full-blown Can Am Porsche or any other racing car ...." Out in the country, the "science-fiction silhouette proved more effective than anything I have yet known at shifting even the more tenacious Topolinos from the fast lane....The Countach breathes naked aggression from every pore: just to look at it is either to want to climb in and thrash the living daylights out of it, or else to run."

Mel Nichols opined in Australia's *Sports Car World* that "if the success

of a car's styling is measured by the attention it gets and the effect it has on people, then the Countach ranks supreme. It is an outlandish vehicle, almost unreal. Seeing it stark and alone on a deserted road made you feel as if you'd been transported to another time and another planet."

Outlandish, unreal, otherworldly. That was how most everyone viewed the Countach. As an expression of the stylist's art, Lamborghini's new ultracar was a triumph. Yet oddly enough, that far-out styling did an injustice to the car beneath it. On the road, the LP400 was brilliant in a way its coachwork was not.

Though undeniably dramatic, Marcello Gandini's body design made for a very awkward, even

The original Countach brochure (opposite) made allusions to a jet aircraft, and with a 375-bhp 3.9-liter V-12 pushing the car to 180 mph, it didn't seem inappropriate. The evolutionary LP400S of 1978 (this page) is identified by the fender flairs needed to clear its fat Pirelli P7 tires.

Countach was the very definition of "high-performance exotic" inside and out. The steeply raked windshield could turn the cabin into a furnace on sunny days and only the bottom portion of the side windows went down. The seats were race-car low and climbing in meant clambering across wide door sills. Visibility was excellent to the front and nonexistence to the rear; the mirrors were filled with air scoops and bodywork. One had to open the door and sit on the ledge to see when backing up. But this was a fast-forward machine, a car for those times you had no particular place to go and wanted to go there quickly.

160

Lamborghini for two decades represent a rebellion against oppressive common sense—a joyous exaltation in something created purely for fun?

"As a roadgoing automobile, the Lamborghini Countach is absolutely useless for anything a citizen of America is allowed to do," wrote Pete Lyons. "It's guaranteed, therefore, to bring lust swelling up in your heart. It's the sort of object you long to possess for all the wrong reasons. It's a seven-year-itch car, an illicit weekend in Lugano... sort of car."

Yet when doing what it was built to do, the immense competence of the thing banishes all thoughts of everyday absurdities. The Countach is surely one of the greatest pure-performance road cars ever to carve a corner or attack an *autostrada*. Driven the way Paolo Stanzani and Bob Wallace intended—hard and sharp, with spirit but with feeling—it is a marvelous ride: perhaps the most exciting one outside a race course.

Like so many great performers, the Countach demanded certain skills from those who master it. Not

the least of these was decisiveness. Said *R&T's* Bryant: "It became apparent quickly that this was not a fragile car to be treated with teacup-and-watercress-sandwich fingers, but a sturdy, high-performance machine that needs a touch of muscle and an aggressive attitude."

Given that, the Countach would reward you with what Blain termed "perfection in performance and behavior [that] brings fast driving to the level of squash or fencing as an exhilarating and highly exacting but at the same time rather exhausting activity." Exhausting? Yes, if the car was used to its limits. "To be effective, you must get in there and boss the thing, using muscle but not force, urging it deeper and deeper into corners with little twitches of the wheel, banging the gears home, stamping on brake and clutch till you ache all over."

But that's where the workout ended. Nichols observed that the "suspension is set hard so that [the car] rides very firmly around town. Yet...it is not uncomfortable, merely reassuring. At speed in bends this stiffness means that the car stays extraordinarily flat. It snaps around curves like an electric slot racer, answering the steering with lightning quick response and precision and displaying a honed sharpness....There is never any understeer, and only oversteer when you want it with power." Summing up the enormous satisfaction of

Countach driving, Nichols said the car merely "feels so purposeful, making you drive with an easy precision and a clear, relaxed mind."

It's inevitable with cars like this that someone will ask, "what'll she do?" With the Countach, nobody really knows. Yes, a good many test numbers have been printed over the years, but they've always seemed to be qualified by circumstances: mechanical problems, lack of a suitable test venue, sometimes both. The plain fact is, the Countach has generally been faster than most available roads and more than a few drivers.

The original 3.9-liter Countach V-12 was supposed to belt out 375 horsepower at 8000 rpm. That was 10 bhp less than the output quoted for the Miura SV, a difference that's been blamed partly on the use of sidedraft rather than vertical carburetors, though the Countach's were larger. Against that, the Countach was aerodynamically steadier at high speed than the Miura, and made it "easier" to hold one's foot in the throttle longer.

Still, one quickly ran out of room. Hutton reported that Wallace had once observed 290 km/h—180.2 mph—at 7600 rpm in the green No. 2 prototype on a timed 5-kilometer stretch of Fiat's private superhighway. Given a few more klicks, Bob thought he could have reached 7800 rpm and an even 300 km/h—186.4 mph. Wallace later told Nichols that he saw 297 km/h—a tad

161

With its beetle-wing doors sprung, headlamps up, and engine-cover open, the Countach looked even more otherworldly than usual. There was no lack of sound engineering behind its appearance, however. The welded-tube space-frame **(opposite top)** was extremely rigid and formed a stable platform for the all-independent suspension. The aluminum body **(opposite middle)** got lots of hands-on attention. The add-on nature of the S model's fiberglass wheel and chin flairs is exposed in this pre-paint state. The cabin **(opposite bottom)** also was the scene of much painstaking work during the slow-moving assembly process.

under 185 mph (presumably in a production car)—and that "there was a little more to come."

Acceleration is similarly problematical. In testing their first Countach, *Road & Track*'s crew clocked 0-60 mph in 6.8 seconds and the quarter-mile in 14.4 seconds at 105.5 mph, but confessed that their privately owned loaner had been babied. Then they added that colleagues at Britain's *Motor*, "by suppressing their feelings of mechanical sympathy" and dumping the clutch at 7000 rpm, got 5.6 seconds to 60, 14.1 seconds in the quarter and "two black lines 50 yards long." Perhaps we should simply state that Countach acceleration was more than adequate from the start.

Ah, but to Sant'Agata, such damning with faint praise would be as a red flag to a bull. Like other Lamborghinis, the Countach arrived with a lot of development potential, though that potential would take time to be fully realized. Yet even as the first customer cars were being delivered, the desire was stirring to make the Countach better.

By some accounts, Walter Wolf got production Countach No. 1, having taken delivery as soon after Geneva '74 as the factory would release a car to him. A Canadian of Austrian birth, Wolf was not unlike Ferruccio Lamborghini himself: a burly, life-loving entrepreneur who enjoyed getting what he wanted and had the means to do it. He had a strong presence in the oil industry at a time when that was a very good thing to have, and was thus able to indulge his passion for auto racing by forming his own team (Jody Scheckter drove for Walter Wolf Racing in Formula 1 during '77 and '78 before becoming World Champion in '79). Reflecting his interest in Automobili Ferruccio Lamborghini, Wolf even considered buying the firm from its Swiss owners of that period, Georges-Henri Rossetti and Rene Leimer.

Before that, Wolf's involvement with affairs Lamborghini was as a very enthusiastic customer who wasn't always content with the factory issue. He thus somehow talked the engine shop into building him a 5.0-liter V-12 like the one Wallace had blown up in 1971, and had it installed in his first Countach. When he sold that car, Wolf had the engine transplanted into a new Countach, done up in his competition livery (deep blue with gold pinstripes) and sporting a prominent racing-style wing atop the rear deck. The same engine later

Pressed by tightening emissions rules, Lamborghini went to a 4.75-liter twelve to keep its power up. This so-called LP500S, or "5000S" model, introduced in 1982, was rated at the same 375 bhp as the older, less-restricted 3.9, but it was achieved at only 7000 rpm, not 8000, and the car simply was not as lively as before.

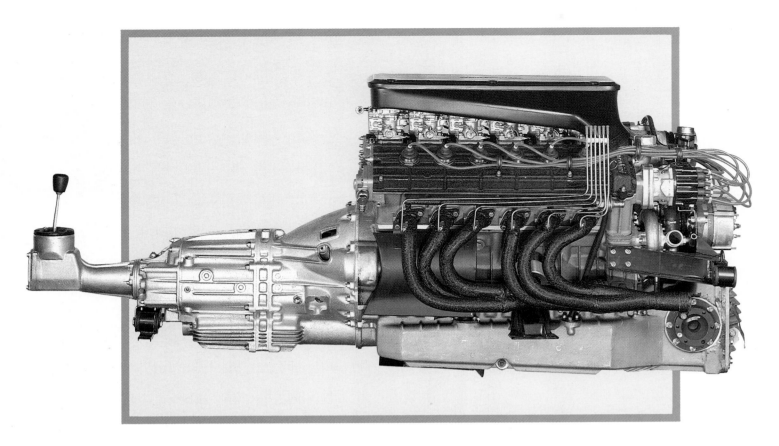

The real answer to the choked-Countach problem was the all-new, four-valve or **Quattrovalvole** cylinder heads (below). Their secret was an ability to pass more air into and out of the combustion chamber for a given amount of valve lift. Put into production in 1985 on a stretched 5.2-liter block, they helped raise output to 455 bhp.

Above: Note the new, "flat-top" heads, as well as a simpler sump casting—probably aluminum now, no longer magnesium.

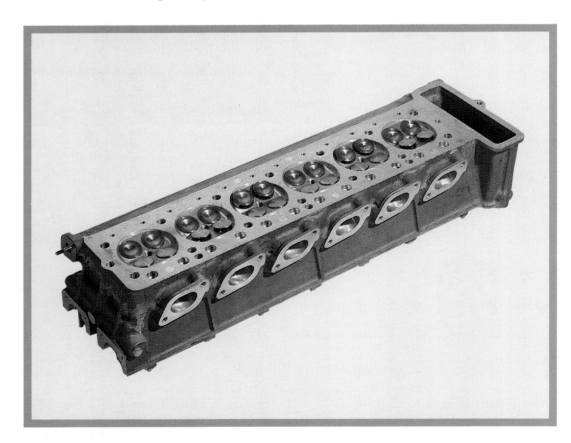

went into a third Wolf Countach. It's likely that this big-bore experience, rather more rewarding the second time around, helped give Lamborghini the confidence to go ahead with a similar production engine a few years later.

Wolf was definitely behind the adoption of Pirelli's low-profile high-tech P7 tire for the evolutionary LP400S of 1978. He'd already had one of his own cars altered to suit the wider, grippier rubber, and it worked so well that he insisted the factory look into it. "It's true," says

Wallace, for once not cutting down a favorite Lamborghini fable. "Wolf paid for Dallara to come back and work out the revised suspension geometry, and also for all the testing they did up on Fiat's freeway."

To accommodate the squat tires, rather graceless fiberglass fender flares were tacked on, the front ones connected by an aggressive chin spoiler—all of which only made the S look even more menacing than earlier Countachs. Wheels were also changed, again following Wolf's example, the relatively plain original rims giving way to a much bolder (and suitably wider) five-hole "telephone dial" type (as first seen on Bertone's Urraco-based 1974 Bravo show car).

Lamborghini finally got around to a "five-liter" production engine in 1982. It was initially offered as an option, perhaps with the hope of using up existing 3.9 stores. So equipped, the car was officially designated LP500S, same as the original Countach prototype of 11 years before, though some later examples were curiously badged "5000S" on the tail.

The new engine wasn't quite the same as the original 5.0-liter. Designed to meet ever-tightening emissions limits, it differed in displacement (4754 cc/290 cid), bore and stroke dimensions (85.5 x 69 mm/3.37 x 2.72 inches), and in having lower, 9.2:1 compression. It thus claimed only 375 DIN horsepower, same as the 3.9, but achieved it at a more relaxed 7000 rpm.

Fuel injection, added in '86, lowered the output to 420 bhp, but helped meet U.S. regulations. European cars retained carburetors, which required a bulge in the engine cover (right). Both versions are visible in the photo below; the tilted engine has the FI.

Highlighting the Countach's third major revision, announced in March 1985, was four-valve cylinder-head architecture, by then almost universal in racing and spreading rapidly among the better road cars. Engineers also stretched stroke to 75 mm (2.95 inches) to bring total capacity up to 5167 cc (315 cid), tightened compression to 9.5:1, and reinstated downdraft Weber carburetors. In European tune, DIN horsepower climbed to a healthy 455, again peaking at 7000 rpm. The car was rebadged LP5000S *Quattrovalvole* ("four-valve," 48 in all on this V-12).

A number of other alterations—some good, some not so good—occurred along with and in between these model changes. For example, there were useful periodic detail revisions to suspension and brakes—and patchwork solutions to U.S. safety standards (most depressingly, the blocky bumpers slapped on in the 1980s by the U.S. importer, then by Sant'Agata itself). Equipment was gradually upgraded, too; even air conditioning was usually installed nowadays.

But while all this fiddling evolved a more civilized Countach, it also made for a larger and heavier Countach. "They raised the body on the frame, and also cut and welded bits and pieces into the body," groans Bob Wallace, who with some disgust has seen his original compact, super-light supercar put on as much fat as muscle over the years.

"And all the original magnesium is gone now," he adds. "It was good on a pure performance vehicle, if the owner would look after it properly, but it's just impractical in everyday service. It corrodes too easily. You can't expect most owners to wash down the underside of the car in the winter. People keep driving it in the snow...."

So even after 15 years, the Countach still had plenty of flaws—perhaps too many for The Ultimate Exotic. Yet it's fair to say that the efforts lavished on it by Wallace, his colleagues and their successors is one reason Lamborghini still exists as an

automaker. Despite an impractical design, rampant inflation and a painfully slow production pace, unflagging demand for this one model is what kept Lamborghini from teetering into the abyss during its long period of economic darkness and labor union enmity in the Seventies. In short, the Countach singlehandedly saved Lamborghini. The Urraco, Silhouette, and Jalpa couldn't do it; nor could the Cheetah, and certainly not the BMW and Fiat contracts undertaken in those desperate years.

That Lamborghini has survived is nothing short of miraculous, all things considered—let alone that its founding spirit still burns bright. Even today, visitors to the now-faded Sant'Agata factory come

back amazed that the firm's original commitment to building the finest roadgoing sports cars imaginable is as strong as it ever was.

No wonder, then, that the handcrafted Countach has become practically synonymous with "Lamborghini" in the minds and hearts of enthusiasts and non-enthusiasts all over the globe. Yes, it's now very much an old-timer by auto-industry standards, yet it was so far out to begin with that time has not dimmed its luster—and likely never will. The Countach is not only unique but uniquely Lamborghini, and that made all the difference.

The exquisite Quattrovalvole engine, a much-altered V-12 but still a direct descendant of Giotto

The optional tail wing (below and opposite) may have added even more impudence to the Countach's attitude, but it contributed only weight and aerodynamic drag to its body—and thousands to its price tag. The Countach's unadorned shape (above) did not suffer aerodynamic lift at high speeds. Controls and engine bay were always no-nonsense.

Bizzarrini's 1963 original, played a big part in Lamborghini's resurgence, especially in America. When the Countach was first schemed, the factory didn't intend to bother with modifications for the special requirements of the world's largest car market. Americans would have to dream from afar. But of course, Americans wanted this spectacular flyer as much as anyone, even though a car capable of two- and three-mile-a-minute velocities made no sense whatsoever in a land with a blanket 55-mph speed limit.

Nevertheless, Lamborghini responded directly for a time, selling a few Countachs under an exemption from federal safety and emissions standards for low-volume producers. When that special dispensation ran out, various independent shops—part of the so-called gray market—stepped in to "federalize" individual cars for wealthy individuals who would not be denied. Washington eventually cracked down on this, too. But by then, there were new owners in Sant'Agata more willing and able than prior regimes to tackle the problems of compliance.

Americans unwilling to truck with the gray market missed out on the Countach from the mid-1970s through about 1982. But then came Jasjit Rarewala, proprietor of California-based Lamborghini Cars of North America, who decided to make the Countach fully U.S.-legal and asked Sant'Agata for help. He got it. By the time the QV engine was ready, the success of Rarewala's interim conversion efforts—plus an upturn in Lamborghini's fortunes—had prompted the factory to build a federal version entirely in Italy.

The result was a 1986 U.S.-spec 5000S QV with "crash" bumpers and specially engineered Bosch KE-Jetronic fuel injection to satisfy the respective demands of the DOT and EPA. SAE net horsepower was a rousing 420—less than eight percent below the output of the carbureted European engine, a difference hardly anyone noticed—developed over a broad 7000-7500-rpm range. Torque was equally impressive: 340 pounds/feet at 5000 rpm.

In the November 1986 issue of *Automobile*, the peripatetic Mel Nichols stated that this federal QV had run 0-60 mph in "a shade over" five seconds, 0-100 mph in 10.8 and the quarter-mile in precisely 13

Lamborghini marked its 25th year in automaking with the Anniversary Edition Countach (opposite). The 5.2-liter V-12 was unchanged, but the body got rocker-panel strakes and air intakes that were more gracefully integrated with the rear fenders. Composite plastics replaced aluminum for these and some other exterior components.

seconds in the hands of factory testers. Still, it took a trip to Italy's high-speed Nardo test track to confirm that even a "clean" Countach could reach upwards of 180 mph. Comparing the *Quattrovalvole* to the 1982 American-spec S-model, *Road & Track* reported 0-60 at 5.2 seconds (versus 5.7) but saw "only" 173 mph flat out (versus 150 before).

There was more good news, as Nichols relayed in the aforementioned *Automobile* piece: "Like the '87 European Countach, the new U.S. model is a better car than the early four-valves in other ways.... Chief experimental engineer Massimo Ceccarani says proudly, 'We've made the Countach better throughout and not just developed the new U.S. engine.' To improve steering response and stability, he's tweaked the front suspension geometry, moved the location of the steering rack, and changed the rate of the rear springs. The oil and water cooling is better, the air conditioning is more effective, and the build quality is finer."

While they were sorting out the Quattrovalvole, Lamborghini engineers also were working on what came to be known as a "super Countach." A test bed for future technology, the car had some composite exterior body panels and also ran four-wheel drive. Both ideas would eventually bear fruit.

It was a pleasant surprise in September 1988 when Lamborghini celebrated its 25th year as an automaker with a special Anniversary Edition Countach. It was even more pleasing when the car was not just a cosmetically enhanced Countach and emerged instead as probably the finest all-around Countach ever.

Most obvious was substantially new exterior styling—the most sweeping change in the car's look since its introduction. Straked air intakes appeared on the lower body in front of the wheel arches. New panels over the engine compartment and rear fenders were highlighted by gracefully integrated radiator grille units that replaced the tacked-on-looking scoops. Besides softening the Countach's lines, the new ducting increased airflow through the engine bay and, along with a larger radiator fan and a beefed up water pump, cured the Countach of its propensity to overheat in traffic. The panels that formed these intakes, plus the new front fender surrounds, trunk lid, and engine cover, were made from

composite materials pioneered on the super Countach. They were lighter than the previous aluminum components. And since they were molded, they could be manufactured to finer tolerances than the hand-formed aluminum pieces.

The anniversary edition's engine was unaltered from its *Quattrovalvole* specification; Lamborghini apparently didn't want to risk having to recertify the V-12 for certain markets. The European version retained its sextet of Weber two-barrel carburetors, while the U.S. variant used Bosch K-Jetronic fuel injection. Both versions now had some of their accessories attached before the engine was installed, however, so reliability was theoretically improved. The engine bay was substantially cleaned up, with wires and hoses rearranged for a tidier look and easier servicing.

U.S. safety regulations were quite evident on the nose of the 25th Anniversary car, where the unsightly front rubber bumper blocks were retained for the American market. A new composite tail panel, however, met federal

crash standards without modification. Complementing the suspension and steering revisions given the '88 model were the Anniversary Countach's new Pirelli P Zero tires with their asymmetrical tread design and use of two rubber compounds across their width. The size remained at 225/50ZR15 in front and 345/35ZR15 in back, but new two-piece aluminum wheels with forged alloy rims were supplied by OZ.

A major goal of the Anniversary exercise was to make the Countach a more habitable supercar. Gone were the previous seats, which looked as if they had been swiped from the *Star Wars* set; in their place were less dramatic looking buckets that were more comfortable and featured a power-seatback recline. The steering wheel also was replaced. A new, more powerful air conditioner that could hold its own against the greenhouse effect of the steeply raked windshield was fitted, and the front-door half windows got electric lifts, at last. Finally, there was so much additional sound insulation that, to the dismay of some Lamborghini purists, gearbox whine

superceded the song of the V-12 as the Countach's principal auditory signature.

While the changes did shave off some of the car's rough edges—and hinted at the character of its successor—they did not alter the Countach's basic bare-knuckles approach. This was confirmed by Gordon Murray, whose evaluation of a 25th Anniversary Countach, Ferrari F40, Porsche 959, and Lotus Esprit Turbo SE was recounted in *Motor Trend* in July 1990. Murray designed Brabhams and McLarens that won four Formula 1 World Championships in the 1980s and was at the time of the article researching the design for a new roadgoing McLaren supercar.

"Simply sitting in the Lambo, there's a supercar feel, a sense of occasion missing from the Porsche," Murray said. "The way the...doors open, and particularly the way they close, is wonderful: They scythe down and shut you in with a solid 'clomp.'" Visibility anywhere other than forward remained terrible, and Murray recoiled at the closeness of the A-pillars, but he lauded the steering, tire grip, and lack of body

Compare the unsullied nose and trim tail of the European-spec 25th Anniversary car on these pages against the bumper-block besmirched bow and spoiled stern of its U.S. cousin on page 171. Which do you like? Regardless, the factory said enough firepower was aboard to get from 0-60 mph in 4.7 seconds and through the quarter-mile in 12.9 seconds. Top speed was 183.3 mph.

roll. Unfortunately, his initial efforts to go fast smoothly were thwarted by the Lamborghini's controls.

"When I first tried to drive away, I had to open the door and ask if the throttle had a lock on it!" he said. "The throttle's about the same weight as a 911's clutch, and the clutch is even heavier than a 911's, which is saying something. The combination of these things and the stiffness and balking of the gear change actually prevent you from

driving the Countach properly. On the track, I was always worried about getting the gear before the next corner." Ah, but that V-12, " a *real* engine," Murray said. "Okay, it doesn't have that electrifying surge that startles you the first time you reach the [twin-turbo] Porsche's powerband, but it revs freely and has a much more punchy feel right through the range. And I think that's important."

Factory acceleration figures for the

25th anniversary edition—0-60 mph in 4.7 seconds and a 12.9-second quarter-mile—eclipse those obtained by outside testers of previous Countachs. The factory's top speed of 183.3 mph (in 5th gear at 7300 rpm) was only a tad slower than the 185 Bob Wallace said he saw in an early model.

So the anniversary edition not only was the most comfortable Countach ever, it very likely was the fastest production example. And with 650 built by the end of production in July 1990, it also turned out to be the biggest seller. In fact, Lamborghini had planned to produce only about 300 anniversary Countachs, but sales benefited from a combination of factors, including a red-hot supercar market, collector interest, quality and driveability improvements wrought with Chrysler's help, and delays to the Countach's successor. Continued improvement is what kept the Countach viable in increasingly hostile times. That's another reason demand for it never abated, even though 15 years of inflation and mechanical alterations more than tripled its original U.S. price of

More comfortable seats, stronger air conditioning, a new steering wheel, and added sound insulation made the Anniversary car's cabin (right) cushier than before. Some of this was evidence of new-owner Chrysler's influence, but it only enhanced the appeal of this, the last, the best-selling, and probably the finest Countach of them all.

around $45,000.

But the fact remains that cars like this should simply not exist in the modern world. As ever, the Countach is an utter contradiction. An awesome, stunning, entirely useless, absolutely incredible racer-for-the-road. A futuristic machine built the old-fashioned way. An expression of frankly medieval social and personal values restated—loudly—in the latest of technological terms. An impossible creation in an unlikely age, yet always a genuinely "wondrous, sensuous thing."

And that, in the end, is why it endures. *R&T* ably expressed the heart of this matter in concluding its 1985 test of the then-new

Quattrovalvole:

"...By any standard, the Countach is bigger than its performance figures, bigger than the sum of its automotive qualities. Approve of the car or disapprove, as you must—and there are plenty who disapprove—but the Countach's sole reason for existence is that somehow, according to some magic formula, it's bigger than life. The fact that after all these years that is still true, that this car still works the same soul-stopping spell on nearly everyone who sees it, is testament to the success of the Lamborghini concept and the original Bertone design. In fact, if you think it over, it's just a bit miraculous."

Like the car itself.

CHAPTER 18
The Devil's Due: Diablo

It was the spring of 1985, and Lamborghini's artisans and engineers were once again working on a sequel to the world's most charismatic supercar. They had last embarked on such a journey around 1970, to lay the groundwork for the Countach.

At that time, their assignment seemed relatively straightforward. The Miura of 1966 had broken the mold with sensuous styling, inspired engineering, and a barbaric lust for speed. It was a product of designers who had unreined their imaginations. In one sense, those gathered at Sant'Agata back in '70 needed only to duplicate that feeling. Indeed, it could be said the Countach they conceived for 1971 retained the ingredients that made the Miura so special, only in a different mix. Now the styling was barbaric, the name sensuous, and the performance inspired.

But simply unleashing their

An automobile so savage, so idiosyncratic, so palpably alive that, just like the best of its beastly forbears, it opens heaven by raising hell. Upon its public debut at the Chicago Auto Show in February, 1990, a claimed top speed of 202 mph made it the fastest production car the world has ever known. It is a new word for hyper-speed exotica. It is the Diablo.

Compared to its Countach predecessor, Lamborghini's supercar for the '90s is longer, wider, heavier, and more powerful. Diablo's styling is less severe, but no less stimulating. Inside are more luxury and convenience features, but not nearly enough to mask the car's ferocity when provoked.

creativity would be of little use to the Lamborghini team in '85. The world had changed. No longer was it enough that each supercar be merely faster and more outrageous than the last. Emissions concerns and safety issues were now part of the blueprint, so were reliability, assembly quality, even a certain degree of refinement. To this demanding manifest Lamborghini management added yet another requirement: Not only must the Countach's successor meet the regulatory standards of every market in which it sold, its performance had to be the same world-over. The European version would no longer be allowed outrun its U.S. cousin. About the only thing that *hadn't* changed was that the new Lamborghini must enflame the senses. This had to be an automobile so savage in sound and manner, so idiosyncratic, so palpably alive that, just like the best of its beastly forbearers, it could open heaven by raising hell.

Behold the Diablo. Its very name means "devil," but it also is an illustrious breed of Spanish fighting bull. Lamborghini knew better than to wander from its roots in

nomenclature, and it stuck to a proven formula in engineering, as well. Thus, the Diablo, like the Countach, has a longitudinally mounted midships-V-12 with the gearbox located ahead of the engine. The Diablo, however, is a larger, heavier two-seater than the Countach. It has a bigger engine, additional amenities, and more sophisticated componentry. In fact, no other Lamborghini has struck so heady a balance between high technology and high speed.

"It was no easy task to replace the world's most famous supercar," said Lamborghini President Emile Novaro. "When we began the program back in June 1985, my instructions to the team were to make it better than the Countach. Better performance, safety, comfort, visibility, accessibility, and emissions. And give me at least 315 km/h (196.5 mph)."

Whether the Diablo is a "better" car than the Countach is problematic, given all the shades of emotion probed when a question like that is asked about cars like these. That it is faster there is no doubt. Lamborghini says the Diablo's top speed is 202 mph, 19 mph above that of the 25th

Anniversary Countach. That also betters the Ferrari F40, for which its maker claims a 201-mph top speed, and the Porsche 959, with its manufacturer's rating of 197 mph. Ferrari's Testarossa, the only other exotic in the mid-engine 12-cylinder idiom, tops out at 178. There were other supercars on the horizon—proposals from Jaguar, Bugatti, Cizeta-Moroder—and their builders professed even higher velocities. But when the Diablo was unveiled to Lamborghini dealers in Monte Carlo on January 20, 1990 (and to the public on February 9 in a special presentation during the Chicago Auto Show), no car had a more secure claim to the title of the world's fastest production automobile.

With the Diablo, Lamborghini closed a debate about the style and substance of the Countach's successor that had simmered at Sant'Agata since the Patrick Mimran days of the early 1980s. Work on the project didn't begin in earnest, however, until Novaro's cannon of '85. That's when Lamborghini brought in as technical director Luigi Marmiroli, whose credentials included his own independent design company and stints in the

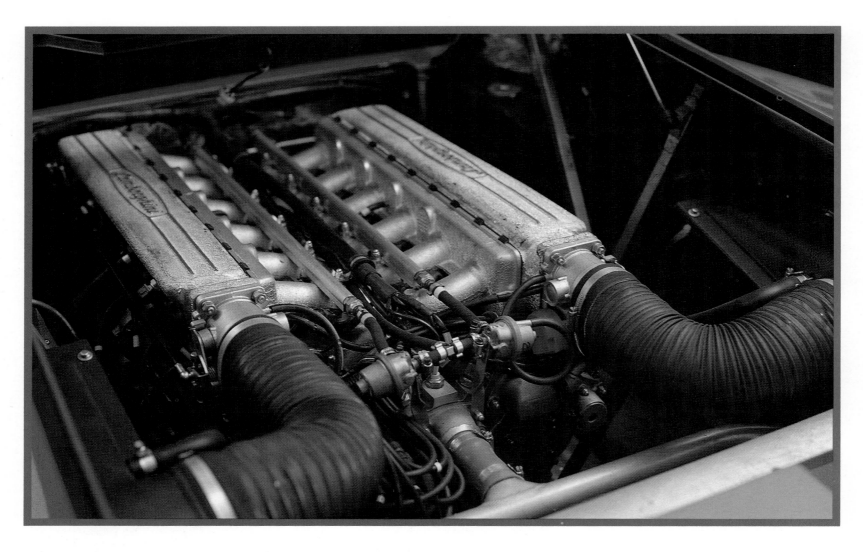

For the Diablo, Lamborghini increased displacement of its dohc 48-valve V-12 (above) from 5.2 liters to 5.7. Compression is up from 9.5:1 to 10.0:1, and an electronic engine management system replaces the previous distributor. The result is 485 bhp at 7000 rpm, 65 bhp more than the four-valve Countach twelve. The Diablo engine burns unleaded premium fuel and routes its exhaust through catalytic converters. It meets emissions standards in the U.S. and in every country in which it is sold and its performance is uniform, no matter the market.

upper management of the Ferrari and Alfa Romeo Formula 1 teams.

For the basic design of the new car, Marmiroli turned to the man who had fashioned both the Miura and the Countach, Marcello Gandini. Gandini started work in November of '85 and by May '86 had set down what he envisioned as its final shape. The creation retained its predecessor's bloodthirsty spirit, but where the Countach celebrated the wedge, Gandini's new machine showed a decidedly a cab-forward silhouette with an even briefer nose. It retained the quirky asymmetrical rear-wheel openings, but added to the profile dramatic plunging A-pillars.

If the design was breathtaking, so was the challenge to a cash-strapped Lamborghini. Given the ambitious target, delivering this car would be more difficult than bringing forth the Miura or Countach. But as the work proceeded, Lamborghini's resources suddenly became formidable. Chrysler Corporation bought the Italian company in April 1987 and soon was involved in Marmiroli's project. This turn of events had many ramifications, not the least of which was that the vast technical power of a mass-market automaker was now available to the tiny band of Lamborghini craftsmen. Gone, for instance, were the days when Sant'Agata learned of the

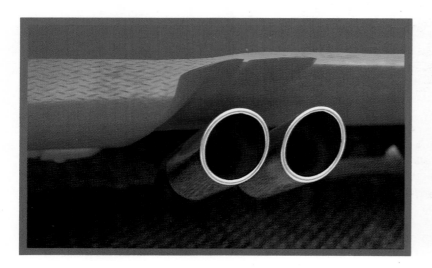

structural failure of early Miuras after production had begun. For the Diablo, Lamborghini could do structural engineering via finite-element analysis with the help of Chrysler's state-of the-art supercomputers in Detroit.

Gandini's first design, however, was rejected by Chrysler soon after it took control. His revamp didn't quite make it either, and Lee Iacocca ordered in his U.S. styling staff. Under the direction of Tom Gale, Chrysler's vice president of product design, the Americans worked with Gandini on the final evolution. It proved a new way of doing things at the small boutique automaker. Where Gandini had drawn his Miura in an ad-lib stroke of genius and refined his Countach with seat-of-the-pants data from test drivers, the Diablo was honed in the wind tunnel. It emerged with some of Gandini's creases planed away for a more organic look. The front spoiler was refined, the air intakes over the rear wheels were changed, and Gandini's original fastback gave way to a tunnel-roof design for improved cooling and better visibility.

In the past, the sound of hammers pounding out aluminum echoed through the halls of Sant'Agata. The hammers were still there, but now they helped nudge into place fully formed body panels for selected pieces of the Diablo's skin. This was another advance over the Countach, which had stamped body panels, but ones that had to be flanged by hand once delivered to the factory. On the Diablo, they were shipped fully flanged and ready for installation. This eliminated considerable hand-fitting, improved quality, and saved time. What was lost in Old-World technique was gained in uniformity and closer tolerances. Likewise, an increased number of tooled pieces made the cabin substructure more sophisticated than the Countach's. Where the older car had aluminum patches to close gaps in the cockpit shell, Diablo has molded panels. Both are hidden from the eye by hand-stitched leather, but guess which will rattle less?

Diablo's space-frame chassis is an evolution of the Countach's, but square- and rectangular-section steel tubes replace the Countach's round ones. It's stronger and the flat surfaces are better for mounting components. A variety of steel-alloy tubes, together with the aforementioned composites, helps the car exceed both American and European collision-impact standards.

Lamborghini parlayed the Countach's scissor-opening doors into an evocative marque trait and they're back in all their glory on the Diablo. A button atop the exterior sill releases the lock, and the door must be hoisted open by its edge. It's pulled closed by a padded grab bar, visible above.

179

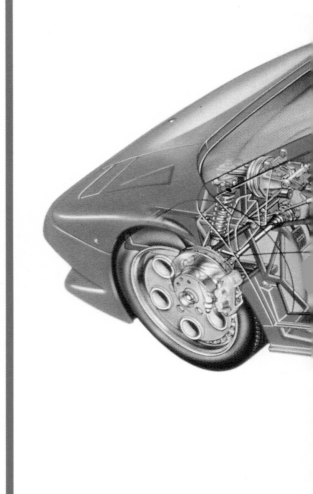

Chrysler oversaw design of the interior (below). There's no airbag, but the steering column tilts and telescopes and the gauge pod is height-adjustable. The space-frame (right) evolved from Countach's, but has flat-sided tubing for easier component attachment. The longitudinal V-12 still rides "backwards," but for better cooling the radiators are in the rear corners, not in the flanks as were Countach's. The fuel tank is behind the seats. The Diablo has no spare tire. Note the quad rear shocks.

Parts of the front and rear structures are designed to crumple in an accident, creating crush zones. And some tubing is intentionally malleable to absorb impact in a front or rear crash; other pieces are grooved to direct the way they'll bend in a collision.

For more durability outside, Diablo's doors and quarter panels are of a stouter aluminum alloy than the pliant pure aluminum hung on the Countach. In addition, the pressed steel door frames and the steel roof are welded directly to the chassis, integrating the entire structure in the name of torsional stiffness. Body rigidity is enhanced

by the use of composite plastic panels in the center tunnel and in the passenger compartment. For light weight, composite materials developed by Lamborghini are used for the front decklid, the rocker panels, bumpers, spoilers, and engine cover. And for a more uniform finish, the composite and metal panels are painted as a unit. It was obvious Lamborghini had a trademark feature in the Countach's scissor-opening doors and so this design is carried over for the Diablo. The new car, however, has power-operated door windows that can be raised and lowered completely—unlike the half-panes on the

Countach.

A 26.4-gallon fuel tank nestles behind Diablo's seats. Aluminum radiators are placed in the rear, at the extreme outboard edges of the car, and are mounted at roughly a 70-degree angle. It's easier to supply air to them there than to direct flow into the flanks just behind the cockpit, where the radiators in the Countach rested horizontally.

Diablo's competition-style four-wheel independent suspension uses upper and lower A-arms front and rear, coil springs, two tubular shocks in front and four in back, and anti-roll bars front and rear. Adjustable damping to improve ride quality is

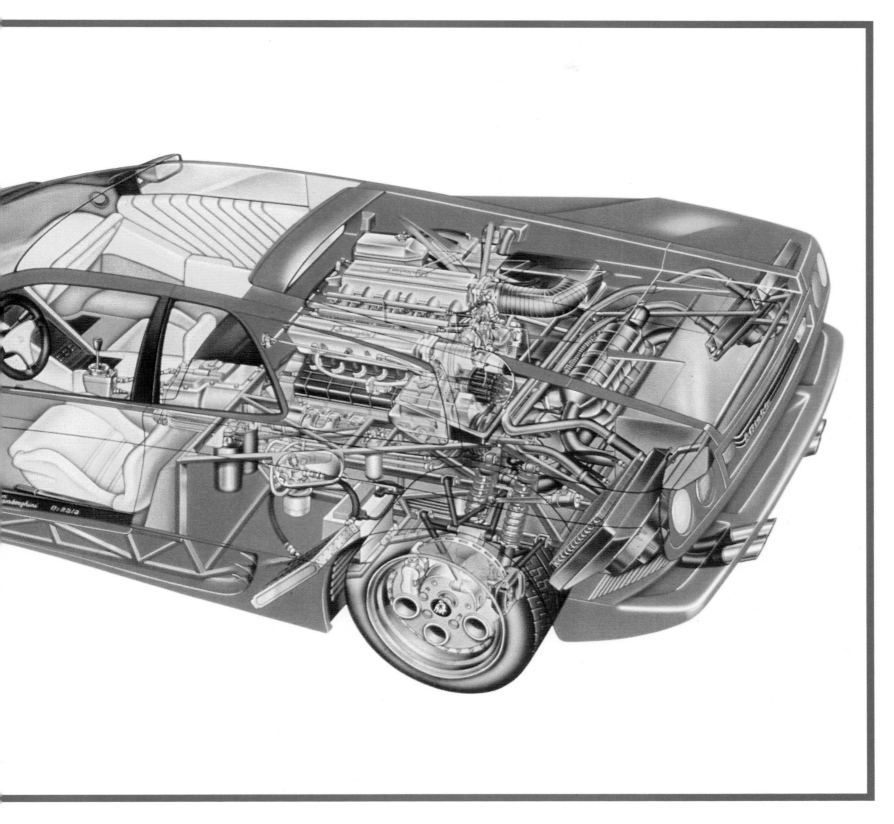

planned for the future. Steering is rack and pinion and is manual.

The 17-inch diameter O.Z. Racing three-piece aluminum wheels are evolutions of the 15 inchers introduced on the 25th Anniversary Countach. The fronts are 8.5-inches wide, the rears 13. Tires are special, hand-made Pirelli P Zeros, 245/40ZR17 in front, 335/35ZR17 in back. A low-pressure warning system and a small can of compressed air substitute for a spare tire. Braking is done with massive ventilated discs; the fronts are 12.99 inches in diameter, the rears measure 11.2. Diablo does without an anti-lock system. Lamborghini acknowledges

that very skilled drivers can achieve superior control in stops without anti-lock brakes, but says ABS is not on the Diablo because it was prohibitively expensive to develop for such a low-volume car.

Compared to the Countach, the Diablo's 104.3-inch wheelbase is longer by 5.9 inches, its body longer by 5.1. Overall beam is broader by 1.5 inches, at 80.3 inches, and with a roof that's 43.5 inches off the pavement, Diablo is an inch taller than the Countach. The new car tips the scales at 3640 pounds, 208 more than the Countach. With driver aboard, Diablo has a front-rear weight split of 40/60, versus 42/58

on the Countach. Aerodynamically, the Diablo is far more efficient, its 0.30 coefficient of drag quite good in light of the airflow fight put up by the steamroller tires. By comparison, the Countach's 0.41 Cd saddled it with the aerodynamics of a bungalow.

Lifting the engine cover reveals Diablo's 48-valve double-overhead cam aluminum V-12. Shouldering its big intake plenums with their 12 baseball-bat-diameter runners, it looks quite similar to the Countach's Quattrovalvole. Lamborghini has, in fact, extensively redesigned its evergreen twelve.

Displacement grows from 5.2 liters

True to tradition, the newest Lamborghini is named for a fighting bull, but Diablo also is another word for devil. Sure enough, it can sometimes feel possessed. With 60 percent of its 3640 pounds on the rear tires and 428 pounds/feet of torque on tap, however, agnostics blame its maleficence on too much throttle in a turn.

to 5.7. Bore and stroke increase, from 86 x 75mm (3.37 x 2.95 inches) to 87 x 80mm (3.39 x 3.12 inches)—a ratio more suitable to the displacement. The cylinders have pressed-in steel liners with Nikasil faces. Forged steel is used for the crankshaft and the connecting rods. Compression is up from 9.5:1 to 10.0:1. The intake manifold gets twin throttles for sharper response in all running conditions. Single-row timing chains with dampers and an automatic tensioner system drive the dual overhead camshafts, replacing the Countach's manually adjusted double-row chains. Lubrication is by an integrated oil pump. The engine runs on unleaded premium fuel and routes its exhaust through catalytic converters, which are the standard now in Europe as well as the U.S.

Lamborghini has always regarded a car's engine as its soul, to be engineered with deference and assembled with respect. It's no different with the Diablo. James D. Sawyer saw the new 5.7 under construction and recorded in *AutoWeek* that, "The bottom of the V-12's aluminum heads are machined so precisely that even from six feet away you can see your face in them. Parts are weighed at the start of assembly to ensure that each engine is in balance. And all engines are sent to a dyno room where they are run-in for two-and-a-half hours."

Electronics are used much more extensively in the Diablo than in the Countach and play a vital role in equalizing the new supercar's performance the world-over. The principal advance is an up-to-date electronic engine-management system developed by Lamborghini and called Lamborghini Injectione Electronica (LIE). It has talents the Countach's single Marelli distributor could only dream about. LIE integrates the ignition and multipoint sequential fuel-injection systems for much more exact engine control. Plus, it governs each cylinder bank individually with separate electronic control units. To top it off, Diablo's press material asserts that LIE "increases performance at high speeds similar in character to the twin barrel carburetors that played such an important role in Lamborghini's history."

All this helps put Diablo's V-12 at the very top of its class in muscle. Lamborghini says the engine makes 485 horsepower at 7000 rpm. That's 65 more horsepower than the four-valve Countach twelve produced at its 7000-rpm peak. By comparison, Ferrari claims 478 horsepower for the

F40's twin-turbo V-8 and 390 for Testarossa's flat-12. Diablo delivers 428 pounds/feet of torque at 5200 rpm, up from the Anniversary Countach's 369 pounds/feet at the same rpm. In addition to claiming a top speed higher than any of these rivals, Lamborghini credits Diablo with a time of 4.09 seconds 0-100 kph (0-62 mph). The Countach took 4.7 seconds.

Getting this potential to the rear wheels is again the job of a five-speed manual transmission. Marmiroli told *Car and Driver* that the Diablo eschews the six-speed gearboxes now fashionable in such

cars as the BMW 850i and the Chevrolet Corvette because "with all the torque we have, a six-gear unit would add only weight and complexity." The final-drive ratio is 3.55:1, compared to Countach's 4.09:1.

Lamborghini planned to introduce an automatic clutch for the five-speed manual transmission. The Valeo-supplied option will allow the driver to move the gear lever through the standard shift gate, but will dispense with the traditional clutch pedal.

As in the Countach, Diablo's power is fed forward through a

single-plate dry clutch, then through the transmission, and back again via a driveshaft to the limited-slip differential. In the Countach, however, the driveshaft was routed through a passage in the engine oil sump. Diablo has the shaft alongside the engine to ready the powertrain for four-wheel drive. Due in 1991, the all-wheel-drive version will be offered alongside the rear-drive model and will be called Diablo VT, for *Visco* Traction. It takes its name from the viscous coupling at the heart of the all-wheel-drive system. When the rear tires begin to lose their grip because of road

Marcello Gandini, whose pen shaped the Miura and Countach, also was hired to style the Diablo (above). However, his first two designs were nixed by Chrysler, which then sent its own stylists to work with him. Changes were made to the front spoiler and the air intakes over the rear wheels, and Gandini's original fastback gave way to a tunnel-roof for better cooling and visibility. He was said to be upset at first, but he did sign the finished car (right).

Gandini's first Diablo design is said to
closely resemble the prototype shown
above, which was used as the basis for the
Cizeta-Moroder (below). This mid-V-16
exotic, proposed by an independent
concern, bowed first. But Lamborghini
says Gandini submitted his Diablo design
before he penned the Cizeta-Moroder. They
share many elements.

Diablo's roof is steel, its doors and quarter panels are of a stouter aluminum than used on the Countach, and its decklid, bumpers, rocker panels, spoilers, and engine cover are of composite plastic. The car is painted as a unit, then the doors are removed for subassembly steps. Main body panels require less hand fitting than on previous Lamborghinis, but with only 10 Diablos built per week, mass-production shortcuts are rare at Sant'Agata.

conditions or the amount of power being applied, the viscous coupling will automatically send up to 17 percent of the engine's torque to the front wheels until traction is restored. The system adds 97 pounds to the Diablo and consists of the coupling itself, a carbon fiber forward drive shaft, a limited-slip front differential, and new front half-shafts. The VT model will have no more horsepower than the regular Diablo and will be available with the automatic clutch.

Lamborghini's plan for the Diablo called for major improvements in interior amenities and ergonomics. For this, Chrysler sent one of its designers, Bill Dayton, to take up residence in Italy and supervise design work on the passenger cell. The result is a thoroughly modern cockpit, with softer, rounded shapes replacing the Countach's squared edges. The center of the instrument panel slopes gracefully toward the windshield in a binnacle that holds controls for the climate system, stereo, and trip computer. Miura had a passenger-side grab bar on the center console and Diablo pays homage with a similar handle, hefty and leather-padded, on the right side of the dashboard.

Serving the driver is a steering column adjustable for height—as were columns on later Countachs—but now it also telescopes 2.8 inches. Plus, the instrument cluster itself can be moved vertically about half an inch. The designers thoughtfully kept the angle between the instruments and the horizon near zero for quicker, safer reads at triple-digit speeds. The seats recline and are again separated by a railroad-tie-sized center tunnel on which sits a gated shift plate. Diablo wasn't engineered to accept a driver's airbag; each occupant is instead restrained by a motorized shoulder belt and an active lap belt.

Automatic climate controls are

standard, as is an Alpine sound system with a cassette or compact disc unit. Supplied with the car is a four-piece set of Italian-made luggage (retail value, about $3000) tailored to fit the five-square-foot cargo hold in the nose. As on the Countach, $5000 buys an ostentatious rear-wing spoiler of dubious aerodynamic benefit. Even more indulgent might be substituting the standard electronic clock for the special-edition removable, wind-up Breguet Swiss timepiece. That option costs $12,000. Still, all is relative. Early reports had the car selling for about $211,000, but by the time it came out, the list had risen to $220,000; no price had been set for the VT version. Chrysler says there was a rolling prototype ready for launch in '89, but that it took roughly 12 months of refinements before it was the automobile everybody wanted. Sant'Agata finally started production in July 1990, building slowly to about 10 Diablos per week, for a goal of 500 annually. About 35 percent of the production is scheduled for the U.S.

Despite its undeniable intervention, Chrysler seems well

The pride is back at Lamborghini, say plant visitors. Assembly of Diablo's cabin (below) benefits from molded panels, but remains daunting. A five-speed manual (below right) was deemed sufficient in place of the six-speed transmissions on some rivals, though an optional system that will do away with the five-speed's clutch pedal is in the works. Pirelli hand-makes the car's special tires (right). The fronts are 9.6 inches wide, the rears measure 13.1 inches across.

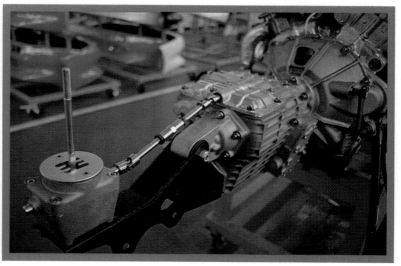

"It lacks the carnal, carnivorous presence that made its predecessor, the Countach, a favorite poster subject for feeding the fantasies of adolescents with rampant hormones," one writer said of the Diablo. Countered another: "The visual impact is awesome. By comparison, the angular old Countach looks like it's mocked up out of cardboard boxes, and a Ferrari F40 looks like an injection molded kid's toy."

Diablo's ergonomics drew mixed reviews in the first round of media test drives, with placement of the pedals—too close together and offset toward the center of the car—roundly panned. Handling was marked by meaty steering and intimate contact with the road. The nose tended to plow through tight corners, and while the tail could be coaxed into controlled oversteer, too much throttle snapped the tail out violently. Acceleration was celestial: 0-60 mph in 3.9 seconds, said Lamborghini. "Driven hard," one writer observed, "the Diablo simply obliterates traffic."

aware that it's but a neophyte in Lamborghini's exotic-car domain. At Diablo's debut, for example, Chrysler Vice Chairman Gerald Greenwald was exuberant about the car, but measured about his company's part in it. "Chrysler played an important role in Diablo," he said, "but it was the role a good accompanist plays behind a virtuoso."

As for Gandini, he reportedly was displeased early on with the design changes wrought by Chrysler. But he was present at their implementation, he posed with the car at its introduction, and he did finally OK the use of his *disegno* signature on its flanks. The stylist did not, however, scrap his initial drawings. Many of their key elements surface again in the Cizeta-Moroder V16T. This proposed supercar is the product of a collaboration between Claudio Zampolli, formerly of Lamborghini's dealer management arm, and Georgio Moroder, a highly regarded musical composer and the project's major financier. Built in Modena with help from a cadre of former Lamborghini employees, a running prototype of the two-seater carries a transverse mid-mounted 6.0-liter V-

16 wrapped in some familiar bodywork. Sure enough, here are Gandini's angular lines and bold air intakes. Here's his diving A-pillar, his fastback roof, even his asymmetrical rear-wheel openings. Some sources insist Gandani penned the Cizeta-Moroder *after* he submitted his original Diablo design to Lamborghini. But the V16T was unveiled months before the Diablo. So interwoven are the spirits of the designs that *Motor Trend* teased its readers in March 1989 with a photo of the Cizeta Moroder and the question, "Could this be the next Countach?"

That the answer was "no" frankly did not disappoint the automotive world. Nonetheless, where critics immediately went agog over the Miura and Countach, early reviews of the Diablo were ambivalent about the styling.

"It lacks the carnal, carnivorous presence that made it's predecessor, the Countach, a favorite poster subject for feeding the fantasies of adolescents with rampant hormones," wrote Sawyer in *AutoWeek*.

Countered Jeff Karr in *Motor Trend*, "The visual impact is awesome. By

comparison, the angular old Countach looks like it's mocked up out of cardboard boxes, and a Ferrari F40 looks like an injection molded kid's toy."

"Say what you will about the styling of Lamborghini's new Diablo," concluded Giancarlo Perini in *Car and Driver*, "but when the car is coming straight at you, no shape is more arrogant, bold, and compelling. . . . The latest Lambo, as it snorts past, actually has the curious effect of causing passers-by to hold their breath."

Driving one could have an alarming effect on respiration, as well.

Press the shotgun-shell sized chrome button below the B-pillar to release the door, then lift the door by its edge. Negotiate the sill—wide, but not as broad as the Countach's—drop over the tall lower side bolsters, and into the firmly padded bucket seat. Shoulder room is very good, and you'll be most comfortable if you're under six feet tall, though how your height is apportioned may make a difference. One six-foot-two-inch driver said he barely fit, another with a six-foot-three frame had no complaints.

Diablo was the first Lamborghini introduced under Chrysler's ownership. At Diablo's debut Chrysler Vice Chairman Gerald Greenwald was exuberant about the car, but measured about his company's part in it. "Chrysler played an important role in Diablo," he said, "but it was the role a good accompanist plays behind a virtuoso."

Overall ergonomics are an improvement over the Countach, but things here are far from perfect. Deep in the footwell, the pedals crowd close enough to one another to cross-up footwork that's the least bit imprecise. More annoying, they're offset toward the center of the car to clear the suspension. At its lowest setting, the rim of the tilt steering wheel hides some of the gauges, and if you're long of leg, it won't adjust high enough to keep your knee, hands, and the center console from meeting during right turns. Reaching the controls for climate and stereo systems requires a stretch forward. If the day is sunny, you might find, as did early test drivers, that the air conditioner is insufficient in capacity and that

there are too few dash vents to cool the cabin comfortably. Your view of the road ahead is excellent and if you adjust the power mirrors, visibility over the shoulders is adequate. Not much can be done about the view aft, which is like looking through a portal and down a gorge formed by those huge haunches. It doesn't help that the rearview mirror vibrates under throttle.

Time to go. Don't touch the accelerator pedal, just twist the key. "The starter engages with a high-pitched metallic whine, and then the V-12 erupts into life with a deep bass thrum," wrote Nicholas Bissoon-Dath in *Car and Driver*. "It idles with the slightly uneven and temperamental flair of a thoroughbred, gently rocking the car as the revs rise and fall. Blip the throttle and the needle swings around the tach, accompanied by the *zizzing* of the cam chains; yet the revs die just as quickly after you lift off. This engine has a light flywheel."

Get a feel for the controls. The clutch pedal is heavy, the shift action is stiff and the lever demands a firm hand to move it through the slotted gate. Despite a thick firewall that divides the engine bay from the cabin, the noise level is quite high, not diminished noticeably from the Countach. Unlike the Countach, which often stumbled at low speeds, Lamborghini's electronic engine controls keep the Diablo's V-12 tractable under virtually any condition, though the power comes on most smoothly in any gear above 3000 rpm. It was at this engine speed and in third gear that *Motor Trend*'s Karr pulled out to pass a

truck on the *autostrada*.

"With the application of full throttle, the Diablo's V-12 instantly snapped from serene to savage," he wrote. "A ragged, hammering wave of sound erupted from the firewall just behind our backs. My chest rumbled at a sympathetic resonant frequency. At this low engine speed, the sound was at first more startling than the acceleration; the engine gathered itself up and the wicked racket grew in intensity. I simply couldn't imagine an engine note more appropriate for a car called Diablo. Nor could I imagine one more sinister."

Bissoon-Dath takes it from there: "As the revs reach 7500, you shift into fifth and keep the pedal buried. The car still surges forward with pure authority, and the road unreels before you like a videotape on fast forward. The speedometer keeps climbing: 175, 180, 185. But the traffic ahead causes you to lift off. As the speed fades, like exhaling a held breath, you find yourself smiling...Driven hard, the Diablo simply obliterates traffic. It eats up gaps between cars in quick, effortless gulps."

Steering and handling are not so facile. The wheel is alive in your hands. There's lots of feedback from the road surface. Some describe the steering effort as meaty; others find it quite physically demanding. Even on center things are happening. This is an early test car and its nose hunts nervously at speed. Lamborghini says the P Zero tires needed more breaking in and that while each car is supposed to pass a 150-kilometer test drive before delivery, maybe this particular one

Diablo was engineered to accept an all-wheel drive system called **Visco Traction.** *Due in 1991, its viscous coupling reacts to rear-wheel slippage by sending up to 17 percent of the engine's torque to the front wheels until traction is restored.*

got by with a steering rack that's too tight.

Get off the freeway. Charge down a twisty road. The Diablo is far from ponderous, but it's so wide and you sit so low that it's difficult to anticipate the line through corners. Handling is typical of a high-powered mid-engine car. With so much mass in back, it wants to push the front tires through turns. Add more throttle—or lift off abruptly—and understeer quickly turns to oversteer. Careful, the wrong mix will snap the tail out. In fact, two journalists, one European, the other American, neither inexperienced, have crashed Diablos. This is a car that demands your attention and concentration.

"In every respect," Bissoon-Dath cautions, "the Lamborghini Diablo is a beast to be tamed. It requires a deliberate and firm hand, and it is a formidable machine that leaves those behind in amazement and awe. It may not be a civilized as an [Acura] NSX, but in terms of all-out performance it is a supercar of the very highest order. The king still reigns from Sant'Agata, and his name is Diablo."

It's safe to say that everything out of Sant'Agata Bolognese has been formidable. But one also could argue that precious few cars from there have enjoyed the symmetry founder Ferruccio Lamborghini held as his motoring ideal. It's a lofty goal, one few automobiles could satisfy. Lamborghini's car "without faults" would have to please both sides of his personality: the serious industrialist and the passionate enthusiast. On the surface, the Diablo doesn't seem to be the be the kind of machine he had in mind, either. But in reconciling the demands of Chrysler's hard-nosed technocrats with the dreams Lamborghini's automotive

expressionists, it strikes a balance that Ferruccio himself embraces. And it has that tribal rage.

"Refinement isn't on the Diablo's list of strengths, and neither is slavish attention to detail design," noted *Motor Trend*'s Karr. "In the grand and romantic tradition of the Italian Supercar, the Diablo is a thundering, fuel-sucking exercise in excess. As close to useless a car as you might ever hope to conceive. If that doesn't appeal to you on some level, strike some sort of cosmic chord in the back of your brain, then there's nothing I can say here that will make you understand.

"Only a mind-altering blast through third gear can do that."

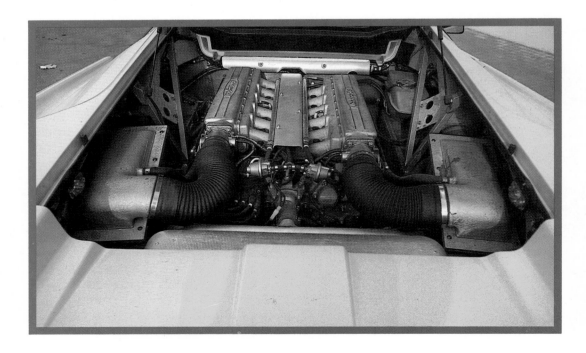

Just as it did in 1964 with the 350 GT, in '66 with the Miura, and in '74 with the Countach, Lamborghini has stepped ahead of arch-rival Ferrari in supercar technology. But the Diablo is not everyman's exotic. It is its own force of nature, as irrational as the matador's taunt, as irrevocable as the bull's charge.

CHAPTER 19
Lovely Loser: Urraco

Lamborghini's first small car was satisfying in many ways. It combined four-place seating with mid-engine placement, and in its later versions, was positively brisk, with handling to match Europe's best sports cars. Trouble was, it always seemed slightly off target. Part of the problem was that Lamborghini's resources were never as vast as its public image implied, so the car was denied the development attention it required. As it turned out, however, the truth was that the Urraco was ill-conceived from basic design to projected sales. In fact, it was largely the squandering of so much time and money on this one project that eventually brought the company to its knees.

Though Lamborghini had established itself with big, world-

class GTs for the very wealthy, the firm had shown interest early on in a smaller, less costly and more widely saleable car. Guests at *Il Cavaliere's* first major open house, at the time of the 1963 Turin show, were told of plans for either a V-8 or perhaps an inline slant-six derived from his 3.5-liter V-12, suggesting that a "junior" model would be offered one day. As we know now, big cars would continue to take precedence for several more years, though the one-off Miura-based Marzal and its 2.0-liter V-6 (see Chapter 21) showed that the notion was still alive in 1967.

Beside simple ambition and the natural urge for growth found in any organization, the basic rationale for a "budget" Lamborghini was survival. A more affordable, higher-volume offering would be the

great leap forward by which a small, relatively vulnerable "boutique" automaker could become a larger, more broadly based concern better able to weather economic storms. The example was Porsche, the once-tiny German sports-car maker that by 1969 had become a growing force in the European military/industrial complex. Sant'Agata's managers apparently envisioned Lamborghini following suit, perhaps establishing a similar engineering consultation business and supplying components to other automakers, and certainly fielding a wider product range of its own. While these were not unreasonable goals given the firm's already high design and manufacturing standards, there would be just too many obstacles to achieving them.

Nevertheless, once the mid-engine

196

Bertone made up two design studies for the new Lamborghini mid-engine V-8 2+2. The first (below) was rejected, but reportedly was later picked up by Ferrari as the basis for its 308 GT4. The second (bottom) was used by Bob Wallace for his Rally Urraco. The finished car (opposite) resembled No. 2, but with slats added for engine cooling.

Lamborghini designated its first V-8 car the P250: P for posteriore, 250 for the 2.5-liter engine. Its given name, however, was Urraco, or "young bull." It debuted at the Turin show in 1970, but production and design snafus delayed its delivery to customers for two years. Just as the concept of a mid-engine 2 + 2 was rather unique, so too was mounting the gauges in the very center of the dashboard, as was done on the prototypes (below). Urraco's rear seats (below, right) best suited those small of frame.

Miura was making money and the big four-seat Espada was launched, it seemed the time had come to pursue the expansionist dream. Paolo Stanzani took over as head of both engineering and plant management in 1968, and it was soon afterwards—certainly during 1969—that he and his staff began drawing up the new "volume" model. What emerged—a compact 2 + 2 with a new small-capacity V-8 mounted amidships—would be Lamborghini's first direct entree into the lucrative market inhabited by cars like the Porsche 911 and Ferrari's Dino 246 GT.

For Stanzani, this was the first chance to create an all-new car of his own, and he made the most of it. Jean-Francois Marchet has described him as "a wise and clear sighted man" who "likes very clean designs and direct solutions, even if this sometimes makes them more complicated to achieve...." Lamborghini's new baby thus arrived with a distinct design elegance about it inside and out, especially in its engine and chassis.

Rather than starting with the Bizzarrini-designed V-12, Stanzani had a completely new engine drawn up. His aim was a powerplant that

198

would be easier and less costly to build, tractable in give-and-take traffic, easier to maintain in extended service, and adaptable for the pollution controls then being mandated. He settled on a 90-degree V-8 with a displacement of 2462.9 cubic centimeters (150.2 cubic inches) on an 86-millimeter (3.39-inch) bore and a 53-mm (2.09-inch) stroke.

This "L240" unit was a graceful piece of work, and very light (375 pounds fully dressed) thanks to an aluminum block and heads. It wasn't especially exotic, though. Rubber belts drove a single overhead camshaft per head, and the two valves for each cylinder were parallel and in line with the cylinder axis. Combustion chambers were formed via concave piston crowns, the so-called "Heron head" that offers certain benefits for both manufacturing and emissions control (Jaguar's production V-12 has a similar arrangement). Compression ratio was set at 10.4:1.

On the dyno, the L240 thrummed out 220 DIN horsepower at 7500 rpm and 166 pounds/feet torque at 5750—impressive numbers that amounted to the same 89 bhp/liter produced by the more elaborate quad-cam 3.9 V-12 tuned to a typical 350 bhp. Assuming the accuracy of these data, it was apparent that Lamborghini engine efficiency had come quite some way in the previous half-dozen years.

The neat little L240 power package was designed to mount sideways ahead of the rear wheels—much like the Miura installation except that the V-8's shorter crankshaft allowed the five-speed transmission to extend beyond the engine on the left, in line with the crank. This, in turn, allowed a direct run for shift linkage to the selector mechanism, a distinct improvement on the Miura's through-the-sump arrangement. The one oddity was the way the shift gate was necessarily angled, so the linkage could run back to the transmission on the car's left. Like senior Lambos, the new junior

Allowing room for four people in a mid-engine layout was no easy task. Stanzini innovated by using MacPherson struts at all corners. Illustrated in the original P250 brochure (right), the struts weren't ideal for a high-performance car, but their compactness helped free enough space to place four seats in a wheelbase shorter than the Miura's.

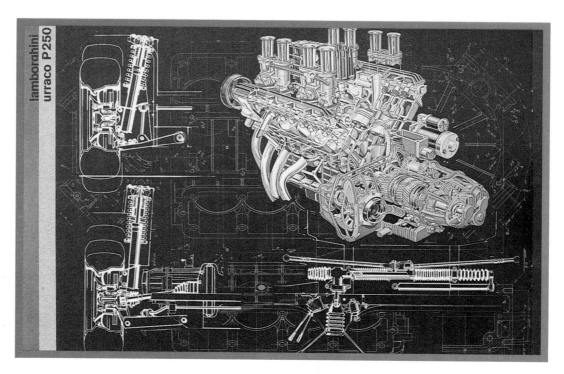

The P250 Urraco was a bridge between the successful V-12 Lamborghinis and several satisfying V-8s to come. But on its own, it was a disaster in nearly all respects, ill-conceived from basic design to projected sales. European versions had 220 bhp at 7500 rpm, and were better at high-speed touring than flaunting quick acceleration. Later U.S. cars ran on only 180 bhp and were much slower.

edition had synchromesh for reverse as well as all forward ratios.

That selector mechanism was on the bottom of the transmission because the two gearshafts were on the same level, the output shaft to the rear. As the output shaft in turn engaged the final-drive gearwheel (which extended out to the rear, Miura-fashion), there were only three basic rotation centers— crank, second transmission shaft, and final drive. The crankshaft thus rotated

"forward" in the same direction as the rear wheels.

Designated P250 (P again denoting *posteriore*), the new chassis was a sheet-steel unibody structure like the Espada's. Within a wheelbase of 2450 mm (96.5 inches)—same as on the 350 GTV (and the forthcoming Countach)—Stanzani found room for two human beings in front and two short-term (or maybe just short) guests in back. He managed this despite the fact that at 26 inches, the sidewinder V-8 was five inches "longer" across the heads than the Miura's V-12. Front-seaters had to angle their legs a bit because of wheelarch intrusion, and some of those in back might start muttering about "2-crush-2" seating; otherwise, the people packaging was quite efficient.

Suspension design was part of the trick. Like many other automakers, Lamborghini realized that the compact MacPherson strut freed up a lot of valuable volume, and decided to install one at each corner. (In Japan, Nissan had just done the same for its nifty little Datsun 240Z.) But all-round struts are less than ideal for a high-performance car, as they force the wheels to lean with body roll, and suffer friction and rigidity problems. Lamborghini was determined to make the geometry work, however, and Bob Wallace did. The struts, by the way, were borrowed from Fiat's top-of-the-line

130. Brakes came from BMW. Lamborghini made many of its cars' components, but bought a lot too.

Body design was still an out-of-house matter. As Lamborghini wanted something special for its new baby, it commissioned Bertone to make up not one but two separate prototypes. Both were good, but not quite good enough, so there was a third attempt. That proved to be the charm, and the production P250 emerged as a genuine beauty—that rare blend of balance, delicacy, grace, innovation, and *passion* that never seems to age. As a finishing touch, someone came up with another bullfighting name: Urraco (oo-RAH-koh)—appropriately, "young bull." So christened, the car was first unwrapped at the Turin show in late 1970.

Response was highly favorable and orders started coming in right away. Unfortunately, this all-new design proved to be full of all-new bugs, which prompted a rethinking and remaking that would stretch to nearly two years. Meanwhile, disgruntled customers began canceling.

Which was doubly unfortunate, because everything was starting to fall apart for Automobili Ferruccio Lamborghini. The man whose name graced the factory was losing his interest as fast as his money, and the workforce was increasingly restive. Worse, because the Urraco program had been predicated on much higher sales volume than previous Lamborghinis, the firm had invested heavily in new machine tools and factory space for it. Alas, the sales forecasts quickly proved optimistic, which meant that unit cost would go nowhere but up. We should also not forget that the early 1970s brought powerful new governmental interference in what had always been a much freer, simpler industry.

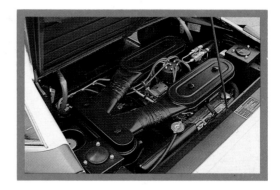

The complete Urraco power package (top) *was a triumph of space-efficient engineering. Note how snugly the V-8 fits between the MacPherson-spring/strut assemblies. The rear subframe facilitated engine removal; good, because access to the engine from outside* (above, right) *was poor. Front hatch vented air from the nose* (top, left) *and led to the spare tire* (above, left).

But in the end, it was the many and major teething problems that hurt the P250 most. Beside engine and suspension failures (recounted by Bob Wallace in Chapter 5), there were difficulties with cam-drive belts, transmission and cooling system, even the tires. And as if all that weren't enough, it was decided at the 11th hour to redo the interior to facilitate assembly of the right-hand-drive version.

When production finally got underway, it did so at a snail's pace: 35 units through the end of 1972 and 285 for all of '73—a far cry from the hoped-for 1000 a year. As for the few "lucky" buyers who took delivery, they discovered that not all the gremlins had been exorcised from their long-awaited Urracos. Those cam belts were particularly troublesome.

But Lamborghini had invested too much to just drop the Urraco. With Ferruccio's full departure, effective in 1974, new Swiss owners Rossetti and Leimer gave Stanzani the go-ahead to implement fundamental revisions. Because sales volume was down, price would have to go up, which dictated that quality and performance would, too.

Meantime, a new "mini-midi" Ferrari, the 308 GT4, had arrived in 1973 with a transverse 3.0-liter V-8

and—unusual for Maranello—a Bertone body. (An interesting aside: Trefor Thomas, president of the former Lamborghini Cars of North America, claimed the 308 GT4 body was based on the first Urraco prototype). Replying to this more direct competition, Sant'Agata enlarged the Urraco V-8 to the same level—actually 2997 cc/182.8 cubic inches—via a longer 64.5-mm

Time and money squandered on the Urraco project dealt a near-fatal blow to Lamborghini as an automaker. Many buyers were lost during the two-year gestation between prototype and production. Redoing the cabin for the right-hand-drive version, shown below with the oddly organized dashboard given all P250s, added to the delay.

(2.54-inch) stroke, and completely revised its top end via new heads. Camshafts doubled to four, all driven by good old reliable chains, and combustion chambers were now in the heads, but the result was more modern than the V-12, the included angle between valves being a fashionably narrow 34 degrees (versus the 60 Bizzarrini had used over a decade before). On slightly reduced 10.0:1 compression, this reworked L300 unit pumped out a claimed 250 bhp DIN at 7500 rpm and 195 pounds/feet of torque at 3500.

Replacing the P250 on its 1974 Turin debut, the P300 was a much-improved Urraco in other ways, with numerous detail changes to transmission, suspension, and bodywork. The factory pronounced it good for more than 160 mph flat out, and those with experience believed it. Automotive journalist Pete Lyons took a brief drive in a British-owned example and found it a delightfully sparkling little car for twisty English lanes, with a bright, revvy motor that didn't remind him at all of the V-8 in the '74 Corvette he was then driving in Europe. Thanks to years of hard flogging by the sensitive and determined Bob Wallace, many European connoisseurs judged the P300 one of the best-handling cars around. At last, the Urraco's promise seemed fulfilled.

Except that the car was still off-target and out-of-favor. Worse, Lamborghini's declining fortunes precluded the modifications necessary to legalize the P300 for the American market, once considered the firm's savior. Instead, U.S. Urracos continued with the sohc 2.5, detoxed to an anemic 180 bhp. Beginning in 1975, there was also a P200 Urraco, a home-market special created in response to new Italian tax laws that levied very heavy penalties on cars with engines above 2.0 liters. This carried the original sohc L250 engine debored to 77.4 mm (3.04 inches) for a displacement of 1995 cc (121.7 cubic inches). Claimed power was 182 DIN at 7500 rpm. Obviously, neither of these was in the spirit of what *Lamborghini* was supposed to mean.

But there was an Urraco fully worthy of the marque—one so unique that Sant'Agata workers gave it a special name: "Urraco Bob." Yes, it was the third of Bob Wallace's personal hot rods.

Like the all-out Miura-based Jota and the highly modified Jarama that came before, this "super-sports" Urraco was never an official factory project, but one that Wallace built on his own time. It was, however, the most elaborate and far-reaching of the three, ultimately encompassing a new *quattrovalvole* cylinder head. This work coincided with Stanzani's departure after increasingly serious clashes with the new owners, and Giampaolo Dallara's return as a consultant after getting some Formula 1 under his belt. One can imagine Wallace and Dallara huddling together to think ...*Racing!* Yet this special was never known as anything but a "rally" car, and Wallace took it racing only once.

With a leftover pre-production prototype as its starting point, the Rally Urraco piece-by-piece became a very thoroughly honed

All Urracos had sheet-steel unibody construction (above). Reacting to the new 3.0-liter Ferrari mid-engine 2 + 2, Lamborghini enlarged its V-8 to the same displacement for 1974 and issued the Urraco P300 (left). Its cams doubled to four and were driven by chains, not troublesome belts, and the combustion chambers moved to the heads. Output was 250 bhp at 7500.

Headlamps moved further forward are one of the few outward signs that distinguish the P300 Urraco (above and opposite) from the P250. Side marker lights and heavy black bumpers identify this as a U.S. version. The P300 was by far the finer Urraco, with more power and a better transmission and suspension. It was more reliable and agile and was assembled with more care. Top speed was over 160 mph. Considerably slower were the Italian-market P200s, powered by a pretty single-cam V-8 debored to 2.0 liters (opposite top) and rated at 182 bhp.

competition instrument. Much as with his Jarama special, Wallace stripped it of all weight not strictly needed, then added a judicious bit back by welding stiffeners and a roll cage into the structure. Steel was replaced with aluminum paneling wherever possible. To sharpen handling, he solidly bolted in the powertrain/rear suspension subframe, discarding its rubber isolation mounts, and rebuilt the suspension front and rear to incorporate the adjustments found on race cars. A large fuel tank went in where the useless rear seats had been, and some of the more florid exterior bits were scrapped. Fenders were flared to match wider wheels and tires, and there was an aggressively deep front spoiler. Painted the startling orange-red with black trim popular on Miuras, "Urraco Bob" was a very businesslike little missile. And with 310 bhp in final form, it was very fast.

Stung by criticism that the Urraco was overweight and underpowered, test czar Bob Wallace showed what could be done when serious speed was the goal. His ideal (both pages) had modifications to body, engine, and suspension. The interior (below) was gutted and race-ready. Nice Urraco, Bob.

"Over the years it ended up with a variety of odds and ends," Wallace recalls now, "including a six-speed transaxle and a dry-sump, four-valve, three-liter engine, and we even put a wing on it. It was an extremely quick and extremely good-handling car. In fact, the one and only time we ever raced it, at Misano, down by the Adriatic coast, I lapped everyone, including the Swiss national Porsche champion, in nine laps. Everyone had said we couldn't build a race car, and that was basically the only reason I built it, to show people the thing could go damn quick."

If Wallace still harbored hopes for a full-on Lamborghini racing program, he was again doomed to disappointment, as Swiss partners Rossetti and Leimer were more likely thinking of selling out by then. In fact, the mood in the once-happy Sant'Agata plant became so gloomy by 1975 that Wallace followed Stanzani out the door toward a change of career.

Though the Rally Urraco he left behind never led to anything, it may have contributed to the shift in marketing emphasis by which the P250/P300 was abandoned as a "2-crush-2" and reformatted as a strict two-seater. Lamborghini's V-8 experience was far from over.

207

CHAPTER 20
Try, Try Again: Silhouette and Jalpa

Ferruccio Lamborghini's original automotive ideal—the production of fleet, stylish four-seaters and 2+2s—left Sant'Agata along with Ferruccio himself in 1974. Disinterest within the company for such Lamborghinis had caught up with the growing indifference the buying public was showing toward them. It thus was easy for new Swiss owners Georges-Henri Rossetti and Rene Leimer to conclude that the Urraco would be more salable as a two-seater, in the vein of Ferrari's new 308 GTB. The transformation was only partly successful.

The big change to the car was a roof reworked into a "targa" style. The panel above the seats was made removable and could be stored behind the seats. Thus was created Lamborghini's first open-air production model. The Urraco's fastback became a notched "tunnelback" design and rear side windows were deleted. Stylish side scoops finished in a contrasting color were added to provide visual relief for the resulting massive rear quarters. Squared-up flared wheel arches shrouded Pirelli's state-of-the-art P7 tires on wider-than-Urraco wheels (much wider at the rear) with the five-hole "telephone dial" design first seen on Bertone's Urraco-based 1974 Bravo one-off (see Chapter 21). Further disguising the Urraco lower body were a more

When Ferruccio Lamborghini departed Sant'Agata in 1974, so did the firm's interest in four-seaters and 2+2s. By '76, the new Swiss owners had turned the Urraco into a car they hoped would sell better. It still said "Urraco" inside (above, middle), but the Silhouette (left) was a strict two-seater. It had a more aggressive look, better gauges (top), and a real rear trunk (above). It also was Lamborghini's first open production model. Seven seconds to 60 mph and a top speed of 147 mph were recorded.

With its well-tuned suspension and P300 V-8, Silhouette (above and opposite, top) was lively, but suffered quality defects. It died in '78, after only 52 were built. In '80, Lamborghini went into the hands of the French Mimran family, which tabbed an updated Silhouette as their volume-sales hope. The Jalpa that bowed in '82 (right and opposite, bottom) was still a targa-topped two-seater, but its styling was less angular, it had a new interior, a larger engine, and 16-inch wheels instead of the old ''telephone-dial'' 15-inchers. It was more successful than the Silhouette, and 410 were produced through 1988.

angular nose and a deeper front spoiler incorporating an oil-cooler duct and front-brake air scoops. Inside was a new, more ergonomic dash.

Underneath was a P300 unit body chassis structure suitably strengthened to go topless, including a safety roll cage within the rear roof "hoop" area. The P300 powertrain was carried over unaltered. Weight didn't change significantly, so performance and road manners promised to be at least the equal of the P300's, if not better.

Inspired for once by the track rather than the bullring, Lamborghini called its newcomer

Silhouette, a glancing reference to the production-based race cars that resemble their street counterparts only in basic appearance. Introduced at the 1976 Geneva show in March, it met a generally favorable reception, many people finding the looks to their liking. "From most angles, it's a very pretty car," wrote Sue Ransom of Australia's *Modern Motor*, "and, in my view, more attractive than the Urraco.

"In fact," she continued, "the Silhouette has changed its basic Urraco design quite drastically from being just another pretty Italian 'special' to having the aggressive good looks of a fast car which knows its business and does it well."

Like most other reviewers, Ransom also admired the blend of practicality with performance. In particular, there was now useful luggage space not only behind the engine but behind the seats (though the Urraco's cramped aft compartment was most often used this way), and roadholding was "far in excess of anything you'd ever need."

Although the Silhouette would never come to America under official factory auspices (more of which in a moment), *Car and Driver*'s Pat Bedard tried one modified to appease the EPA and found a lot for a car-nut to like, its color for one thing: "Harlot Red. Scarlet Harlot Red. No car has ever been redder than this Lamborghini. If you look too long at the finish, your temperature begins to rise." The suspension pleased him, too: smooth, supple, and bereft of harshness despite the wide super-performance tires. "Somebody at Lamborghini knows about suspension."

As for the engine, "The catalytic converter smothers the exhaust note, choking it right down to civilized volumes, but the sound is still pure high-calorie Italian: whirring cam drives, sucking carburetors, rattling transmission bearings....The eight carburetor barrels sing like organ pipes, and the patter of all those valves opening and closing blends together into a sweet, mechanical moan....It's *Sounds of Sebring* all over again, live and in color. We are red and we are on the move."

With all this, plus open-air appeal, the Silhouette should have sold well. But it didn't, and the reasons weren't hard to find.

Even though dumping the Urraco's back seat made for a "purer" sports car, the designers were unable at the same time to reconfigure the cockpit for the sort of space around the pedals that Miura drivers enjoyed. There was no money for that. So the two-seater had to retain the Urraco's floorpan and basic bodyshell, including windshield and surrounding structure. That meant it inherited not only most of the Urraco's design faults, but the same indifferent workmanship and suspect reliability. While this might have been expected in a car from a small, troubled company, it did nothing to ease buyer wariness in the face of Lamborghini's continuing, well-publicized financial and management problems. Then too, there was little about the Silhouette that shouted, "Buy me anyway!" as did the Countach.

The same strut suspension that gave the Silhouette surprisingly good handling was used for the Jalpa (opposite, top). The newer car's fat steering wheel (opposite, middle) blocked some of its instrumentation, but that didn't dim one customizer's vision (top). The quad-cam P300/Silhouette V-8 was stroked to 3.5 liters in the Jalpa (above), for a rated 255 bhp at 7000 rpm. In European-spec trim, it did 0-60 mph in 7.3 seconds and the quarter-mile in 15.4 at 92 mph.

Razor-sharp steering, a sure clutch, firm controls, poise in traffic, and a suspension that gave excellent control over virtually any surface were high points of the Jalpa, which listed for $58,000 in 1983. The seating position, poor vent system, and reflections bounced about by the windshield, rearview mirror, and vertical back glass were among the criticisms. Still, wrote journalist Pete Lyons, "In essence, this is a Practical Exotic—a super-expensive automotive playtoy that's willing to work for its living."

Yet a third factor: Lamborghini was in no position to certify Silhouette for the American market, where it might have sold in respectable numbers despite a stiff price. Inevitably, then, demand never approached hoped-for levels, and the creaky Sant'Agata line ground out a grand total of 52 Silhouettes before sputtering to a halt as corporate arteries hardened in the late '70s.

But, miraculously, the patient did not die. Giulio Alfieri came over from Maserati and, after a transfusion of new financial blood from the Mimrans, he had the little Lamborghini back on its feet. Picking up where Stanzani had left off a few years earlier, he lengthened the V-8's stroke to 75 millimeters (2.95 inches) for a new displacement of 3485 cubic centimeters (213 cubic inches). That bumped power to 255 DIN at 7000 rpm and peak torque to 231 pounds/feet at 3500.

In addition, some internal transmission ratios were juggled to suit, suspension details revamped, and even lower-profile P7s were specified on larger, 16-inch-diameter wheels (versus the previous 15s). Cosmetic alterations were made to the fender flares, nose, and "hunchback," and there was another new interior treatment. There was also a new name: Jalpa (YAWL-pa), another breed of *toro*. The new-breed junior Lamborghini went on sale in 1982.

It was well received. "As a model for rebuilding Lamborghini's reputation, it stands a good chance," was J-F Marchet's optimistic assessment. Although the steering was heavy at low speeds, he continued, "The Jalpa was very easy to drive in varied conditions, and... it was suitable for city traffic."

And the open road. Writing about a trans-European jaunt in a new Jalpa for Britain's *CAR* magazine, Steve Cropley complained about the seating position and very distracting reflections in the windshield and—via the interior mirror—in the vertical rear window. But he appreciated the easy handling on difficult surfaces and raved about overall feel: "The rifle-bolt firmness of the Lambo's controls, the brilliant razor-sharpness of the steering, the short-travel sureness of the clutch bite and the long-travel precision of the throttle...." One got the impression that though he didn't entirely love the Jalpa when driving it, he missed it afterward.

Road & Track judged the Jalpa "one of the most exciting cars to drive

we've come across in recent years... an exotic car that demands a firm and knowledgeable hand at the wheel—then it delivers more driving excitement than many of us experience in a lifetime." Said excitement translated to 7.3 seconds for the 0-60 charge, and to 15.4 seconds at 92 mph in the standing quarter-mile. Fuel "economy" was an estimated 12 mpg. Oh, and the price quoted in that 1983 test: a cool $58,000.

Auto writer Pete Lyons logged some time in a Jalpa that same year, also in California, and was inspired to record that, "The grandest cars

have a real Mediterranean flavor and feel, a color and a contrast that, somehow, make you think of sun shining on a wine-dark sea, of old tile-roof villages, of flower-bedecked roads winding along mountainous coastlines. A car bred in such a clime brightens the scene no matter how grey and cold the elsewhere it may travel."

But blended with the holiday mood of this vivid red car was a solid sense of everyday value. "In essence," wrote Lyons, "this is a Practical Exotic—a super-expensive automotive playtoy that is willing to work for its living. As sensuous to

An all-steel body for durability **(above)** and a V-8 mounted amidships for balance **(right)** helped account for some of the Jalpa's appeal. Plus, unlike the Silhouette, the Jalpa would be certified for U.S. sale. But it never achieved the hoped-for volume sales. Jalpa had exclusivity and a relatively attractive $65,000 price by '88, but it was surpassed in performance by the likes of the Porsche 928 and 911 Turbo and the Ferrari 308 Quattrovalvole and 328—not a good showing for such a vaunted pedigree.

look at as an Italian starlet, its bodywork is of sturdy steel. Low-slung as a stalking cat, it's comfortable and content in civilized traffic streams. Its motor, mounted midships like a racer, is a wondrous, raucous thing of many camshafts housed in light alloys; yet its personality is docile, broad-shouldered and friendly." The engine, virtually 2/3 of the Countach unit, provided plenty of horses for the real world; "They are remarkably smooth-mannered horses, sturdy, healthy, thrilling, but not wild....This is one of those point-and-pull-the-trigger cars, but it is not a Magnum; its discharge does not bruise the hand."

The Countach was "willful" and "wanton," altogether "not a lady of the real world," Lyons concluded. "The Jalpa, though; you could live with her. Go places, suffer through traffic, park. And love every minute with her....And yet, for all the studied practicality, this is a car that captivates. Driving it brings back, irresistibly—who would resist?—sunny mornings along the *Costa del Fiori*, golden afternoons above the sea at Amalfi."

Alas, sales, never strong to begin with, tailed off through 1987 and new owner Chrysler decided the Jalpa wasn't really the companion the Countach needed. The inventory of parts was used up and production of the Jalpa was quietly halted in July 1988.

"Harlot Red. Scarlet Harlot Red.... If you look too long at the finish, your temperature begins to rise," said one writer about a Silhouette, and it was as true for the Jalpa (above). Jalpa production ended in July '88; it had aged poorly, sales lagged, and Lamborghini needed line space for the Diablo. Its baby-Lamborghini role will be filled by a new mid-V-10 two-seater due in 1992.

217

CHAPTER 21
Showstoppers: The Concept Cars

How an automobile looks has always been vitally important to Lamborghini, even if the styling of its cars is sometimes disappointing. The results have consistently been interesting, though, for there's a spirit to the machines from the sign of the bull that seems to inspire an extra measure of creativity among Italian *carrozzeria*.

The vitality and imagination of their efforts has been seen throughout this book in the development of the various production Lamborghinis. In particular, some of the first attempts at a new design have been quite intriguing, even if they didn't make it to the assembly line.

We also have noted special bodies built on various Lamborghini chassis at various times for various reasons. An important example was the Scaglione-designed 350 GTV, commissioned by *Il Cavaliere* as his first car. It was not an entirely successful shape, nor was the car as a whole ever really finished. But the GTV did attract attention, alerting the world that here was an ambitious new enterprise worth watching. Later, working mainly on their own, the houses of Bertone, Frua, Neri & Bonacini, Touring, and Zagato applied their skilled artistry to create some very special Lamborghinis.

Four other very special Lamborhinis have been built by the company itself or at its direct behest. More than the usual exhibitions of the Italian flair for body design, they also explored engineering concepts. Today these cars stand as serious and daring efforts by Lamborghini and its coachbuilders to advance the state of the entire automotive art. Their names: Marzal, Bravo, Athon, and Portofino.

The Marzal, another Lamborghini named for a fighting bull, burst upon a startled world in March 1967, a year after the Miura. Though clearly based on the same chassis concept as that very advanced, very powerful mid-engine two-seater, the Marzal was Lamborghini's first attempt at establishing a new line of grand-touring sedans.

Originally, head engineer Giampaolo Dallara must have concluded that a longer-wheelbase version of the sheet-steel Miura platform would be a good starting point for a four-seater. And indeed, a sedan built like that would have some intriguing theoretical advantages. For one thing, mid-engine placement would allow a low, sloping nose for excellent vision forward. For another, it would put rear seaters near the middle of the wheelbase, so passenger loads would be distributed more equally between the front and rear tires than is the case in front-engine sedans

Lamborghini was born with a show car—the 350 GTV—and some of its greatest triumphs have come on the salon circuit: witness the stir caused by the unveiling of the Miura chassis at Turin in '65. The future foretold by these dream machines can be fanciful, or quite factual. But it's always captivating. The Portofino (left) *announced the Lamborghini/ Chrysler union in '87.*

219

Sometimes inspiration comes from show cars commissioned by other sources. A London newspaper had Bertone restyle a Jaguar E-Type 2+2 into the 1967 Piranha (above). Its body buck was later used for Lamborghini's Espada prototype. Sometimes others' ideas were rejected; the factory never followed up on Bertone's 1968 Miura targa proposal (left) or on Touring's graceful 350 GT ragtop from 1965 (bottom).

(especially those with front drive). Finally, it could permit the car to have a trunk at each end. This opened up some interesting weight-tailoring possibilities for augmenting handling and roadholding that already promised to be uncommonly good, thanks to the midships layout's low polar moment of inertia.

But even mounted transversely, the big V-12 would have made a Miura-based sedan needlessly large and unwieldy. Reason: it simply occupied too much space. The Miura's rear axleline is 26 inches distant from its firewall at the level of the exhaust camshafts. The firewall slants even farther forward at its base, and insulation ahead of it adds another four inches. In short (or should we say "in long?") the Miura had no hidden nooks or crannies for cramming in extra seats, as there might be in a front-engine

car, and splicing in enough length to fit them in would have meant a wheelbase of 130 inches or more.

Well, why not simply sling the motor out behind the rear axleline? Answer: Because several hundred pounds of metal, oil, and water back there would make the car unduly tail-heavy, to the detriment of handling and straightline stability. Owners of early Porsche 911s knew this only too well.

But then Sant'Agata's head engineer was inspired to take a hacksaw to the Miura motor. Lopping off its "front" cylinder bank left a shorter, lighter inline six still in unit with the end-on transaxle. By turning the resulting package around 180 degrees, the remaining cylinder bank slanted forward, thus minimizing rear overhang. It also freed up that 26 inches for accommodating an extra pair of passengers, which meant that wheelbase could be a manageable 103.1 inches. Early Miura development had already proved how easy it was to make the crankshaft turn the "wrong" way to get the final drive right. Halving the

Lamborghini aimed to build a gentleman's GT, but others kept trying to make something else out of his basic product. Zagato turned a 350 GT into the 3500 GTZ (below). The 1965 one-off had strong Ferrari overtones. Later, an American customer had Neri & Bonacini build a two-seat coupe from a 400 GT 2 + 2. Called the Monza 400 (above), it had a Ferrari windshield and a phony side vent.

3.9-liter V-12 created a slant six of 1964.5 cubic centimeters (119.8 cubic inches), which was tuned for 175 horsepower, more than most normal Eurosedans had in those days.

Ferruccio Lamborghini asked Carrozzeria Nuccio Bertone to do the body design for this concept vehicle, but he got more concept than he wanted. The ears of young Marcello Gandini, newly established as Bertone's chief stylist, were still ringing with cheers for his Miura, which may be why he went all-out with the Marzal.

Legend has it that the finished work simply appalled *Il Cavaliere* (the Emilian farmer's son probably uttered something worse than

''*Countach!*''). His main objection seems to have been those glassy doors. In fact, they were almost *all* glass, top to bottom, front to rear. Well, no customer of *his* would be caught dead in such a fishbowl. Why, every peasant would be able to ogle a great lady's legs—or so his comments have been reported.

Regardless, Mr. L. flatly declared that this was nothing like the sedan he wanted, and that there would never be a second one. Sorry, boys, try again—and this time make me *a real* car. With this began the development effort that would culminate in the front-engine Espada of 1968.

Meantime, *Il Cavaliere* allowed the

mesmerizing Marzal to appear on his stand at the '67 Geneva show, where public reaction proved to be something he could abide happily. As with the Miura the year before, this far-out fantasy inspired magazine articles galore and put the Lamborghini name on everyone's lips. Two months later, the Marzal had the honor of "closing the circuit" for the Grand Prix in Monte Carlo—driven on that great occasion by His Royal Highness, Prince Rainier, and his Princess Grace, the former Ms. Kelly of Philadelphia and Hollywood. A very good show it was, and very good press.

Though flashy in the best ''dream-car'' tradition, the Marzal

Among the most thrilling Lamborghini show cars was the Marzal. Ferruccio was pondering a four-place GT and Bertone's Marcello Gandini, fresh from the Miura, gave it life in '66. The rear-engine wonder had glassy gull-wing doors that gave the desired rear-seat access, but also promised to be highly impractical. A grille-less nose and narrow headlamps predicted late-'80s design, however. The glass doors were too much for Il Cavaliere, but the seeds planted by the Marzal would blossom two years later as the Espada (left).

was a serious exercise. The use of gullwing doors—a single large one per side, each counterbalanced by a strong spring across the engine compartment—gave access to the entire seating area, so entry/exit was as easy aft as fore. Answering the head man's objections about "unintended visibility" would be as easy as deleting some glass, which also would allow for the roll-down windows that were missing on the Marzal. Of course, there remained the potential difficulty of opening the huge doors in the event the car wound up on its head, but you can't have everything.

At only 175.2 inches long and 43.3 inches high, the Marzal was seven inches shorter and the same amount lower than Lamborghini's contemporary 400 GT 2+2. And startlingly low it was—in fact, a bit *too* low in front for adequate suspension movement or for meaningful luggage space, despite the fact that the radiator was in the tail. Like most handmade prototypes, this one came out heavy—half again heavier than a Miura. And with only half a Miura engine, potential performance was less than grand, even for touring.

Then there was Gandini's unfortunate fondness at the time for hexagons that left the Marzal awash in honeycomb appliques, notably on the dash and the matte-black engine hatch/backlight. As a design theme it was distinctive, bordering on bizarre.

Still, these and other lapses would likely have been corrected with a production Marzal—which in a sense they were, with the Espada. But Ferruccio Lamborghini was the boss, and though he gave his creative "kids" a lot of scope, the Marzal was just too far out as it stood. The silver flash was shown around Europe for another year or so, then retired. In retrospect, it contributed to the evolution of production Lamborghinis only as a pattern for certain elements of Espada styling, though something of its basic layout would eventually appear in the transverse V-8 Urraco.

Lamborghini's next "official" show car appeared in 1974. Called Bravo in public and internally designated project 114, it was a sort of scaled-down Countach, though built on a P300 Urraco chassis shortened 7.9 inches (200 millimeters) for a wheelbase of 88.6 inches (2250 mm). Body design, predictably executed by Bertone under Gandini, continued two Countach themes: a large, steep windshield raked right on forward through the nose, and asymmetric rear wheelarches as on the original LP500 prototype.

Overall, though, the Bravo was a good deal stubbier and plumper than the Countach, measuring just 147 inches long but nearly 70 across—wide enough for embracing fat roadwear without fender flares. A quite glassy greenhouse featured predictive semi-concealed A-pillars plus large triangular panes ahead of the door shutlines and tiny quarter windows aft. For decorative detail, Gandini contented himself with mere rectangles and circles. The former showed up in the angular nose and a heavily louvered "fasthatch" (so much for rear vision, again). The latter took the form of wheels with big lug holes arrayed "telephone dial" fashion, an item that would be applied to later Countachs and the Silhouette. The interior was notably spartan, the dashboard having little more surface development than a plank.

In this, his last chassis for Lamborghini, Paolo Stanzani installed a hopped-up Urraco engine rated at 300 bhp, plus different gearing and wider tires. Claimed weight was about 2400 pounds, top speed over 160 mph.

Sant'Agata apparently had thoughts of offering this car for sale, as the original show model, the only Bravo built, is believed to have covered over 40,000 hard highway miles. But as Jean-Francois Marchet observed, 1974 was the wrong time for a new car of this type. The first energy crisis had just hit, and "anti-performance car feeling was such that Bertone felt obliged to

Bertone's Miura roadster proposal of '68 was turned over to the International Lead-Zinc Research Organization, which transformed it into a rolling exhibition for its metals' automotive applications. Called the ZN 75, this targa-topped one-off had a tunnel-back roofline (above) in place of the production car's fastback slats.

A Miura made of lead and Zinc? What a concept. The ILZRO could not have chosen a higher-profile auto to showcase its products, though ultimately, the ZN 75 was more noteworthy as an open-top Miura than as a use for specific metals. Note the arty gear lever **(above)** and absence of the production car's rocker-panel vents **(below)**.

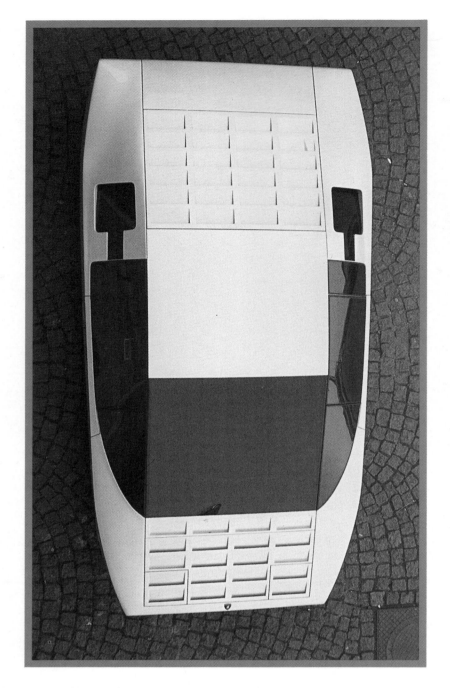

apologize and justify its design...." Hopes of producing the Bravo bravely lingered on into the 1980s, according to historian Rob de la Rive Box, then seem to have evaporated. The name, however, has resurfaced as the rumored moniker for the Jalpa successor due in the early '90s (see Epilogue).

Bertone was primarily responsible for another special based on the Urraco—or more precisely, the Silhouette. This was a captivating little topless toy called Athon (AH-tawn), first shown at Turin in 1980. As noted in Chapter 4, the name was taken from ancient Egyptian mythology and generally reported as meaning "Hymn to the Sun." That was appropriate, because the Athon was a hymn of support for an automaker whose sun seemed to be setting. A Bertone press release, quoted by Box, read in part: "At such a testing moment [for Lamborghini], it is Bertone's intention to once again lend its support to a name that it does not want to die." And as Lamborghini didn't, maybe the name possessed

Gandini's Bravo of 1974 **(both pages)** *was to be the junior Countach. Its shortened Urraco chassis carried a 300-bhp V-8. The Bravo was well finished for a show car and might well have seen series production had not Lamborghini's money woes and the first energy crisis interfered. The Silhouette was introduced instead.*

some ancient magic of the Pyramids.

The car itself was certainly an encouraging omen. Designed by a Bertone staffer named Deschamps, the Athon had no top and no provision for one. It did have a more orthodox hood/windshield transition than either the Countach or Bravo, but was a very futuristic little roadster all the same—the kind of thing Luke Skywalker might have used for a date with Princess Leia. Interior design was typical Italian *haute couture*, with a single-spoke wheel and a large "satellite" control-switch pod projecting from the dash to the left, ideas likely picked up from Citroën. Electronics abounded, including a trip computer.

Riding the standard 96.5-inch-wheelbase Silhouette chassis, the Athon measured 156.2 inches long and 74.3 inches wide. Though built in a hurry, it was fully driveable and was even made available to the press. But lack of funds doomed any possibility of production, and the Athon had no discernible influence on the Silhouette's Jalpa successor that came out the following year. Still, this dramatic little device was a definite ray of sunshine in Lamborghini's darkest hour.

Fortunately, Lamborghini would survive that hour, and by 1987 it not only had a much rosier outlook, courtesy of new owner Chrysler Corporation, but was apparently tilting anew at the four-seater market, abandoned almost a decade before with the end of the Espada.

Hinting at the prospect was a shapely show car that, according to a report in the March 1988 *Motor Trend*, was built to celebrate Chrysler's takeover of Lamborghini.

A year earlier, 1986, Chrysler stylist Kevin Verduyn had developed a concept for a possible future sedan. Dubbed "Navajo," it was well received but looked a dead end—until the Lamborghini buyout. Refined in detail and set on a Jalpa platform stretched 26 inches in wheelbase, the clay-and-fiberglass

Compare Gandini's sketch of the Bravo (opposite, top) with the running car on the previous page. Which is more remarkable, that his vision was translated nearly intact, or that the design looks fresh even today? Some concept cars mark specific points in Lamborghini's history. The Portofino (above) celebrates Chrysler's buyout. Bertone's topless Athon (left) was a ray of sunshine in 1980, when the Lamborghini forecast was quite bleak.

Navajo became the metal-and-plastic Portofino, finished as a running demonstrator by Coggiola of Turin and unveiled at the Frankfurt show in late '87, soon after the Chrysler/Lamborghini deal was announced.

At this writing, it seems doubtful that the Portofino or anything like it will ever see production as a Lamborghini, though its cab-forward silhouette was borrowed for the Eagle Optima, a Chrysler show car that sets the pattern for the Detroit company's sedans of the 1990s. Still, the four-place four-door Portofino achieves much of what the Marzal did, albeit on a much longer wheelbase, and has a definite high-tech look to it that seems perfect for the '90s. Though the rounded body is perhaps a bit heavy-handed compared to the purely Italian designs in Lamborghini's past, it does reportedly accommodate four six-footers. It also nicely accommodates the midships Jalpa V-8 without being obvious about that. It's probably no coincidence that asymmetric rear wheelarches are on hand once again, and they work even better here than on the first Countach.

However, we suspect that the vertical-opening scissors-action doors, another deliberate Countach tie-in, may be a little extreme for the real world. Access is good, as the design completely eliminates the need for B-pillars just like the Marzal's gullwings did, but accident egress must surely be no better. And we can imagine unwary passengers bumping their heads on them when getting out.

Symbolizing the new Highland Park-Sant'Agata connection, the Portofino arrived with badges in which the Lamborghini bull was penned in by the Chrysler pentastar. Company officials say that the logo will remain one-of-a-kind—and that Lamborghini will retain its independence. Let's hope they keep their word.

Rather than predicting a Lamborghini four-door, the Portofino (opposite, top) foreshadowed the shape of Chrysler's mid-1990s sedans, as suggested by the Eagle Optima concept of 1990 (opposite, bottom). Turn back to Chapter 18, however, to see how Portofino's dashboard and sloping center console (top) resemble those of the Diablo. Note Portofino's bull-in-a-pentastar steering-wheel logo.

231

CHAPTER 22
Fractious 4x4s: Cheetah and LM-Series

Build a Countach six feet tall. Keep the Jules Verne styling and quad-cam V-12, but give the thing four-wheel drive, enormous tires, dwarf-clearing ride height, four doors, and an open rear cargo bay. Take it to the desert. Make tracks. Put it on the road. Make trouble. How does 6700 pounds going 118 mph sound? See what we mean about trouble?

The company that brought you that outrageous exercise in automotive excess, the Countach, has also let its unmatched penchant for social deviance wreak havoc on everything off-roaders have known for the past 40 years. Run for cover,

folks, for here comes the Lamborghini LM, the world's one and only $126,000 Jeep.

Of course, it's not a real Jeep, even though Lamborghini has lately become part of the same Chrysler family as Jeep. But it *is* a genuine Lamborghini.

The LM originated in 1977 during the period when Lamborghini was desperately scratching to find enough work and money to stay alive. One result was a contract with the American firm Mobility Technology International to design and produce an all-terrain runabout for sale to the U.S. military under its High Utility Mobile Military Vehicle

program. Better known by its acronym "Hum-Vee," the program was set up to devise a replacement for the veteran World War II-vintage Jeep.

Alas, Mobility Technology ran into patent infringement trouble with FMC Corporation, maker of the eventual HUMMV, and had to abandon the project. But it was no great loss because the single prototype—built by Lamborghini with a rear-mounted, 360-cubic-inch Chrysler V-8 and automatic transmission—was apparently not that good. Called Cheetah (FMC might have thought "Cheater" a better name), it was written off in a

Built to conquer nearly any terrain, the fearsome LM machines boast the V-12 soul of a Countach and the unstoppable heart of a Lamborghini tractor. The current LM002 model (opposite) shows its U.S.-spec side marker lights, while the version below is in its element among the shifting dunes of North Africa.

233

234

The antecedent of today's LM002 was the Cheetah of 1977 (opposite, bottom). *Lamborghini built it for an American company as a replacement for the U.S. military Jeep. It had a rear-mounted 360-cid Chrysler V-8 but never was mass produced. It was followed by Lamborghini's own LM001* (opposite, top), *also with a rear engine, but this time a 360-cid AMC V-8. Neither design worked well, prompting development of the front-engine LMA in '82* (this page).

crash during tests somewhere in the California desert.

Under normal circumstances, that would end the story—and maybe Lamborghini, which had diverted funds advanced by the Italian government for the BMW M1 program (described in Chapter 4) to the Cheetah project. But circumstances have seldom been normal at Sant'Agata, and the idea of a super off-roader was still a flickering ember when the Mimran brothers arrived with their financial fuel. Thus stoked, the fire flared up at the 1981 Geneva show with an all-new, all-Lamborghini all-terrain vehicle.

Well, almost all-Lamborghini. This second iteration, called LM001 (the letters are variously explained as meaning "Lamborghini Military" or "Lamborghini-Mimran"), was supposed to be available with either a 4.75-liter Countach V-12 or another chunk of Detroit iron, a 360-cid AMC V-8—a bit closer to a Jeep. Either way, it was still a rear-engine design and still not that great. The main problem seemed to be that weight transfer in acceleration made the front end too light for best steering control. The solution was a third vehicle with the engine in front—a Lamborghini engine.

The result, called LMA (A for *Anteriore*, referring to the front engine), appeared in 1982. Besides significant revisions to suspension and chassis, it also had power steering (which its predecessors didn't) and was able to carry extra people where the engine had been in the Cheetah and 001. All this worked much better in testing and the LMA began looking like a promising commercial prospect—so much so that it was redesignated LM002 in anticipation of series production.

A further front-engine version was developed with a 3.0-liter turbocharged diesel six supplied by

Italy's VM, but with only 150 bhp to carry nearly three tons, this LM003 literally went nowhere. Accordingly, Lamborghini took the opposite tack, and in 1983 introduced an LM004 with a 7.3-liter gas engine.

This was no NASCAR big-block but a 7.3-liter Lamborghini V-12—aluminum block and heads, four cams, six big Webers, the works. We haven't talked about this unit before, but it had been lying around the Sant'Agata shop since the early 1970s. Bob Wallace recalls that Paolo Stanzani had designed it

for boat racing. Lamborghini's original Bizzarrini-designed V-12 found great favor with watercraft folk, and it has won numerous races and a couple of championships. So there was a market, and Stanzani was allowed to create an all-new powerplant in initial sizes of 6.0 and 8.0 liters.

These days it's offered in 7.3- and 8.0-liter forms for installation in both offshore racing boats and luxurious marine cruisers. It owes nothing at all to the 3.9, being bigger in every dimension and having a narrower

After toying with a 3.0-liter turbocharged diesel six and then with V-12s of 7.3- and 8.0-liters, Lamborghini settled upon a 5.2-liter V-12 for its production LM002 (below). A cabin of leather and wood inlays (left) contrasts with the utilitarian exterior.

valve angle. You can tell it from its 5.2-liter "baby sister" by very square-cut cam covers with small raised blocks.

Yes, we have asked Wallace the inevitable question: Did he ever hanker to stuff The Big One into a car? His hot-rodder's eyes lit up. "Oh, yeah!" But he never did.

As used in the LM004, this powerhouse displaced precisely 7257 cubic centimeters (443 cubic inches). Claimed power output is 420 DIN at 5400 rpm, torque an "adequate" 435 pounds/feet at 3500 rpm. Lamborghini built only one LM004, a prototype, in 1986. Production of the LM002 continued, though, with the latest Quattrovalvole version of the "small" twelve for power. With 5167 cc, Weber carbs, and 9.5:1 compression, it packs 444 bhp at 6800 rpm and 368 pounds/feet of torque at 4500 rpm.

As did the LM004, the LM002 has a wheelbase of precisely three meters (118.1 inches). Track measures 63.6 inches front and rear. Overall length is 192.9 inches, width 78.7, and height a rangy 72.8 inches. Ground clearance is 2/5 of an inch less than a foot. A bridge-strong steel-tube space frame supports an all-independent coil-spring suspension. Rolling stock comprises 17-inch steel wheels mounting 325/65VR tires. Brakes are discs at the front, drums in back.

Because this is a Lamborghini, the LM's four-door notchback body is made of lightweight aluminum and fiberglass. Belying the square-rigged utilitarian styling are interiors upholstered in fine leather and furnished as to give the uncanny impression of a giant, upright Countach. Fuel capacity is a camel-like 76.6 gallons U.S.—and that's for the *little* LM. The big one took 84.

Naturally, both LMs have four-wheel-drive, via a very heavy-duty ZF five-speed gearbox and two-speed transfer case. The front hubs must be locked manually for 4WD operation, which seems a bit old-fashioned. On the other hand, we understand that the transfer box has a very cunning design that allows the front wheels to turn one percent faster than the rears, which enhances stability and traction in the dirt.

Though Lamborghini sells a few LM002s to various armies each year—which was the original idea, after all—it's developed a decent civilian market for the LM—wealthy

clients who'd really rather drive a Countach but live in places with few paved roads. This means sheiks and the like—even a few Americans.

Car and Driver's Brock Yates experienced the range of LM capabilities in an American-spec 5.2 model during the summer of 1987. "Rambo Lambo," he called it, and he loved it. "Meet the closest thing to a street-legal Tiger tank known to man," he wrote. "Never before in recent memory have we driven a vehicle that has turned as many heads, blown as many minds, freaked as many citizens, or been as much insane, outrageous fun...."

Yates went on to point out the LM tested had "the standard Italian exotic's complement of wacky contradictions and absurdities," everything from non-canceling turn signals to air conditioning that pumped hot air. He also complained that steering and clutch effort were heavy at low speed.

But on the prowl, "Rambo" was a savage joy: "Once the tach needle sweeps past 5000 rpm, the LM002 sheds its street clothes and begins to operate like something out of DC Comics. The big engine howls unearthly tones through its dual exhausts, and suddenly one is seeking out 3-series Bimmers, 300E Mercs, and unready Z28 Camaros. To shock and humiliate their hapless drivers is one of the more civilized urges one gets behind the wheel of this leviathan."

As for handling and stick, it did surprisingly—no, astonishingly—well on curvy roads, and braking power was amazingly high. Off road, "the surprisingly supple Lambo suspension soaked up the impacts like a sprinting tiger. The brute is pure feline when it comes to rapid off-road transit—truly the best such machine we have ever encountered."

Against *C&D*'s computerized test gear, Yates' 002 did 0-60 mph in 7.7 seconds, the standing quarter-mile in 16.0 seconds at 86 mph, and 118 mph all out. The full-throttle sound reading was 97 dBA, not quite as loud as the vintage Miura the magazine tested a few months later. Oh, and observed mpg was 8.

Even more incredible was the big-inch 004 tested by Britain's *Autocar* in May 1986. Theirs was a military version demonstrated in part by a factory driver "who clearly enjoyed his work. He showed the wheel travel of over 20 in....Driving

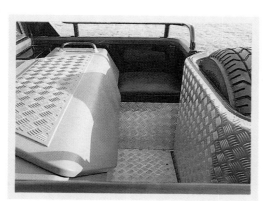

It takes some effort to tread lightly in a vehicle that's as wide as a Countach, stands six feet tall, and weighs nearly 6800 pounds. But that's the LM002 (left). Under its quaking hood is a 455-bhp doch V-12 topped by a sextet of Weber carbs (top left). The gear box is a five-speed manual. On dry pavement, power is to the rear wheels. The front hubs (left) must be locked manually to engage 4WD. Two 4WD systems allow the torque to vary automatically among the wheels or to lock and favor the rears with 75 percent. The tailgate forms a step to the cargo/passenger bed, which is lined in non-skid aluminum (middle left).

The LM002's aluminum and fiberglass body covers a steel-tube frame. Only four seats are inside, but occupants are treated royally in this most exotic of utility vehicles. Power steering, power windows, and air conditioning are standard. Even the headliner is upholstered in leather and suede. The two levers left of the console allow the driver to select among the drive systems.

through a water basin [that deep] proved no problem, no water entering through the doors, although they were under water."

With typical British understatement, *Autocar* noted that the LM's "ability to take steep hills is unprecedented....It can take a single angle of 70 degrees without falling over, although that isn't very comfortable for passengers.

"With the works driver, something of a Kamikaze pilot, we drove up a hill with an angle of 30 degrees, which the LM took with great ease. It was followed by a 50-deg. hill. In

either case, the car just climbed. One has to depend very much on the car, since the only thing you can see [in that situation] is the [hood]. Now on to a 70-deg. hill. We aren't sure if we would like it but, once again, the car just climbed upward. Bystanders reported the front wheels coming off the ground. We should be in the *Guinness Book of World Records* by now."

LM004 performance certainly should. *Autocar* wasn't able to run its usual tests, but quoted the factory-claimed top speed of over 200 km/h (125 mph) and 0-100-km/h

(0-62-mph) time of "no more than 8.5 seconds."

Summing up, the editors noted that the "Lamborghini people think the Countach has no competition among cars. One might argue with that. Most certainly, there is no car that can even come close to the LM."

Production of the LM002 is scheduled to cease in late 1992 or early '93, when Lamborghini begins to retool for the P140 Jalpa replacement. As of late 1990, only 250 LMA/LM002s had been assembled since the 4×4's introduction in 1982. The final 60 to be built will be tagged the LM/american. They'll share the LM002 mechanical specification, but will be dressed out in commemorative badging and body stripes, and roll on MSW/OZ Racing alloy wheels.

Though the market for the LM series has always been small, this outrageous vehicle's impact has always been large. Sometimes good things do come in *big* packages.

Depending on the source, LM stands for "Lamborghini Military" or, in honor of the owners at the time of its inception, "Lamborghini-Mimran." The factory lists its 0-60 mph time as 8.5 seconds and its top speed at 125 mph. "Insane, outrageous fun..."

EPILOGUE
The Road Ahead

Lamborghini grids for the '90s with two landmark vehicles. The Diablo (top in the photo above) *succeeds the most successful and most famous Lamborghini, the Countach. Next to it is the first true Lamborghini racing car, a Formula 1 engine/chassis combination for the 1991 season. The Diablo was completed under the stewardship of Lamborghini's new owner, Chrysler Corporation, and the F1 effort was begun by Chrysler shortly after its 1987 takeover. Both projects have helped renew enthusiasm at the Lamborghini plant in Italy* (opposite).

When *Lamborghini* was purchased by Chrysler Corporation for $30 million in 1987, it not only was a timely rescue for the troubled Italian concern, it was yet another helping of European car company for a hungry American auto industry. Chrysler earlier snacked on 16 percent of Maserati S.p.A., and in the period surrounding the buyout of Lamborghini, Ford consumed the remains of Britain's tiny A.C., then dined on Aston Martin and Jaguar. General Motors, meanwhile, was making a meal of all of Lotus and half of Saab.

Each buyout came with its own questions and unresolved issues. For Lamborghini, the immediate uncertainty was how Chrysler would handle completion of the Diablo project. This would be an important bellwether of things to come. But it alone would not resolve the broader issue: Could the agenda and management style of a mass-market U.S. company be compatible with those of a low-volume Italian producer that survives as much on passion as on money?

In acquiring Lamborghini, Chrysler Vice Chairman Gerald Greenwald said his company sought insight into its craftsmanship and high-performance engineering. In turn, he said, Chrysler would reciprocate with capital resources, advanced electronics, testing facilities, and marketing expertise. Greenwald pledged not to change Lamborghini. But Greenwald quit Chrysler in June 1990 to head a proposed employee buyout of United Air Lines. Michael Hammes, who ran Chrysler's international operations, also left the company at about the same time. Whether Lamborghini will be as autonomous under Greenwald's successors as he had vowed to keep it remains to be seen.

What is evident is that Lamborghini was obviously influenced by Chrysler on the Diablo. Whether the car is better or worse for Chrysler's hand can never be known. But the American presence certainly didn't turn the Diablo into a dullard. Nor did it take the car far afield of the Lamborghini ethic. Indeed, some powerful people inside Chrysler clearly are sensitive to the special place Lamborghini holds in the upper reaches of the automotive cosmos. And the Americans seem cautious about disturbing this orbit. "It would be nonsense to go in and change anything," said Anthony Richards, head of Chrysler's Lamborghini

244

Lamborghini's legacy embraces a range of products and emotions, from the unconcealed aggression of the Countach to the renaissance ambition of the 350 GT (above) to the deleteriousness of the Urraco (opposite bottom). Athleticism, demonstrated by the Jarama below, is their bond. Among Lamborghini's most successful creations are its marine V-12s (opposite, top right).

division. "You would rapidly destroy what you bought."

One good sign was that Chrysler seemed willing to promote from within. Emile Novaro, who joined Lamborghini in 1980 as managing director and who helped guide the company through some very dire straits, was named president of Lamborghini Automobili in '87 upon Chrysler's purchase. Similarly, Gianfranco Venturelli was promoted from production manager to general manager in '87. Further, Chrysler said it would increase the Lamborghini workforce and so it has, boosting employment by more than 100 people, about 30 percent, as of mid-1990. Morale is said to be high again, and visitors are impressed to see a happy coexistence between the hand tools of Lamborghini's past and the computerized machine tools of its future. Chrysler acknowledges plans to greatly enlarge the plant itself and early reports had it spiking production to 5000 units annually in imitation of the 4000-per-year Ferrari builds under its parent, Fiat. But Richards said Lamborghini will be kept smaller and more exclusive, with production not to exceed 2500 per year. Diablo accounts for about 500 of this number. It's the cars that will make up the remaining 2000 that give a glimpse into the future.

First off for mid-1992 is an all-new mid-engine two-seater, smaller than the Diablo and aimed squarely at the Ferrari 348. Lamborghini hasn't had an entry in this class since the Jalpa, but unlike that V-8 sports car, the new model is to run a V-10. It's code named P140, and some reports say it will be called the Bravo, a label also carried by the Urraco-based Bertone concept car of the mid-'70s. Richards, however, said the Bravo tag is unavailable and that Lamborghini probably will stay with tradition and name the car for a fighting bull. Little else is known about the P140, except that Lamborghini hopes to broaden its appeal by offering the optional automatic clutch that's set to debut on the Diablo. The P140 will account for the lion's share of future Lamborghini production, but tentative plans also call for a very-limited-edition grand-touring coupe later in the decade. It'll be a front-engine V-12 two-door with either two seats or a 2+2 setup. There's also talk of another mid-engine supercar in the mid- to late-1990s to slot above the Diablo. And rumors percolate about a possible V-12 Lamborghini minivan by 1995.

246

With such libidinous exteriors (above) it's little wonder the control layout of Lamborghini cars sometimes seemed to get overlooked. An evolution is clear in these four views. Top row: the classicism of a '65 350 GT and the virtuous—if slightly disheveled— simplicity of a '68 Miura. Bottom row: Countach's cold angularity and finally, the synthesis of several influences in the more organic Diablo. Ferruccio remains active in his mid-70s. Shown at La Fiorita in 1990 (right), he's building a recreational complex and overseeing a vineyard and winery. He also was rumored to be part of an attempt to take over Bugatti.

While Chrysler's capital and resources are the foundation upon which Lamborghini will build its future, Lamborghini, in turn, is designing and developing for Chrysler the aluminum 8.0-liter V-10 engine that will power the Dodge

Viper sports roadster due in 1992. Its design efforts on the Portofino four-door also have been picked up by Chrysler as the styling theme of the American automaker's cab-forward sedans of the 1990s. But Lamborghini's main role in Chrysler's game plan for early '90s is not necessarily to funnel expertise across the Atlantic. It is instead to supply something less tangible: an image boost. And it starts with the Diablo.

While the American company's pentastar appears nowhere on the Diablo, Chrysler wasted little time in capitalizing on the hot new supercar. "If Chrysler isn't the performance company, then I'm Joe Isuzu, [signed, Chrysler Chairman] Lee Iacocca," read the tag line to one of Chrysler's boldest print ads since the muscle-car era. The four-page fold-out appeared in U.S. car-enthusiast magazines during the last part of 1990. As the eye traveled across the pages it picked out an Eagle Talon and various other Dodges and Plymouths, and then the Viper. On the far right, as if to punctuate a lurid sentence, was a blood-red Diablo. This is the automobile upon which a smiling Iacocca rested his hand. Of course, the ad does promote the Diablo. But that clearly is not its intent, leading some lovers of the marque to wonder whether a proud heritage is shamed when a Lamborghini is forced to shill for Dodges and Plymouths.

The reality, of course, is that both sides are getting something here. For if marketing has cost Lamborghini a small fraction of its pride, it is marketing that has allowed Lamborghini to go racing.

One of Chrysler's very first acts upon taking over was to establish a wholly owned subsidiary, Lamborghini Engineering, expressly to develop a Formula 1 engine. In a reversal of the official policy set down by Ferruccio Lamborghini himself, the powers in Highland Park, Michigan, decreed that track competition was vital to enhancing Lamborghini's image. And only Formula 1, they decided, had the world-wide prestige to impress the clientele Lamborghini must reach.

To design its racing engine, Lamborghini Engineering acquired the services of Mauro Forghieri, who in 1969 designed the flat-12 that would power Ferrari to four Formula 1 manufacturers titles and some sports-car wins. Also brought on board was Danielle Audetto, who managed Ferrari's Formula 1 team in the early '70s, when World

Champion Niki Lauda was its premier driver. The crew also includes Sandro Munari, a champion rally driver and former member of the Ferrari sports-car racing team.

Secrecy is the rule in Formula 1 engineering, and so little was made public about Forghieri's engine other than its basics: a 3.5- liter, 80-degree V-12 with four camshafts and four valves per cylinder. The engine did buck the trend in having 12 cylinders at a time when Honda set the tone for naturally aspirated F1 engines with its V-10. Lamborghini decided to sacrifice some fuel economy and weight savings for the higher-rpm capabilities of a V-12. It produced an estimated 650 horsepower and innovated by mating its Lamborghini-built six-speed gearbox to the engine, thus keeping the length of the powerplant about the same as the conventional engine/transmission package of rival V-10s.

Ready in time for the 1989 season, the Lamborghini V-12 debuted in two Lola chassis for the team owned by Gerard Larrousse, a former two-time LeMans winner and ex-Renault F1 racing director. Driven by Aguri Suzuki of Japan and Frenchman Eric Bernard, the Larrousse-Lamborghinis finished only five of the 23 races they started, with no wins and just a single championship point. But the team showed signs of progress.

"Lamborghini's magnificent-sounding V-12 had a year of steady refinement, aided by probably the most elaborate engine management and monitoring along pit row," wrote Jonathan Thompson in his review of the '89 F1 season for *Road*

With Chrysler came the resources to build an F1 engine for '89, and for '91, Lamborghini has an F1 engine/chassis combo **(below)**. **Below right:** *The car's designer, Mauro Forghieri, poses with a test driver. Racing promotes Lamborghini, but as part of the bargain, the Diablo must cast the glow of its prestige over other Chrysler products, as evidenced by this advertisement* **(bottom)**.

"IF CHRYSLER ISN'T THE PERFORMA

Eagle Talon TSi AWD.
Zero to sixty in 6.3 seconds.**
Faster than Toyota Celica All-Trac.*

Dodge Daytona ES Turbo.
Zero to sixty in 7.8 seconds.†
Faster than Nissan 240SX.†

Plymouth Laser RS Turbo.
Zero to sixty in 6.6 seconds.†
Faster than Mazda MX6 GT.**

D
Zero
Faster

*Motor Trend Magazine. †USAC test. **Car & Driver Magazine. ††Manufacturer's data.

& *Track.* "Bosch and of course Chrysler involvement helped to bring this engine a long way from its early image of leaking oil around the circuit, then steaming if off next lap."

For '90, the V-12 went into two additional F1 cars, Lotuses driven by Britishers Martin Donnelly and Derek Warwick. The Lotus chassis were hardly competitive, and while the Larrousse team improved, none of the Lamborghini-engine cars could stay with the Honda- or Ferrari-powered machines. The high-water mark was Suzuki's third-place finish before 145,000 cheering countrymen at the Japanese Grand Prix in October.

Lamborghini took a major step for the 1991 season by introducing a Forghieri-designed chassis to go along with the improved "Step 3" version of its V-12. Again, few details were shared, but the chassis did break some ground by using a single, horizontally positioned shock absorber front and rear; other mono-shock applications have been confined to the front. Among revisions to the Step 3 engine was a

shorter stroke for more revs and more power. Lamborghini thus joined Ferrari as the only manufacturer to field both an F1 chassis and an engine. But while Ferrari's is a factory team, the Lamborghini cars would be campaigned by Team Modena. Two cars were planned. Nicola Larini, just over from the Ligier F1 team, and Eric Van Der Poele, moving up from Formula 3000, would drive. Neither Lotus nor Larrousse re-upped for '91, but the Lamborghini engines did go into a pair of Ligier chassis. Thierry Boutsen moved from Williams to Team Ligier and was joined by Formula 3000 star Erik Comas. Lamborghini also made some of its F1 engines available for evaluation in Spice Engineering cars for Group C sports-prototype competition. Lamborghini super-fan Walter Wolf was considering a Group C effort with this combination under a team bearing his name. It's thus quite possible that the Lamborghini name would now be seen at places like LeMans as well as Monaco. The

dream of the early Sant'Agata hotbloods was coming to pass.

All this suggests that the pieces are in place for a solid, uninterrupted ascent of Lamborghini Automobili. But nothing is assured, of course. In mid-1990, for instance, chief engineer Luigi Marmiroli was rumored to be leaving Lamborghini to become technical director of Bugatti Automobile SpA. The Bugatti group planned to revive the famous European marque in 1991 with an exotic supercoupe designed by none other than the man who penned the Miura, Countach, and Diablo—Marcello Gandini. Here, the intrigue thickens. The job Marmiroli was said to be in line for at Bugatti was open because Bugatti's board had fired Paolo Stanzani, the former Lamborghini technical director and a father of the Countach. Stanzani was ousted because he was attempting a takeover of the Bugatti company. A rumored partner in the foiled takeover attempt was none other than Ferruccio Lamborghini. It looks as if *Il Cavaliere* has the itch again. World, look out.

LAMBORGHINI SPECIFICATIONS 1963-91

Model[1]	350 GTV	350 GT	400 GT	400GT 2 + 2	Islero 400GT/GTS	
Years Built	1963	1964-66	1966-67	1966-68	1968-69	
Production	1 (+ 1 chass.)	120	23	224	225	
Engine/Drive	front/rear	front/rear	front/rear	front/rear	front/rear	
Seats	2	2 (some 2 + 1)	2	2 + 2	2 + 2	
Engine	dohc V-12	dohc V-12	dohc V-12	dohc V-12	dohc V-12	
Displacement, cc/ci	3465/211	3465/211	3929/240	3929/240	3929/240	
Horsepower @ rpm (DIN)	360 @ 8000	270 @ 6500	320 @ 6500	320 @ 6500	350 @ 7500[2]	
Torque @ rpm (lbs/ft)	240 @ 6000	239 @ 4000	276 @ 4500	276 @ 4500	289 @ 5500	
Suspension, front	A-arms, coils	A-arms, coils	A-arms, coils	A-arms, coils	A-arms, coils	
Suspension, rear	A-arms, coils	A-arms, coils	A-arms, coils	A-arms, coils	A-arms, coils	
Steering	worm & roller	worm & roller	worm & roller	worm & roller	worm & roller	
Brakes, front/rear	disc/disc	disc/disc	disc/disc	disc/disc	disc/disc	
Overall length (mm/in.)	4500/177.2	4640/182.7	4640/182.7	4640/182.7	4525/178.1	
Overall width (mm/in.)	1630/64.2	1730/68.1	1730/68.1	1730/68.1	1730/68.1	
Overall height (mm/in.)	1220/48.0	1220/48.0	1220/48.0	1285/50.6	1300/51.2	
Wheelbase (mm/in.)	2450/96.5	2550/100.4	2550/100.4	2550/100.4	2550/100.4	
Track, front (mm/in.)	1380/54.3	1380/54.3	1380/54.3	1380/54.3	1380/54.3	
Track, rear (mm/in.)	1380/54.3	1380/54.3	1380/54.3	1380/54.3	1380/54.3	

1 Except for 350 GTV, Cheetah and LM001/4, all models listed are production.   2 "S" version.

	Jarama 400 GT/GTS	Espada	Miura P400	Miura P400S	Miura P400SV	Countach LP400
	1970-76	1968-78	1966-69	1970-71	1971-72	1974-78
	327	1217	475	140	150	150
	front/rear	front/rear	mid/rear	mid/rear	mid/rear	mid/rear
	2 + 2	4	2	2	2	2
	dohc V-12	dohc V-12	dohc V-12	dohc V-12	dohc V-12	dohc V-12
	3929/240	3929/240	3929/240	3929/240	3929/240	3929/240
	345 @ 7800[2]	345 @ 7800	350 @ 7000	370 @ 7700	385 @ 7850	375 @ 8000
	280 @ 5500	280 @ 5500	271 @ 5100	286 @ 5500	286 @ 5000	286 @ 5000
	A-arms, coils	A-arms, coils	A-arms, coils	A-arms, coils	A-arms, coils	A-arms, coils
	A-arms, coils	A-arms, coils	A-arms, coils	A-arms, coils	A-arms, coils	A-arms, coils
	worm & roller	worm & roller	rack & pinion	rack & pinion	rack & pinion	rack & pinion
	disc/disc	disc/disc	disc/disc	disc/disc	disc/disc	disc/disc
	4485/176.6	4738/186.5	4370/172.0	4370/172.0	4370/172.0	4140/163.0
	1820/71.7	1860/73.2	1760/69.3	1760/69.3	1760/69.3	1890/74.4
	1190/46.9	1185/46.7	1050/41.3	1050/41.3	1050/41.3	1070/42.1
	2380/93.7	2650/104.3	2504/98.6	2504/98.6	2504/98.6	2450/96.5
	1490/58.7	1490/58.7	1412/55.6	1412/55.6	1412/55.6	1500/59.1
	1490/58.7	1490/58.7	1412/55.6	1412/55.6	1541/60.7	1520/59.8

Model	Countach LP400S	Countach LP500S	Countach LP500S QV[3]	Countach 25th Annv. Ed.	Urraco P250	Urraco P300	
Years Built	1978-82	1982-85	1985-88	1988-90	1972-76	1975-79	
Production	235	323	610	650	520 (+ 66 P200)	205	
Engine/Drive	mid/rear	mid/rear	mid/rear	mid/rear	mid/rear	mid/rear	
Seats	2	2	2	2	2 + 2	2 + 2	
Engine	dohc V-12	dohc V-12	dohc V-12	dohc V-12	sohc V-8	dohc V-8	
Displacement, cc/ci	3929/240	4754/290	5167/315	5167/315	2462/150	2996/183	
Horsepower @ rpm (DIN)	375 @ 8000	375 @ 7000	455 @ 7000	455 @ 7000	220 @ 7500	250 @ 7500	
Torque @ rpm (lbs/ft)	286 @ 5000	302 @ 4500	369 @ 5200	369 @ 5200	166 @ 5750	195 @ 5750	
Suspension, front	A-arms, coils	A-arms, coils	A-arms, coils	A-arms, coils	struts, A-arms	struts, A-arms	
Suspension, rear	A-arms, coils	A-arms, coils	A-arms, coils	A-arms, coils	struts, A-arms	struts, A-arms	
Steering	rack & pinion	rack & pinion	rack & pinion	rack & pinion	rack & pinion	rack & pinion	
Brakes, front/rear	disc/disc	disc/disc	disc/disc	disc/disc	disc/disc	disc/disc	
Overall length (mm/in.)	4140/163.0	4140/163.0	4140/163.0	4140/163.0	4250/167.3	4285/168.7	
Overall width (mm/in.)	2000/78.7	2000/78.7	2000/78.1	2017/78.7	1760/69.3	1740/68.5	
Overall height (mm/in.)	1070/42.1	1070/42.1	1070/42.1	1070/42.1	1160/45.7	1160/45.7	
Wheelbase (mm/in.)	2450/96.5	2450/96.5	2450/96.5	2450/96.5	2450/96.5	2450/96.5	
Track, front (mm/in.)	1490/58.7	1492/58.7	1536/60.5	1536/60.5	1460/57.5	1450/57.1	
Track, rear (mm/in.)	1605/63.2	1606/63.2	1606/63.2	1606/63.2	1460/57.5	1470/57.9	

3 QV = Quattrovalvolve (4 valves/cylinder)   4 Chrysler   5 AMC

	Silhouette	Jalpa P350	Cheetah	LM001	LMA/LM002	LM004	Diablo
	1976-78	1982-88	1977	1981	1982-date	1986	1990-date
	52	410	1	1	—	1	—
	mid/rear	mid/rear	rear/rear	rear/rear	front/all	front/all	mid/rear
	2	2	4	4	4 + 6	4 + 6	2
	dohc V-8	dohc V-8	ohv V-8[4]	ohv V-8[5]	dohc V-12	dohc V-12	dohc V-12
	2996/183	3485/213	5900/360[4]	5900/360[5]	5167/315	7257/443	5707/348
	250 @ 7500	255 @ 7000	183 @ 4000	180 @ 4000	455 @ 6800	420 @ 5400	485 @ 7000
	195 @ 5750	235 @ 3250	NA	NA	368 @ 4500	435 @ 3500	428 @ 5200
	struts, A-arms	struts, A-arms	torsion bars	torsion bars	A-arms, coils	A-arms, coils	A-arms, coils
	struts, A-arms	struts, A-arms	torsion bars	torsion bars	A-arms, coils	A-arms, coils	A-arms, coils
	rack & pinion	rack & pinion	NA	NA	recirc. ball	recirc. ball	rack & pinion
	disc/disc	disc/disc	disc/disc	disc/disc	disc/drum	disc/drum	disc/disc
	4320/170.1	4330/170.5	4320/170.1	4790/188.6	4900/192.9	4900/192.9	4460/175.6
	1880/74.0	1880/74.0	1880/74.0	2000/78.7	2000/78.7	2000/78.7	2040/80.3
	1120/44.1	1140/44.9	1580/62.2	1790/70.5	1850/72.8	1850/72.8	1105/43.5
	2450/96.5	2450/96.5	3000/118.1	2950/116.1	3000/118.1	3000/118.1	2650/104.3
	1490/58.7	1500/59.1	1520/59.8	1520/59.8	1615/63.6	1615/63.6	1540/60.6
	1550/61.0	1554/61.2	1520/59.8	1520/59.8	1615/63.6	1615/63.6	1640/64.6

BIBLIOGRAPHY

Illustrated Lamborghini Buyers Guide
Rob de la Rive Box
Motorbooks International
Osceola, Wisconsin

Lamborghini
Stefano Pasini
Automobilia
San Francisco, California

Lamborghini, A Source Book
Robert C. Ackerson
Motorbooks International
Osceola, Wisconsin

Lamborghini Collections (5 books)
Brooklands Books
Motorbooks International
Osceola, Wisconsin

Lamborghini Countach
Jean-Francois Marchet and Peter
  Coltrin
Osprey/Motorbooks International
Osceola, Wisconsin

Lamborghini Countach
Graham Robson
Publications International, Ltd.
Lincolnwood, Illinois

Lamborghini Miura
Jean-Francois Marchet and Peter
  Coltrin
Osprey/Motorbooks International
Osceola, Wisconsin

Lamborghini Espada & The 4-Seaters
Jean-Francois Marchet
Osprey/Motorbooks International
Osceola, Wisconsin

Lamborghini Urraco
Jean-Francois Marchet
Osprey/Motorbooks International
Osceola, Wisconsin

Legendary Lamborghinis
Publications International, Ltd.
Lincolnwood, Illinois

The Lamborghinis
Chris Harvey
Motor Racing Publications
London, England

Automobile Quarterly magazine
Vol. 23 No. 1 (Winter 1985)
Kutztown, Pennsylvania

CLUBS

Readers who'd like still more information about Lamborghinis are urged to consult one or more of the following major owners clubs. Many welcome new members, regardless of Lamborghini ownership, and several publish informative newsletters and magazines. Some also stage periodic meets and shows where the public may see the fabulous supercars from Sant'Agata.

Lamborghini Owners Club
Jim Kaminski
St. Petersburg, FL 33734

Lamborghini Club America
Jim Heady
170 Monte Vista Road
Orinda, CA 94563
(415) 254-2107

Lamborghini Club UK
208 Latymer Court
Hammersmith Road
London W6 7JY England

Lamborghini Club Canada
John Paul Coppolino
P.O. Box 3733
Hamilton, Ontario
Canada L8H 7N1
(416) 549-0243

INDEX